── *The* ──

FRANCIS

MIRACLE

The
FRANCIS
MIRACLE

Inside the Transformation of the Pope and the Church

JOHN L. ALLEN, JR.

TIME
Books

Published by Time Books, an imprint of Time Home Entertainment Inc.
1271 Avenue of the Americas, 6th floor • New York, NY 10020

ISBN 10: 1-61893-131-8
ISBN 13: 978-1-61893-131-3
Library of Congress Control Number: 2014952628

We welcome your comments and suggestions about Time Books.
Please write to us at:
Time Books, Attention: Book Editors,
P.O. Box 11016, Des Moines, IA 50336-1016
If you would like to order any of our hardcover
Collector's Edition books, please call us at
800-327-6388, Monday through Friday, 7 a.m.–8 p.m.,
or Saturday, 7 a.m.–6 p.m., Central Time.

To Shannon, for 23 years of love and support.

TABLE
── *of* ──
CONTENTS

Introduction

IT WAS THE KIND OF VATICAN MEETING that normally shuffles along for two weeks without making headlines, but in October 2014 a tumultuous synod of bishops captured both the excitement and the alarm that Pope Francis is generating in the Catholic Church. Roughly 260 bishops, clergy and laity from around the world gathered in Rome to debate issues that have embodied the Church's identity for generations: family life, marriage and sexual morality. There have been 26 such synods since the first in 1967, and they've generally been tame affairs. This time, however, the gathering was filled with intrigue and controversy.

Two sides squared off: traditionalists, unnerved by the new pope, and progressives, hoping to spur Francis on to even greater change. On the right, prelates complained of a plot to suppress their voices and led an internal revolt—one disgruntled cardinal even told the media that the pope was sowing the seeds of confusion and owed the world an apology. Inside the synod hall, another rose to accuse a cardinal advocating a permissive line on divorce of spreading "sickness and disease." On the left, reformers groused about a lack of nerve, and many saw the final document of the synod as a disappointing concession on issues such as a new welcome for homosexuals, recognizing positive values in non-traditional relationships and the possibility of allowing Catholics who divorce and remarry outside the Church to receive communion. Yet both sides could agree on at least one thing: Francis had let loose a battle for the soul of Roman Catholicism.

Given the upheaval and acrimony that surfaced over the two weeks, it was tempting to frame the 2014 synod of bishops as a defeat for the pope, proof that he can't control the forces he's generated—in effect, that his leadership has put the Church in danger of spinning out of control. There were even hints that Francis might rethink his plans to call a second, larger synod in October 2015, on the grounds he was lucky this one didn't fall apart completely and he might not want to tempt fate again.

Then, at the close of the meeting, Francis broke his silence, giving a 15-minute talk that seemed to capture the spirit of the Church he wants to lead. He noted that at the beginning of the event he had called on bishops to speak boldly and hold nothing back and said he would have been disappointed if there hadn't been "animated discussion."

In the most critical portion of his speech, Francis ticked off several temptations that the Church must avoid if it's to resolve its challenges successfully. It must not succumb to a "hostile rigidity," a fussy legalism devoid of compassion and subtlety. At the same time, it must also reject what he called a "destructive do-goodism" and a "false mercy," a touchy-feely morality incapable of calling sin by its name. The Church must not impose "impossible burdens" on people, he said, but it also must not "come down off the cross" by abandoning its core principles in order to win approval. Francis recognized that both sides that emerged at the synod—reformers pushing the Church toward its future and conservatives determined not to jettison its past—had a point, and that each perspective wouldn't be fully Catholic without the other. He drew a five-minute standing ovation, including prelates who not long before had been virtually at one another's throats.

Francis effectively laid out the program of a moderate pontiff, fully committed to the more than 2,000 year old faith of the Catholic Church and equally committed to cajoling the Church into a deeper and more positive dialogue with the world around it. He wants people's first impression of Catholicism to be one not of judgment but rather of welcome; he trusts that whatever verdicts the Church delivers will be better received if they come in the context of a loving embrace. To achieve that, he knows he needs to bring all ideological camps along with him.

For clarity's sake, the labels "right wing" and "left wing" are an inexact fit for the Catholic Church, especially where the hierarchy is concerned. By secular standards, there are no liberal bishops—who would favor abortion rights, gay marriage and playing down the role of religion in public life. In the Church, a liberal bishop usually means someone committed to Church teaching but flexible and accommodating in the way it's applied, while a conservative believes in drawing lines in the sand. The difference is more about attitude than substance. In that sense, there are clearly both liberals and conservatives in the Church Francis leads, and he wants to be the pope for both.

Ultimately, the 2014 synod of bishops signaled Pope Francis's ambition to lead the Catholic Church to the political center, to the geographical and cultural margins of the world and to the heart of the Christian gospel with his message of mercy.

THOSE FAMILIAR WITH Jorge Mario Bergoglio as the cardinal of Buenos Aires in Argentina before March 2013 will tell you his election to the papacy was destiny fulfilled. Bergoglio had been the runner-up in the 2005 papal conclave that elected Benedict XVI and, given the anti-establishment mood after Benedict's resignation, the choice of a Latin American outsider with a reputation as a strong manager seemed plausible. Bergoglio's age at the time, 76, put him on most handicappers' B-list, but since Benedict had been elected at 78, even that wasn't seen as disqualifying.

What utterly astonished even his closest friends, however, is the kind of pope he's turned out to be. This is a pontiff who has been splashed across more magazine covers than Scarlett Johansson, who has been googled almost as often as Justin Bieber and who beat out the likes of

George Clooney when he was named *Esquire's* Best Dressed Man of 2013. He has poll numbers that politicians and celebrities would drool over and more than 16.8 million followers on Twitter. His instantly famous line about gays—"Who am I to judge?"—was among the most-quoted phrases of 2013, earning him "person of the year" honors from not only TIME magazine but also the pro-gay magazine *The Advocate,* which showed the pope's smiling face with a "NO H8" sticker. After it emerged that Francis had briefly worked as a bouncer at an Argentine bar as a young man, NBC's *Today* show breathlessly proclaimed him "the coolest pope ever."

In Argentina, though, both as a Jesuit official and later as a bishop, Bergoglio generally dreaded the spotlight. On the rare occasions he did appear in high-profile situations, he had low-wattage appeal. He was described as "humble" and "shy" by those who liked him and "boring" and "gray" by those who didn't, and neither side would have labeled him charismatic. Pictures of Bergoglio taken prior to his election to the papacy rarely show him smiling. Since becoming Pope, however, Bergoglio has been transformed into a beaming public figure. When the pope's only surviving sibling, 64-year-old Maria Elena Bergoglio, was asked in April 2013 what she made of the change, she jokingly said, "I don't recognize this guy!"

A veteran Latin American cardinal who has known Bergoglio for decades made an appointment to see his old friend over Christmas 2013 in Casa Santa Marta, the hotel on Vatican grounds where the pope has chosen to reside. (He lives in room 201, a slightly larger suite than the one he stayed in during the conclave at which he was elected, giving him enough space to receive guests.) The cardinal, who didn't wish to be named, said he looked at Francis and, referring to the exuberance and spontaneity that are now hallmarks of his public image, said to him point-blank, "You are not the same man I knew in Buenos Aires. What's happened to you?"

According to the cardinal, Francis answered, "On the night of my election, I had an experience of the closeness of God that gave me a great sense of interior freedom and peace, and that sense has never left me."

Perhaps the impression that there's something indefinably novel about Pope Francis, something that can't be understood entirely in terms of human logic, accounts for the paradox that it's far easier to document the popularity Francis enjoys than to explain it. Is Francis a left-wing revolutionary, or is he basically a company man adept at rebranding the same religious product? Is he a real-deal reformer, destined to turn the Catholic Church on its ear, or is he more about PR than substantive change? Is he a wide-eyed country pastor plunked down into the corridors of power who has had a good run of luck, or is he a savvy politician who knows exactly what he's doing? Even his closest friends and allies sometimes find themselves asking this. Amid the chaos of the October 2014 synod, Cardinal Reinhard Marx of Munich, one of the leaders of the reform movement and a member of the pope's council of nine cardinal advisers, said, "I want to believe the pope has a plan . . . but if he does, he's not sharing it with me!"

THE CORE ARGUMENT OF THIS BOOK is that Francis is a man on a mission. He wants to be a change agent, a historic reformer who reorients the Catholic Church decisively across multiple fronts.

There are three main thrusts to his reforming zeal. First, Francis aims to steer Catholicism back to the political and ecclesiastical center, following a period in which it appeared to drift ever more steadily to the right during the twilight of the papacy of John Paul II and the eight years of Benedict XVI. Hard-line bishops who prospered during that stretch, such as American Cardinal Raymond Burke, have had their wings clipped. In their place, Francis has picked men like the new cardinal of Cologne in Germany, 58-year-old Rainer Maria Woelki, who won praise during his years in Berlin for opening lines of communication in the city's diverse cultural milieu, even receiving a Respect Award from the German Alliance Against Homophobia. This new breed of senior prelates also includes Archbishop Blase Cupich in Chicago, who once dismayed aggressive pro-life forces when he discouraged priests and seminarians from praying in front of Planned Parenthood clinics as part of an anti-abortion protest, seeing the gesture as unnecessarily provocative.

Despite his attempts at change, Francis is no doctrinal radical. To date, he has not changed a single word of the *Catechism of the Catholic Church*, the official compendium of Church teaching. Every time he's been asked for his personal views on contentious matters such as abortion and homosexuality, he has replied that they're the views of the Church because he is a "son of the Church." Yet in Catholicism, the official teaching is often less important than how it's applied in real-world circumstances, and that's the level at which the true "Francis effect" is being felt.

Second, Francis wants Catholics to "get out of the sacristy and into the streets." Since becoming pope, Francis has repeatedly astonished people with the various ways in which he breaks through the bubble that ordinarily surrounds a pope. He's sat down for chats with atheists and believers alike, called ordinary people on the phone out of the blue, even invited three homeless men and their dog to join his household staff for his birthday breakfast. (The dog, by the way, was named Marley, for the reggae icon Bob Marley.) These are gestures that reflect the pope's personality, but they're also consciously crafted symbols of the Church he wants to lead. It's a Church that doesn't sit around waiting for people to walk through the door but goes out to meet them where they live.

As Francis understands it, part of this is personal—that is, seeing the person in front of you and reaching out to him. Thus, when he stops the popemobile in St. Peter's Square to embrace a man horribly disfigured by boils or when he invites an Italian teenager with Down syndrome to hop up for a ride, Francis is being a missionary. The other dimension of this outreach is social, and in this sense Francis is a determined apostle of what Christians call the "social gospel": a Catholic who focuses on defending the poor, opposing war, concern for the environment and protecting people at the margins of life, such as immigrants, the elderly and minorities. His emblematic expression of this social commitment came just three days after his election when he said he dreams of a "poor Church for the poor."

Third, Francis is a reforming pope elected on a platform of good governance. He's determined to break the grip of an old guard in the Vatican, which over the years has become dysfunctional and sometimes brazenly corrupt. The choice of a total Vatican outsider as pope was fueled by frustrations among cardinals from around the world over a series of governance meltdowns during the Benedict years, including the bungled response to the sexual abuse crisis in Europe and the "Vatican leaks" affair, which reached its denouement with the arrest of Benedict's own butler as the mole. Francis is delivering on that mandate, beginning with the most sweeping overhaul of the Vatican's financial operations in centuries.

As part of that reform agenda, Francis has proposed a sweeping decentralization in Catholicism by transferring power from Rome to local churches around the world. He also wants to foster a new spirit of humility in the Church's leadership class, so that when people see the symbols of authority in Catholicism—such as the Roman collar of a priest or the pectoral cross of a bishop—their automatic association is with service rather than with power and privilege. When, shortly after his election, Francis made a point of visiting a youth prison in Rome to wash the feet of 12 inmates on Holy Thursday—including two Muslims and two women, in a technical violation of Church rules—he was not just after a photo op. He was providing a visual illustration of what his reform looks like.

It remains to be seen if Francis will succeed in translating his vision into structures and personnel, or if he will end up as no more than a beguiling personality who leaves behind an essentially unchanged institution. It's also not clear if his moderate, flexible approach to Catholic doctrine will produce the more dynamic and attractive community he has in mind, or whether its effect in the real world will be to seed greater division and acrimony within an already fractured Church, turning people away from Catholicism rather than beckoning them in.

INSTITUTIONAL RELIGION has been in decline for a long time, especially in the West, and the Catholic Church in particular has seen its standing slip for a variety of reasons, not least the massive child sexual abuse scandals that have taken an enormous toll on its moral authority. Yet the truth is that the papacy matters, whether one is Catholic or not. Political scientist Joseph Nye reckons the Vatican as the world's most important soft power—that is, a superpower not through military or economic might but by its ability to move hearts and minds. Catholicism claims a global following of 1.2 billion, and the papacy is by far the most visible office of religious leadership on the planet. Anyone who doubts the ability of a pope to influence events ought to consult with former Communist leaders across Eastern Europe, who suddenly found themselves out of work after 1989 because of the role the late John Paul II played in the collapse of the Soviet empire. To cite a less happy example, skeptics of the Vatican's real-world importance might survey still-angry Serbs and European diplomats who blame the Vatican's hasty recognition of independence of both Croatia and Slovenia for triggering the devastating Balkans war in 1992.

The question is not whether a pope—any pope—matters but rather how a given pope plans to wield the influence that comes with the office. On that score, a visit to a Roman parish by Pope Francis offered a vital clue. A pope is also the bishop of Rome, the shepherd of the city's flock, and Francis takes that role seriously. In May 2013, he headed out to spend his Sunday morning at the Roman parish of Saints Elizabeth and Zechariah, located in the Prima Porta neighborhood on the city's northern edge. It was a deliberate choice because, as Francis explained to the crowd, "sometimes you understand reality better from the edges than from the center."

The pontiff was scheduled to arrive at 9:30 a.m., but the pastor, a balding, amiable Romanian immigrant named Fr. Benoni Ambarus, heard the rotor wash of the papal chopper almost a half hour before the appointed time. When the pontiff emerged from the helicopter, he pulled Ambarus aside and explained the reason for the early start.

"I know I'm supposed to meet the parish children and say mass," the pope said. "But would it be OK if I also hear some confessions?"

Confession is the Catholic sacrament in which a believer confesses his or her sins confidentially to a priest and then receives God's forgiveness. It's an important part of the daily ministry carried out by priests all over the world, but it had never before been on the agenda when a pope visited a Roman parish. Neither Ambarus nor Vatican organizers had made any provision for it in the day's schedule, but Ambarus nevertheless grabbed eight people at random and brusquely told them they'd be going to confession. (Ambarus later explained that some of those parishioners protested that they didn't want to lose their spot in line to see the pope. "Trust me," he told them, "you're going to see him.")

After the fact, an Argentine priest who worked for Bergoglio in Buenos Aires and who's now one of his closest aides in the Vatican was asked why his boss decided to add confessions to his schedule, which has since become a staple of Francis's parish visits. "It's important to him," the priest replied. "He wanted the world to see him making a point of celebrating the Church's premier rite of mercy."

Mercy is a traditional virtue, not just in Christianity but most human cultures. It has always been on the books in official Christian teaching and is understood to be the natural complement to judgment. As a minister of the Christian gospel, Francis understands that he has to pronounce both God's judgment and God's mercy on a fallen world, because one without the other would be a falsification. His calculation, however, appears to be that the world has heard the Church's judgment with crystal clarity, so now it's time to witness its mercy.

Francis's commitment to mercy is found in his papal motto, translated loosely as "choosing through the eyes of mercy." In his first Sunday homily as pope, delivered at the Vatican's parish church of St. Anne, he said that "in my opinion, the strongest message of the Lord is mercy."

In all the ways that matter, mercy is the spiritual bedrock of this papacy. It lies underneath Francis's moderation and his insistence that laws are made for people, not the other way around. It's the basis for his missionary drive, especially the conviction that people at the periphery should be special objects of the Church's concern. Mercy is even the core of his reform campaign—the idea that good government is about making an institution serve its people.

It's not empirically obvious that Pope Francis has created a more merciful Catholic Church, or that mercy has taken hold to any greater degree in the wider world because of his example. There's legitimate ground for skepticism that mercy can serve as the basis of a complex multinational religious organization. The drama of the Francis era, however, is surely contained in the effort to make mercy the key—and whether Francis will prove tough enough to make that message stick.

1

Bergoglio's Roots

WHEN JORGE MARIO BERGOGLIO made his debut as the new leader of the Catholic Church on March 13, 2013, he told the crowd gathered in St. Peter's Square that the cardinals had gone "to the end of the earth" to find a pope. The reference was to his origins in Argentina, and it's revealing that it was the first thing he chose to tell the world about himself. This is a pope to whom history matters, including his own, and one can't understand where Pope Francis is going without grasping something about where he comes from, as a child of immigrants and the first pope from the developing world. He believes he knows in his bones what it's like to be driven from home by loss and desperation, what it's like to experience want and fear, because it's part of his own family experience. When he became the first pope to appear on Google Hangouts in September 2014, he urged teenagers from five countries to have both "roots and wings." In many ways he was talking about himself.

The Bergoglio story begins in the 1920s in the northern Italian region of the Piedmont. Fallout from the First World War had left Italy bankrupt and seething, fueling fear among the middle class of a Soviet-style revolution, but it in fact paved the way for the rise of Benito Mussolini's fascist movement. In the context of economic despair and political upheaval, scores of Italians turned to the solution so many of them had embraced in previous decades, pulling up roots and seeking opportunity elsewhere. Argentina was a destination of choice, in part because in the 1920s it had a higher per-capita standard of living than virtually any country in Europe. Between 1860 and 1940, an estimated 1.4 million Italians settled in the country, and today it's believed that up to 24 million Argentines, representing roughly 60 percent of the entire population, have some Italian blood in their veins.

By 1927, two great-uncles of the future pope had already settled in Argentina, founding a prosperous paving company in a port area about an hour outside the capital city of Buenos Aires. Giovanni Angelo Bergoglio, the pope's grandfather, made the decision to join his brothers, preparing to set sail for the New World with his wife, Rosa Margarita Vasallo di Bergoglio, and their six children. Family lore has it that Giovanni's decision wasn't just because of a lack of economic opportunity in the Piedmont in the late 1920s or the desire to raise his family near his brothers and their extended kin, but also because of his political and ideological revulsion to Mussolini's Blackshirts. When the new pope was later accused of having supported Argentina's military junta during the Dirty War of the 1970s, his sister, Maria Elena Bergoglio, testily replied that their family had left Italy to escape one band of fascist thugs and her brother would never embrace another.

Giovanni and Rosa originally hoped to book passage on a cruise ship called the *Principessa Mafalda*, which was the pride of the Italian commercial fleet. It was designed to be the fastest and most massive cruise ship of its day, and the Bergoglios scrambled to complete the sale of a coffee shop they owned in Turin in order to leave home in style on the *Principessa*. In the end, the sale got bogged down and the Bergoglios missed the ship's departure. Not long afterward, news reached home that on Oct. 25, 1927, in waters off the coast of Brazil, the *Principessa Mafalda* suffered a cracked propeller that damaged its hull and caused it to sink, killing 314 of the boat's 1,252 passengers. It was the Italian version of the *Titanic* disaster. Relieved by their narrow escape, the Bergoglios set sail on another passenger ship a month later and arrived in Argentina without incident.

Initially, all went according to plan. Giovanni joined his brothers in the paving company, the family settled in a comfortable middle-class residence and life unfolded in the context of a supportive Italian network of relatives and friends. Two years later, however, the Great Depression hit Argentina. The Bergoglio enterprise foundered, forcing Giovanni and Rosa to move again, this time back to Buenos Aires and into a far more modest home. For a time, the future pope's father, Mario José Bergoglio, supported the entire family with his meager earnings from doing bicycle deliveries around town. In Italy, Mario had trained as an accountant, working as an apprentice at the Banca d'Italia, and eventually he was able to resume that career in Buenos Aires.

Having secured his professional prospects, Mario José felt free to pursue a relationship with a young woman he'd met named Regina María Sívori, who had been born in Argentina to another family of immigrants from the Piedmont. The two fell in love and eventually married, then settled in Flores, a predominantly Catholic, Italian and middle-class neighborhood of Buenos Aires, where their eldest child, Jorge Mario, was born in 1936. He was baptized on Christmas by a local priest, Fr. Enrico, a member of the Salesian religious order founded by 19th-century Italian St. John Bosco.

The family never really moved again, and today the pope's sister still lives near the old family home in the suburb of Ituzaingó, an hour from downtown Buenos Aires. Her house is a small one-level brick building on an obscure street, with blue bars on the windows to ward off the petty crime that occasionally plagues such working-class neighbor-hoods. Asked shortly after her brother's election in March 2013 if she might contemplate relocating to nicer environs, she showed a flash of the family spirit by insisting she didn't need anything else. "I'm a house-wife, for God's sake," she told the *National Catholic Reporter.*

AS THE YOUNG Jorge Mario Bergoglio began to make his way in the world, by all accounts the most significant influence was his grandmother Rosa, who helped raise the future pope while his parents worked to support the family. Today, when Francis talks about women in the Church, insisting that the real action in Catholicism is usually among its women, it's not difficult to hear the echoes of Grandma Rosa in his memory. She was a woman of such tenderness and simplicity that it would be easy to miss the toughness that lay beneath, but it was certainly not lost on her grandson.

Although she was deeply pious, Rosa was no merely devotional Catholic who never asked hard questions about her faith, or someone content to park her religious convictions at the door of her local parish. Back in Italy, the young Rosa had become a leader in Catholic Action, a lay movement encouraged by early-20th-century popes to bring Cath-olic social teaching to bear on the country's political and social life. In the 1920s, Catholic Action members tried to protect the indepen-dence of the Church from the country's increasingly powerful fascist forces. Rosa became a fixture on the lecture circuit, speaking regularly to women's groups. If the fascists prevented her from entering the hall in which she was scheduled to appear, she stood outside on a soap-box, daring them to come after her. She kept up her campaigning after immigrating to Argentina, plugging into the country's already strong Catholic Action network, and became a pioneer in Catholic social teaching, arguing for economic structures that better protect the poor.

Much of what's essential about Pope Francis's view of faith in action was imbibed from Rosa's example. For instance, his insistence on the primacy of compassion over judgment, of striving to see the best in others even when they don't share one's ideas, is something the pope attributes to his grandmother. He tells the story of walking down the streets of Buenos Aires one day holding her hand, when he noticed a couple of women from the Salvation Army. He asked Rosa if they were nuns, since their headgear was similar to what he was accustomed to seeing Catholic sisters wearing. "No, but they are good people," Rosa told him.

The comment left an impression, because it cut in a different direction to the rather severe Catholic ethos of his childhood. A divorced or separated person wasn't allowed to enter the family home, for example, and all Protestants were regarded as automatically destined for damnation. Rosa, however, broke through that rigidity, shaping a more generous faith that later flowered in the Argentine pope's most famous line, "Who am I to judge?"

But Bergoglio's early years weren't all about the Church. His parents also took him to every Italian movie screened in local cinemas; *La Strada* and *Rome, Open City* became personal favorites. He acquired a taste for Italian opera and the tango, especially in a form known as *milonga*. He also became a lifelong fan of the neighborhood soccer club, San Lorenzo, founded by another priest, Fr. Lorenzo Massa, a Salesian. (Much later, as archbishop of Buenos Aires, Bergoglio kept in his office a chunk of wood from the stadium's bleachers, as a reminder of the many happy hours he'd spent there.)

Although Bergoglio felt the first stirrings of a vocation to the priesthood at around age 12 or 13, it didn't take right away. Among other things, he swept floors as a janitor and was a bouncer at a local bar to make some extra money while he worked at a local chemical lab testing nutrients. (There, Jorge Mario developed close ties and a deep respect for a female supervisor who happened to be an avowed communist.)

During that span, he fell in love with a neighborhood girl named Amalia Damonte and told her in a letter, "If I don't become a priest, I'll marry you." Damonte's father wasn't thrilled at the prospect. He beat Amalia and forbade her to see Bergoglio again.

At the age of 16 in 1953, Bergoglio made a firm decision to become a priest, though he didn't actually enter the seminary until three years later. In part, the delay was because of resistance from his parents, who, despite their fierce Catholic faith, had hoped to see their eldest son become a doctor. Two years later, Jorge Mario entered the Society of Jesus, beginning his journey to become a Jesuit priest. In between fell a crisis that left both a spiritual and physical mark on the young Bergoglio: he contracted a severe inflammation of the lungs that proved resistant to antibiotics and left him barely able to breathe. After being rushed to the hospital, surgeons removed three cysts and a small portion of his upper right lung. Bergoglio had to spend the next five days in an oxygen tent, followed by a month of recovery with a catheter in his chest. It was his first real experience of physical and emotional suffering, and he was helped through it by his family and his fellow seminarians, two of whom donated blood for his surgery.

That brush with mortality not only meant that Jorge Mario Bergoglio went through the rest of his life with part of one lung missing, but it also deepened his resolve to devote himself to service as a priest of the frontier—one who wouldn't sit around waiting for hurting people to walk through the door but who would go and seek them out. For him, that vocation had only one natural home: the Society of Jesus, the Catholic Church's legendary order of missionaries and men on the move.

JORGE MARIO BERGOGLIO became a Jesuit novice in 1958, just four years before the reforming Second Vatican Council. Held from 1962 to 1965, the celebrated summit of Catholic bishops in Rome triggered a period of liberalizing reform and modernization in all aspects of Catholic life. Changes included the introduction of modern languages in Catholic worship, outreach to other faiths and, thanks to American Catholic thinkers, endorsing religious freedom and the separation of church and state. Bergoglio was sent to Casa Loyola in Padre Hurtado, Chile, for what Jesuits call the juniorate, studying languages, liberal arts and basic human sciences geared toward ministry. There, he rose each day at 6 a.m. for an hour of meditation, followed by mass, and then spent the rest of the day in studies. As was the custom for aspirants to the priesthood, students were expected to serve their own food, wash their own dishes and clean up after themselves. Most would set those habits aside as they moved up the clerical ladder, but for Bergoglio they lasted a lifetime. When he later made his first visit as archbishop to the seminary in Buenos Aires for dinner, the rector asked Bergoglio if he'd like to say a few words to the seminarians. "Yes," he replied. "I'd like to say that tonight I'll do the dishes." Legend has it that a tradition of faculty helping to clean tables and wash dishes was born that night.

Bergoglio returned to Argentina two years later when he was permitted to make his initial vows of poverty, chastity and obedience, thus officially becoming a Jesuit—though not yet a priest—in 1960.

The organization to which Bergoglio committed his life has, to put it mildly, a storied history. Jesuits were founded by St. Ignatius Loyola and a band of early companions in Spain in 1539. A former solider, Loyola left a quasi-military imprint on the society he founded, which over the centuries has acquired a reputation as a kind of marine corps of the Catholic Church. In the early years, the Jesuits emerged as the foot soldiers of the Counter-Reformation, winning back chunks of Europe from Protestants and holding the line elsewhere. Before long, they also became known as the Church's most ardent band of missionaries, bringing the faith to far-flung locales such as Latin America, Asia, the Middle East and the Pacific Islands.

Jesuits were seen as tough, smart and resourceful, willing to go anywhere and to try anything to plant the flag for their faith. They are also celebrated for their personal daring and their intellectual chops— they are the only religious order in Catholicism to bequeath a special term to the English language to denote their unique brand of reasoning: "Jesuitical," which to admirers denotes a capacity for sophisticated distinctions and to critics a type of hypocrisy and deceit cloaked beneath hair-splitting logic.

Although Jesuit priests actually take a special fourth vow of loyalty to the pope, their independent-mindedness and creativity have sometimes brought them into conflict with their masters in Rome. After getting caught up in the dynastic politics of both Europe and the New World in the 18th century, the Jesuits were formally suppressed by the Vatican from 1773 to 1814. By the 20th century, tensions between the society and officialdom in Rome were less political than theological and intellectual, as daring Jesuit thinkers such as Teilhard de Chardin, Karl Rahner and Jean Daniélou pushed the boundaries of Catholic teaching on multiple fronts. De Chardin laid out the basis for a Catholic theology that not only tolerated the theory of evolution but embraced modern science, while Rahner offered a rationale for recognizing God's presence in non-Christian religions. In Latin America, Jesuits were marking new territory not at the level of doctrine but of practice, trying to upend the order's traditional identification with educating the children of the rich and the elite in favor of a new solidarity with the poor and with victims of the region's military regimes.

After a Jesuit novice is formally accepted for membership, he typically undergoes a long period of formation. In Bergoglio's case, it involved his two years in Chile; three years of philosophy study back in Argentina; three years of teaching in a high school; three years of studying theology; and a year in tertianship, a final period of reflection in which members are asked to pray and to think carefully about whether it is truly the life to which they're called. All told, Bergoglio spent 13 years in formation, all but three of them in various settings in Argentina.

He was finally ordained to the Catholic priesthood in 1969, took his permanent vows as a Jesuit in 1970, and took the special fourth and final vow of papal loyalty in 1973.

From the beginning, Bergoglio's fellow Jesuits marked him as someone destined for leadership, given both his intellect and his deep faith. (It wasn't just Jesuits who felt so—Maria Elena, who is 12 years younger than her brother, said it was clear to her early on that Jorge Mario would do something special with his life. "He's got a strong character and he's also got a deep belief in his convictions that's unbreakable," she said in 2013. "Nobody is going to be able to force him to compromise on what he believes in.") That sense proved prophetic when, shortly after taking that final vow in 1973, Bergoglio was named the provincial superior in Argentina, meaning he became the national leader of the Jesuits.

It was a surprising choice, first because Jorge Mario was only 36 at the time. Decades later, Bergoglio said his youth alone made it "crazy" for him to have the job. It was also a departure from normal practice in another sense, because Jesuits typically do not elect a provincial leader who hasn't had the experience of serving as superior of a local house. In this case, however, Argentina's Jesuits were divided between more traditional members, who wanted to maintain the order's spiritual discipline and roots, and progressive Jesuits pushing the order to go "all in" with regard to attacking unjust social structures and serving the poor. Bergoglio was not clearly identified with either camp, making him a good compromise—but also the man in the middle of competing camps.

That background would have made the assignment challenging under any circumstances, but Bergoglio also stepped into his first leadership role at a uniquely turbulent moment in Argentina's history.

BY 1973 PERONISM, the political movement founded by legendary Argentine politician Juan Perón, had splintered into competing left- and right-wing factions, reflecting the broader divisions in Argentine society. A military government had reluctantly given way to democratically elected President Héctor José Cámpora, who allowed Perón to return from exile in Spain. On the very day Perón returned, however, a massacre took place at the airport amid clashes between rival Peronist camps, leading to Cámpora's resignation. Three years later, Perón's widow Isabel was ousted from leadership of the country by an Argentine general named Jorge Rafael Videla. He initiated the euphemistic National Reorganization Process, basically a right-wing military dictatorship. The Dirty War followed, a violent period in which left-wing guerrillas such as the Montoneros faced off against the country's military government. Tens of thousands of ordinary Argentines were caught in the crossfire, many of them joining the ranks of the "disappeared"— people who simply vanished, presumably murdered.

From 1973 to 1979, Bergoglio served a six-year term as superior of the Jesuits, right in the middle of this national drama. Fairly quickly, he developed a strategy of trying to lead his fellow Jesuits to reject ideologies of all stripes and focus instead on their missionary calling. In a 1974 talk, Bergoglio asked the Jesuits to set aside their "sterile inter-ecclesiastical contradictions" and ignore the division between "progressive" and "reactionary" wings of the Church, embracing instead a "true apostolic strategy" based on their own spiritual roots and the message of the gospel. Bergoglio suggested that the order, rather than taking Marxism or a version of Peronism as its point of departure, look instead to popular Latin American piety, expressed in Marian devotions, pilgrimage shrines, the rosary and other elements that formed the bedrock of popular faith.

"Of course, there are elements you can't just take at face value, but Bergoglio thought [popular piety] was a strong reality present among the people and [that Jesuits] could work with it," said Fr. Humberto Miguel Yáñez, who was received into the order by the future pope in 1975 and who grew up under him as a scholastic during a time when

Bergoglio was rector of the Jesuit-run Colegio Máximo in San Miguel.

Instead of discarding popular faith, Bergoglio believed Jesuits should "build on it, purify it and evangelize it. His idea was to focus on the positive elements of this popular religiosity, because it represents an authentic faith among the simple people," Yáñez said in 2013.

Although Bergoglio was attempting to bring the Jesuits back to the heart of their calling, more liberal Jesuits saw it not only as a rebuff of the new social justice impulses flowing in the Church since Vatican II but also a form of denial in light of the atrocities and chaos unfolding all around them. As a result, Bergoglio's tenure as superior gave him a reputation as a conservative, a description that didn't fade until years later.

Politics aside, the most controversial episode from Bergoglio's period as superior occurred in 1976, when two of his fellow Jesuits, Franz Jalics and Orlando Yorio, were arrested by government security forces and sent to the country's largest detention center, housed at a navy mechanical school known as ESMA. Both had been serving in the *villas miserias*, the sprawling slums that ring Buenos Aires, and were suspected of supporting left-wing guerrilla movements. Jalics and Yorio spent five months chained and blindfolded in a cell, wondering if each day would be their last, until they finally resurfaced, drugged and semi-naked, in a local field. In part because Bergoglio had tried to warn them of the dangers they faced, and also because of his general reputation for being leery of adopting an overly partisan anti-government stance, the two Jesuits initially suspected Bergoglio had turned them in, or at least that he hadn't done enough to protect them. (Friends of Bergoglio from the time came forward in 2013 to testify to his efforts to save people, including both Jalics and Yorio, from the regime. Jalics later acknowledged that the two men were arrested not because of Bergoglio but rather because of a female catechist who had joined the guerrillas and been arrested and who confessed under torture to contacts with the two Jesuits. Unaware of that, Yorio died in the winter of 2000 still believing his former superior was at fault. Jalics released a statement in March 2013 from the German monastery where he resided, saying, "These are the facts: Orlando Yorio and I were not reported by Fr. Bergoglio.")

Beyond the specific case of Jalics and Yorio, Bergoglio made no public statement against the Dirty War. His old friend Yáñez said the future pope was swimming against the tide by struggling to maintain order at a time when the Jesuits were embracing liberation. "For instance, he gave us a fixed schedule," Yáñez said. "When I entered the novitiate, there was no such thing. As rector, he ordered that we should have a schedule. At the time, things like that seemed like going back to the past. Obviously, this isn't the most important thing in the world and you can discuss whether it was a good idea."

In a conversation in August 2013 with fellow Jesuit Fr. Antonio Spadaro, editor of the order's Rome-based journal *Civiltà Cattolica*, Bergoglio conceded that while his intentions for those measures may have been noble, his method of imposing them was excessively "authoritarian." He said the experience had taught him the importance of governing in collaboration, cultivating the ability to listen as well as to speak.

In 1980 Bergoglio was for a second time named rector of the philosophical and theological faculty at the Colegio Máximo in San Miguel, about 30 miles from Buenos Aires. Some saw the move as a kind of exile to allow the tensions he had created to calm. Six years later, Bergoglio was still uncertain about the next chapter in his life, heading to Germany to consider possible dissertation topics that might lead to a professorial career. Academia didn't take hold, however, and he was soon back in Argentina serving as confessor and spiritual director for a Jesuit community in Córdoba. That job lasted from 1986 to 1992, when Bergoglio once again found himself thrust into an unexpected position of leadership.

AS THE 1990S DAWNED, it wasn't a smart bet for most observers in Argentina that Jorge Mario Bergoglio would rise up the ecclesiastical ladder. He had spent the prior decade in a series of fairly obscure positions inside the Jesuits, but what people missed was Bergoglio's friendship with a wide range of people, including an increasingly strong rapport with Cardinal Antonio Quarracino of Buenos Aires. Quarracino was an Italian-born prelate who had served in a couple of smaller Argentine dioceses before taking over as the shepherd of the capital city in 1990. A gifted churchman, he had attended Vatican II and was later elected president of the Latin American bishops' conference, CELAM, a role in which he came to the favorable attention of Pope John Paul II. Shortly after he became cardinal, John Paul agreed to Quarracino's request to make Bergoglio an auxiliary bishop, an assistant to the cardinal.

Looking back, it's clear that the approach to leadership that Bergoglio carried with him into the papacy began to take shape during his years as an auxiliary bishop. For one thing, he opted not to live in the comfortable apartment provided for a bishop in Buenos Aires. He originally wanted to remain in his Jesuit residence, but the local priest told him it wasn't appropriate, perhaps fearing that having a bishop in-house would allow Bergoglio to challenge his authority. Instead, Bergoglio found a modest residence in a Buenos Aires parish, and that became his base of operations. And although many bishops are assigned a priest to serve as their personal secretary, Bergoglio preferred to keep his own calendar, carrying around a small black notebook in his shirt pocket—a habit he still has today.

People who worked with Bergoglio in those years said he rose each day at 4 a.m., and it was generally known that if anyone needed something they could start calling him at 6 a.m. He moved around the city on his own, taking the bus or the subway, visiting parishes, schools and hospitals. His style was hands-on and can-do, with priests and laity alike noting that when he was involved, the usual lag in the Church between encountering a problem and deciding on a solution narrowed considerably. He also began his outreach to the *villas miserias* and encouraged talented young priests to serve in the slums. After 18 months, Quarracino decided to make Bergoglio his vicar general, effectively the CEO of the archdiocese.

By the middle of 1996, Quarracino was approaching 73 years of age and was suffering from serious heart problems. Knowing that when he submitted his resignation to the pope in about 18 months' time it would likely be swiftly accepted, Quarracino wanted to have Bergoglio named his coadjutor, meaning he would have the automatic right of succession to the position of archbishop of Buenos Aires whenever the incumbent either died or retired. Quarracino feared that President Carlos Menem's government would try to block the appointment as a way of limiting the influence of the Church, since the Menem administration had been criticized by many bishops for its neoliberal economic policies that were thought to exacerbate poverty. Initially, Quarracino's plan ran into opposition in Rome—perhaps stoked by Menem allies with Vatican ties—but eventually he appealed directly to John Paul II and got his wish. Bergoglio was named coadjutor in June 1997, and when Quarracino died eight months later in February 1998, Bergoglio found himself the de facto leader of Argentina's Catholic Church and governor of one of the most complex archdioceses anywhere in the world. It was a position he held for the next 15 years.

THE BOY WHO HAD LEARNED his faith at the knee of his grandmother, Rosa, entered the College of Cardinals in February 2001, part of a bumper crop of 42 new princes of the Church. (For the record, he was not the superstar of the bunch, not even among the Latin Americans. That distinction belonged to the handsome, charismatic and multilingual Cardinal Óscar Andrés Rodríguez Maradiaga of Honduras.)

During that long run in Buenos Aires, Bergoglio developed a unique pastoral style and a vision for the Church. His approach can be characterized in terms of four pillars. First, Bergoglio emphasized personal closeness and service to the poor, while avoiding partisan political overtones. Second, he had a strong focus on popular faith and devotion as the best expression of the "sense of the faithful"—the religious concerns and needs of ordinary believers, especially as expressed in the great popular shrines and festivals of Latin American Catholicism. Third, he had a missionary vision for the Church, striving to change the traditionally passive Latin American way of faith into one that gets out into the street and meets people where they live. Fourth, he rejected clerical privilege, thereby breaking with the Latin American convention of seeing bishops as part of the ruling elite and expecting them to be deeply enmeshed in political affairs.

The heart of Bergoglio's "option for the poor"—the concern for the poor that is one of the basic principles of Catholicism—was found in places such as Villa 21, one of the nameless slums that surround Buenos Aires, in the parish of the Virgin of Caacupé. The parish is named for Mary as the patroness of Paraguay, because most of the residents are poor immigrants from that country. According to Fr. Juan Isasmendi, a Bergoglio protégé who lives and works in the parish, it's the sort of place where the future pope could fill his lungs with the "oxygen" he needed to think about what the Church ought to be.

Service in the *villas miserias* of Buenos Aires is a difficult calling. There are roughly 20 of these slums in the city, often just a block away from gleaming high-rise office towers and luxury apartment buildings. Bergoglio's pastoral revolution was to handpick a cadre of especially strong, dedicated priests to not just visit the *villas* but live and work there. The aim was to make the faith come alive, preaching and celebrating the sacraments while also turning the parish into a comprehensive social-service center by fighting drugs and violence, educating the young and taking care of the old, providing job training and even establishing community radio to give the people a voice. Bergoglio was determined to send a message to the *villas*: even if politics and the economy have forgotten about you, the Church hasn't.

Isasmendi was one priest chosen by Bergoglio to carry out this mission. Isasmendi said that Bergoglio didn't just approve the work—he was intimately involved at the level of detail, including decisions about which priests were picked to become what Isasmendi described as Bergoglio's "infantry" in the *villas*. "He told me he wanted to send me to the Virgin of Caacupé to work with Fr. Pepe," Isasmendi said. "I started talking about something different, just to buy myself some time to think. Bergoglio answered my questions, but he kept coming back to, 'OK, yeah, but are you going to Caacupé?' He did that three times in about 20 minutes, always saying that I [was needed] there. He can be incredibly bullheaded."

Isasmendi added that Bergoglio was so well informed that it sometimes made him hard to deal with. "You couldn't just feed him a line of crap, because he'd see right through it," he said. "You couldn't just say, 'Everything's fine, the parish is going great,' because before long he'd ask a pointed question that made it crystal clear he knew perfectly well what was going on." (When I visited Isasmendi's parish in April 2013, I stopped a woman at random and asked if she had ever met Bergoglio. She scuttled into her tiny shack made of tin and wood, emerging with two prized photos. One showed him as a young auxiliary bishop with her family in the early 1990s and another showed him as a cardinal confirming two of her cousins.)

IN 2007 POPE BENEDICT XVI visited Brazil. To coincide with the visit, the Latin American bishops published their "Aparecida

Document." Bergoglio was the document's lead author and editor, by all accounts pouring everything he had into it. The top note of the document described a great "permanent mission," calling the Church to reach out to all the peoples of the continent, especially the poor and those at society's margins. It called on Latin American Catholics to have a "missionary disciples' outlook on reality," meaning not that of a power broker or a bureaucrat but someone striving to make the Church relevant to a hurting and frequently confused world. The document stressed the need for Latin American Catholics to experience a personal conversion to Jesus Christ, as opposed to going through the motions on the basis of tradition or simply being born into the faith. One crucial line read, "The Church is called upon to go out of itself and go to the periphery, which is not only geographical, but also existential: where there is sin, pain, injustice, ignorance and religious indifference, where there is human misery."

Bergoglio's record in Buenos Aires was not spotless. For instance, vocations to the priesthood fell on his watch, despite the fact that they were up in some other dioceses in Argentina. In 2012 the archdiocese of Buenos Aires ordained just 12 new priests, as opposed to 40 to 50 per year, at the time that Bergoglio took over. Certain conservatives groused that he was too committed to the social gospel and not enough to proclaiming the faith. Some liberals saw him as an enemy of liberation theology and social emancipation. Others complained that Bergoglio could come off as inscrutable and too political. Those who watched him in action during that time frequently remark, "I never knew what he was really thinking . . . he is a Jesuit, you know."

THE TERM "CONCLAVE" comes from two Latin words meaning "with a key," referring to the custom of locking the cardinals inside the Sistine Chapel until they pick a pope. Bergoglio's previous shot at walking out of that storied ritual as the winner was in April 2005, following the death of John Paul II. On top of his reputation as a strong manager and ardent missionary, at 68 years old, Bergoglio was the perfect age for papal candidacy. But Bergoglio was not the front-runner—that title belonged to German cardinal Joseph Ratzinger, even though he was considered a lightning rod because of his reputation as an archconservative. The anti-Ratzinger forces, though, included moderates who knew they couldn't elect one of their own but wanted someone closer to the center, as well as "globalists" who wanted to break the European monopoly on the papacy once and for all. For both camps, Bergoglio served their purposes perfectly.

Like politics everywhere, the run-up to a papal election is not for the faint of heart. If someone pops up as a potential candidate, the knives come out and the rumor mill goes into overdrive about potential skeletons in closets. Bergoglio's candidacy seemed serious enough for Horacio Verbitsky, a prominent left-wing Argentine journalist and longtime critic of Bergoglio, to bring up the case of Franz Jalics and Orlando Yorio in a book, *El Silencio: De Paulo VI a Bergoglio. Las relaciones secretas de la Iglesia con la ESMA*, accusing Bergoglio of acting in complicity with the military junta in Argentina.

What no one realized at the time, though, was that the tidal wave of grief and acclaim for John Paul II that washed through Rome on the occasion of his death led to a "funeral effect" on the choice of a new pope.

John Paul II was seen in the flesh by more people than any other human being who ever lived. He regularly drew millions when he traveled, including 4.5 to 5 million people in Manila in 1995 for World Youth Day and a total of 10 million at various stops in Mexico in 1979. Therefore, many people were expected to pay their respects to John Paul as his body lay in state in St. Peter's Basilica and to attend the funeral mass in St. Peter's Square. What was a surprise was just how many mourners showed up—by some estimates, as many as 5 million in the week after the pope's death until his funeral—and how raw and deep their emotions were.

By the time the doors of St. Peter's were closed for the last time, some pilgrims had waited up to 16 hours just to spend a few fleeting seconds beside John Paul's body. The crowd was a fascinating demographic mix that included the elderly, some of them among the most faithful Roman Catholics of all, and whose hearts were breaking at the loss of a pope who had been their moral compass for more than a quarter-century; couples who were drawn by a sense that, even in death, John Paul could somehow make a difference in their lives and the lives of their children, nudging them toward the good in the world; and the young, tens of thousands of them, driven by a deep awareness that this was *their* pope, a man who loved youth, who believed in youth and who sacrificed for young people as few adult figures of any era ever had. Together, these mourners formed an impromptu city-within-a-city in the blocks around St. Peter's Square, braving the cold in sleeping bags, maintaining an air of reverence as Vatican loudspeakers repeatedly played hymns and litanies to the saints.

None of this was lost on the cardinals. The public response made continuity with John Paul II the dominant voting issue. In that context, more and more cardinals looked to the figure who had been John Paul's right-hand man for almost 20 years, the intellectual architect of his papacy as well as the prelate who presided masterfully over the funeral rites and other public events of the interregnum period. In the end, Ratzinger was elected in just four quick ballots to become Pope Benedict XVI. Bergoglio was the de facto runner-up, by some accounts attracting as many as 40 of 115 votes in the early stages but eventually losing in a landslide.

By the time of the 2013 conclave, following the resignation of Benedict, many observers felt that Bergoglio's moment had passed. Not only was he 76, but he had been president of the bishops' conference in Argentina in 2010 when it became the first Latin American nation to legalize same-sex marriage. His performance at the time had left almost no one satisfied, with conservatives accusing him of being too soft and liberals offended that he challenged the measure at all. This time, however, the stars aligned in the lead-up to the conclave to alter Bergoglio's prospects for the better.

For one thing, there was no funeral effect in 2013. Because the election followed the resignation of a pope rather than his death, there was no eruption of grief in the streets of Rome, no round-the-clock tributes on television, no cycle of largely laudatory obituaries. Whether intentionally or not, by stepping aside while he was still alive, Benedict XVI cleared a psychological and political space in which cardinals could take a more balanced and even critical look at the papacy that had just ended.

As it turns out, many were indeed inclined to be critical. Their beef wasn't with Benedict's teaching—which most regarded as magnificent and destined to endure—and certainly not with the pontiff himself. Most cardinals regarded Benedict as a misunderstood and sympathetic figure, and many felt a degree of guilt for perhaps not coming to his aid with sufficient vigor when his papacy was beset by scandals. (In their daily meetings preceding the election, Cardinal Christoph Schönborn of Vienna, a Ratzinger protégé who had studied under the future pope in Regensburg, Germany, in the late 1970s, invited his fellow princes of the Church to an examination of conscience about whether they had done enough to support him, and they took the plea seriously.)

What the cardinals were inclined to criticize, however, was the management performance of Benedict. They pointed to the disastrous Williamson affair of 2009, when the Vatican lifted the excommunications of four traditionalist bishops, including one, Richard Williamson, who was a Holocaust denier. (In 2009 a German court fined Williamson after he appeared on a Swedish television program expressing his belief that only 200,000 to 300,000 Jews died in Nazi concentration camps, "none of them in gas chambers.") The backlash against Williamson created a tempest so fierce that Benedict was compelled to send a personal letter to the world's bishops apologizing for how it had been handled. The cardinals also cited the bungled Vatican response to the new wave of sexual abuse scandals that erupted in Europe in 2009 and 2010, when tone-deaf comments from senior officials in Rome created impressions of arrogance and denial. They also pointed to a series of financial scandals, including accusations of money laundering at the Vatican Bank that temporarily led to credit card services being frozen at the Vatican museums and post office, as well as criminal probes of several key officials. Above all, they were appalled by the tawdry Vatican leaks mess, which featured a stream of supposedly confidential documents ending up in the press. As it dragged on, "Vatileaks" created the appearance of infighting and chaos within the corridors of power and ended with the surreal arrest of the pope's own butler, Paolo Gabriele, who confessed to stealing the documents and was sentenced to 18 months' incarceration. Two months into his term, he was pardoned by Benedict and is now free.

If continuity was the driving issue in 2005, eight years later it had become discontinuity. The 115 cardinals who filed into the Sistine Chapel in March 2013 wanted a clear break, making it the most anti-establishment papal election of the past 100 years. As a result, while the pre-election dynamics of 2005 helped the front-runner, this time they doomed him.

The man in pole position in 2013 was Cardinal Angelo Scola of Milan, whose victory was considered such a lock by many Italians that when the white smoke began to pour out of the chimney above the Sistine Chapel, the Italian bishops' conference prematurely released an e-mail congratulating Scola on his election. In retrospect, however, and from the cardinals' comments afterward, it was clear that no Italian was destined to end up on the throne of St. Peter that year.

Instead, the cardinals were in a mood to elect an outsider, someone not tainted by association with the recent Vatican regime and who had a track record as a strong leader of a major archdiocese. As a bonus, they were in the market for someone perceived to have unassailable personal integrity, ideally someone who could also put a face on the burgeoning Catholic population outside the West. As they looked around, it occurred to many that they had kicked the tires on just such a candidate eight years ago. He was still there, with the same quali- ties that now seemed even more attractive. If anything, Jorge Mario Bergoglio's advanced age may have helped; some cardinals recognized they were rolling the dice, but drew consolation from the thought that they wouldn't be stuck with the results forever.

The stage was set for the debut of a pope from "the end of the earth," who would soon reveal himself to be a man on a mission.

WHEN JORGE MARIO BERGOGLIO celebrated his first mass as Pope Francis in St. Peter's Square on Palm Sunday 2013, it wasn't a luminary whom he chose to quote in the first of countless ad-lib addi- tions to his prepared texts. Instead, he chose the words of his paternal grandmother, Rosa. Francis often cites her, weaving her into the folksy improvisational flourishes that have become a trademark of his public rhetoric. On that Sunday, he talked about her insight into the fleeting nature of wealth, that "a burial shroud doesn't have pockets."

Perhaps the deepest imprint Rosa left on Francis is the idea that faith in a loving God is bound up with compassion and mercy, and that the rules of religion are meant to serve people rather than the other way around. At some point in her extraordinary life, Rosa Margarita Vasallo di Bergoglio wrote a note for Jorge Mario, Maria Elena and her other descendants—words that in 2010 Cardinal Bergoglio revealed he keeps in his breviary, the two-volume book priests use for their daily prayers. The note read: "May my grandchildren, to whom I have given my whole heart, have a long and happy life. But if pain, sickness or loss of a loved one should fill them with sadness, may they remember that one breath taken at the Tabernacle, where the greatest and august martyr is present, and one glance at Mary at the foot of the cross, will act like a balm that is able to heal the deepest and most painful wounds."

When the cardinals elected Bergoglio to the papacy, they knew they were entrusting the Church to a capable manager, someone who would make transparency and accountability in governance a priority. They also knew they were choosing one of their own, a local bishop who felt the same frustration with a bloated Vatican bureaucracy and had the same sense that seasoned bishops from around the world ought to have a greater voice in running the show than office-bound mandarins in Rome. The cardinals laid out a detailed program of change during their daily meetings in the run-up to the election, and they felt confident that Bergoglio had listened and would act.

What those cardinals didn't quite grasp, however, was that they weren't just electing a CEO who would make the Vatican's trains run on time. They were also electing Rosa's grandson, a believer who derived from her the lesson that real faith is more about compassion than rigidity, more about seeing good in others than finding fault, and that rhetoric is hollow if not backed by action. The cardinals thought they were electing a manager, perhaps a missionary, and what they got in the bargain was the Pope of Mercy.

The Francis mission was under way.

2

Moderate to an Extreme

MANY YEARS AGO, AT A BOOKSHOP in Rome, I attended a small talk by a senior Vatican official, a man who is today a member of the College of Cardinals. Toward the end he took some questions, and an elderly Italian woman rose to say that she was divorced and had remarried outside the Church, which technically disqualified her from receiving communion at Sunday mass. But her pastor had quietly told her it would be all right to come forward at mass to receive the sacrament. She wanted to know from this Vatican official if that was OK.

"Let me answer first as an official of the Holy See," he said, using the technical term for the Vatican as the seat of government in the Catholic Church. "At that level, the answer is clear. The law of the Church says that if you are in an irregular situation, then you are excluded from holy communion.

"Now let me answer as a pastor," he continued. "I can't presume to judge your conscience or what's in your heart, and so I can't make a decision about how that law should apply in your specific situation. You have to make that decision in conscience, with the advice of your own pastor."

In a nutshell, that's the difference between law in Catholicism, which is generally sweeping and firm, and how it's applied, which can leave room for tremendous nuance and flexibility—depending, of course, on who's doing the applying.

Officially, the Church teaches that marriage is between a man and a woman and hence gay marriage is wrong. But what does that doctrine mean for the concrete decisions Catholic institutions have to make about their interactions with same-sex couples? Let's say a same-sex couple has a child in a Catholic school, and the school is holding a mass for families. Does the school's principal quietly discourage the same-sex couple from coming, on the grounds that their presence might risk confusion about where the Church stands? Or are they welcomed with open arms, on the grounds that some contact with the faith is better than none at all? Both options are fully consistent with the teaching, but the different applications create two very different senses of what the Church is all about.

By pushing Catholicism toward more generous modes of pastoral application, Pope Francis can change the Church significantly without altering a single comma in the catechism, its official compendium of teaching. That's why the Catholic street regards this pope as a genuine change agent. Most Catholics honestly don't expect the Church to overhaul its teaching, understanding that the weight of tradition in Catholicism is too strong to make that realistic. Instead, what they see is a Church that not long ago seemed to be growing more rigid, all of a sudden loosening up, embracing a more merciful and understanding attitude toward those who don't share its ideas. In multiple ways, from the leaders he's appointing to the way he's reaching out to those outside the Catholic fold, Pope Francis is proving to be moderate in the extreme.

IT'S A BASIC LAW of corporate management that personnel is policy, meaning that the kinds of people appointed to key positions reveal the priorities and direction of the institution. Given the deference traditionally afforded to clergy, especially bishops, in the Catholic Church, it's even truer that the people a pope names to key jobs is the best bellwether of where he wants the Church to go. In that regard, there's probably no better embodiment of Francis's program than Cardinal Oscar Andrés Rodríguez Maradiaga of Tegucigalpa, Honduras. He was once tipped to be the next pope, but his career in Catholicism had taken a nose-dive and seemed all but finished prior to Francis's election.

Rodríguez had a cosmopolitan upbringing, learning to speak English, German, French, Italian and Portuguese in addition to his native Spanish. Although he dreamed of playing in an orchestra and becoming a pilot, he felt the tug of the priesthood and eventually joined the Salesians in 1961.

The Salesian religious order has a reputation for both loyalty and getting things done at the parish level, and many power brokers in Catholicism have emerged from its ranks. Rodríguez studied theology in Rome and psychology in Innsbruck, Austria. When he returned to Honduras in 1978, he was named an auxiliary bishop of Tegucigalpa at the tender age of 35 and took over the top job as archbishop in 1993. He became a cardinal in 2001 at just 58 years old, making him one of the youngest eminences in the world.

Rodríguez emerged as the attractive, charismatic face of a resurgent Latin American faith. He managed to more than quadruple the number of Honduran men training to be Catholic priests, from 40 in 1989 to 170 in 2007. As president of the Latin American Episcopal Conference from 1995 to 1999, he became a champion of Catholic social teaching and an acerbic critic of the injustices he believed had been imposed on the continent's people by a neoliberal global economic system. He also became a key mediator between adherents of Latin America's liberation theology movement—which sought to place the Catholic Church on the side of the poor—and the continent's traditional and affluent Catholic elite.

"Rodríguez could be a firebrand when he wanted to, hanging out with the *campesinos*," said one Honduran observer in the late 1990s, referring to peasant farmers, "but he could also be a 1930s-era cardinal hobnobbing with the rich and famous."

Rodríguez certainly captured his countrymen's trust. In 1993 a victim of military abuse in the 1980s came forward to denounce the Honduran secret police. A reform government under Carlos Roberto Reina created an independent commission, and Rodríguez was asked to chair it. While the members agreed the secret police had to be abolished, it wasn't clear who would lead a reformed police agency. In 1997, while in Houston for dental surgery, Rodríguez stopped by a parish to say mass and was stunned when someone handed him a Honduran newspaper carrying the headline that he had been appointed police chief! He politely declined the position, but the story illustrates the extent to which Hondurans had come to see him as a leader.

Rodríguez's star began to dim as early as 2001, when he was first inducted into the College of Cardinals. Not long afterward, Pope John Paul II traveled to Latin America, bringing his freshly minted Honduran cardinal in tow. Some felt Rodríguez deliberately overshadowed the Polish pontiff, giving impromptu press conferences in multiple languages. Some Church veterans grumbled that the upstart seemed to be "running for pope." Conservatives also began raising questions about Rodríguez's theological pedigree, noting that he studied moral theology under a German named Bernard Häring, whose liberal views on sexual morality were not in favor during the John Paul and Benedict years.

In 2002 Rodríguez set off a tempest in the U.S. by comparing the "fury" of the American media's coverage of Catholic Church sexual abuse scandals to the persecution inflicted by Roman emperors Nero and Diocletian, as well as to the demonic rules of both Hitler and Stalin. Describing one media mogul as anti-Catholic and several newspapers as acting in "persecution against the Church," he even suggested that their obsession with the scandals was a way to distract attention from the Israeli-Palestinian conflict, hinting that it reflected the influence of a Jewish lobby. His comments brought protests from both sexual abuse victims and the Jewish Anti-Defamation League. Rodríguez said that his intent was to draw attention to the suffering of people in the developing world, not to play down the gravity of the abuse crisis, but that didn't erase the impression of a leader with a tendency to put his foot in his mouth.

In the years to come, there was recurrent whisper that Rodríguez's rhetoric in defense of the poor wasn't matched by a command of policy details, especially in regard to his own country. When the left-of-center Manuel Zelaya became Honduran president in 2006, Rodríguez seemed to support the new leader but later became critical, claiming that Zelaya was becoming radicalized by Venezuela's Hugo Chavez. After the Honduran military seized power in June 2009, Rodríguez at first remained silent, then read a statement on national television that seemed to bless the action. He eventually backpedaled, insisting that supporting the coup was merely a way to avoid bloodshed.

In 2007 Rodríguez was elected president of Caritas Internationalis, a Rome-based international federation of 164 Catholic charitable organizations. In early 2011, Lesley-Anne Knight, a Zimbabwe-born laywoman who served as the organization's secretary-general, was denied permission by the Secretariat of State to stand for a second term. Several senior officials in Catholic charitable groups told reporters they regarded the move as payback for an unacceptable coziness between Caritas and secular nongovernmental organizations, some of which provided birth control and other reproductive services in contradiction of Catholic teaching. A year later, the Vatican decreed a sweeping set of new statutes for Caritas, imposing tighter controls by bishops over the activities of Catholic charities and requiring senior officials to swear loyalty oaths vowing to uphold Catholic principles.

Caritas officials and members assumed Rodríguez could mount a defense, in part because the cardinal secretary of state at the time, Italian Tarcisio Bertone, was a fellow Salesian. Rodríguez first tried to save Knight and then to stave off the new rules, and in both cases he failed. As one American in the Vatican phrased it, "You can put a fork in his career, because it's done."

That history explains why, among Catholic insiders, the most convincing proof of the new winds blowing in the Church under Pope Francis's lead isn't via his celebrated catchphrases like "God is not a Catholic," nor his gestures such as choosing not to live in the papal apartment. Rather, it's the rehabilitation of Óscar Andrés Rodríguez Maradiaga, who has gone from someone whose entrance into Roman salons might have triggered an embarrassed silence, to the second-most-powerful man in Roman Catholicism. He's virtually the vice-pope, because his politics line up with the pontiff's and perhaps because Francis sympathizes with the uneven treatment Rodríguez has received from Rome.

One flabbergasted Vatican official captured the reaction in April 2013, when Francis appointed the Honduran as the coordinator of a new and all-powerful Council of Cardinals. "Dear God," the official said, "Oscar is back!"

RODRÍGUEZ MARADIAGA IS NOT the only out-of-favor moderate whose career has experienced a renaissance under Pope Francis. Pietro Parolin is the son of a hardware store owner in the Vicenza province of northern Italy. He grew up absorbing the concern for workers and social justice that permeated post–World War II Italian Catholicism. He eventually entered the Vatican's diplomatic service and was posted to embassies in Mexico and Nigeria before returning to Italy in 2002 to become the Vatican's deputy foreign minister. For the next seven years, Parolin was the real brains of the Secretariat of State and someone who got things done. He was a quietly moderate voice during an era of increasing vigilance about "Catholic identity."

In 2009 there was a perceived falling-out between Parolin and Bertone, the secretary of state under Benedict XVI. The circumstances remain murky, but the upshot was that Parolin was sent packing to be the pope's new ambassador to Venezuela. He distinguished himself there in his relations with the irascible Hugo Chávez and his aplomb during the transition to a post-Chávez government, becoming a trusted broker for both the ferocious anti-Chávez opposition and hard-core Venezuelan socialists. Parolin's exile ended under Francis, when he was called back to Rome in August 2013 to take over as the new pope's top diplomat.

German cardinal Walter Kasper was another once-rising star of the Catholic Church and considered one of the few theological minds at senior levels who could hold an intellectual candle to Joseph Ratzinger, the man who became Pope Benedict XVI. In 1999 Kasper was named the No. 2 official at the Pontifical Council for Promoting Christian Unity, the Vatican's department for relations with other Christian denominations, and eventually took the top job in 2001. He also became head of the Vatican's Commission for Religious Relations with Jews. As the years went on, Kasper's moderate and open stance seemed increasingly out of sync with the growing concern about maintaining the integrity of Church teaching vis-à-vis the pressures of secularism. This point of difference was crystallized in the early 2000s when Kasper and Ratzinger debated each another in a series of magazine articles about which comes first: the universal church, which was Ratzinger's position, or the local church, which Kasper prioritized, as it appealed to his instinct for flexibility and decentralization.

More and more, Kasper found himself frozen out of the decision-making loop. In 2009 Benedict's team decided to lift the excommunications of four traditionalist Catholic bishops, including Holocaust-denier

Richard Williamson. Kasper was never consulted, even though he was the one who would have to explain the decision to the Jewish world. He made no secret of his unhappiness, both with the decision itself and the way it was presented.

By the time 77-year-old Kasper stepped down from his Vatican posts in 2010, already two years past the normal retirement age, he had become something of an afterthought. But Francis pulled another surprise. When the pope wanted someone to set the stage for an all-important meeting of cardinals in February 2014 to discuss issues relating to the family, he chose Kasper to give the opening address. The pontiff knew full well what he was likely to get, because in 1993 Kasper joined two other German prelates—Karl Lehmann of Mainz and Oskar Saier of Freiburg—in publishing a pastoral letter offering guidelines for cases in which divorced and remarried persons could be admitted to the sacraments. Although a 1994 document released by the Vatican's doctrine office (headed by Ratzinger) shot the ideas in the pastoral letter down, the contrast between the two texts in many ways still frames the terms of debate in the Church. By selecting Kasper to give that speech, Francis not only rehabilitated Kasper's reform position, but he gave the German intellectual a new lease on life. Kasper has since published his February address in book form and has become sought after for media interviews and on the lecture circuit.

Although these cases are different, Rodríguez, Parolin and Kasper were all considered too moderate for senior leadership positions in the John Paul II and Benedict XVI years, when the top papal priority was Catholic identity.

While no one questioned their loyalty to the papacy or to Church doctrine, the sense was that their brand of engaged and adaptive Catholicism had run its course in the period after the Second Vatican Council. By the 1990s, the most serious perceived threat to the faith had become secularization—the fear that non-religious culture was pressuring Catholicism to water down its beliefs. In response to that pressure, both John Paul II and Benedict XVI came to believe that the Church needed a new brand of leadership, one unafraid to assert boldly the truth of traditional Catholic teaching.

American Catholic writer George Weigel coined the term "evangelical Catholicism" for this new ethos, defined by a strong defense of Catholic identity, including the Church's traditional sources of authority, and a robust public expression of Catholic teachings and practices. The evangelical wave reached an apex under John Paul II and Benedict XVI, as the Vatican attempted to rein in dissident theologians by appointing strong "Catholic identity" bishops such as cardinals Francis George in Chicago and Carlo Caffarra in Bologna, and through papal sponsorship of conservative Catholic movements such as Opus Dei and the Neocatechumenate, both originating in Spain with a primary focus on gathering enthusiastic and devout laypeople. It also found expression in papal encouragement of traditional liturgical practices such as eucharistic adoration; the practice of praying before a consecrated host believed to be the body and blood of Christ; and also communion, in which wafers are placed on the tongue, rather than the more common recent practice of receiving it in the hand. They may seem like small points, but they became markers for larger theological and political trends.

At the grass roots, there have been multiple eruptions of evangelical Catholic energy, such as Communion and Liberation meetings in Rimini, Italy, which annually draw more than 700,000 Catholics committed to challenging secularism; and World Youth Day, an international Catholic youth festival centered on the pope, which is one part liturgy and one part rock festival and routinely draws crowds in excess of 1 million. The expansion of evangelical Catholic media and an ever-growing host of Catholic blogs reflect this trend, as does the proliferation of Catholic schools and colleges characterized by biblical fervor. Former Domino's pizza magnate Tom Monaghan has built an entire Florida town, Ave Maria, which might be described as the world's first planned evangelical Catholic community.

Not so long ago, this evangelical Catholic push seemed irresistible, consigning the likes of Rodríguez Maradiaga and Kasper to the margins of the circles shaping Catholicism's future. It was not immediately obvious, not even to some of the cardinals who elected him to the papacy, that Jorge Mario Bergoglio would be the man to apply the brakes to this freight train. In the eyes of many observers, especially those who didn't know him well, Bergoglio's reputation before March 2013 was as a fairly conventional conservative, not someone inclined to steer Catholicism back toward the theological and political center.

IN THE EARLY HOURS of March 14, 2013, I stood on a television platform in Rome after the lights had finally gone out following a long night of broadcasting the news of the election of a new pope. Next to me was a well-known Jesuit priest and media commentator who, like many of his post-Vatican-II-era Jesuit colleagues, identified with liberal positions on most Church matters. As friends, I asked what he made of the election of history's first Jesuit pope.

"Watch out," my friend said. "This guy is a John Paul II bishop," by which he meant a strong conservative. "It wouldn't surprise me if the cardinals elected him to finish the crackdown on the Jesuits that John Paul II started."

His reference was to a controversial episode in 1981, when a legendary Jesuit superior, a Basque named Fr. Pedro Arrupe—a man who had lived through the atomic destruction of Hiroshima while serving in Japan in 1945 and who went on to harbor a lifelong sympathy for suffering people of all stripes, making him an early friend of liberation theology—suffered a stroke and announced his intention to resign. Bypassing the order's constitutions, John Paul II appointed his own delegate to govern the order until they could elect new leadership, which was widely seen as a warning that the Jesuits needed to find someone more to Rome's liking—that is, more evangelical and less given to resisting papal authority.

The man they eventually chose, Dutch Fr. Peter-Hans Kolvenbach, became known for his ability to mediate the tensions between the Vatican and his own order, but the underlying clash of cultures was never really resolved. One wing of the Jesuits always feared someone would come along to complete the unfinished business from 1981 and another has been eager for it to happen.

That night, my left-leaning Jesuit friend—who has since gone on to become a cheerleader for the new pope—assumed Bergoglio was in the other camp for three primary reasons. The first was that while he served as a Jesuit official in Argentina during the 1970s, Bergoglio had appeared to be close to the country's military junta and on the conservative side of debates over liberation theology. Next, he had been in a sort of Jesuit deep freeze until 1992, when John Paul II revived his career by making him an auxiliary bishop of Buenos Aires. Without that act, Bergoglio likely would never have become archbishop (and thus wouldn't have been in a position to be taken seriously as a papal candidate). Finally, in 2010 Bergoglio clashed with the left-of-center Kirchner Argentine government, after it became the first Latin American nation to legalize gay marriage. Bergoglio later emerged as the leader of the conservative moral opposition to legalization.

But a closer examination reveals that each episode gave a false impression of where Bergoglio stood.

FROM 1973 TO 1979, Bergoglio was the provincial superior, essentially the national leader, of Argentina's Jesuits. During that time he was neither an outspoken critic of, nor an apologist for, the country's military government.

"There's almost no record of anything he either said or wrote during that period, either in favor of the regime or against it," Argentine historian Roberto Bosca said in a 2013 interview. "Bergoglio was not really a church authority back then," Bosca went on. "He wasn't a bishop yet in Buenos Aires; he was simply the regional superior of a religious order. The nature of his job didn't lend itself to taking positions for or against the government. It was not a public position, and there's little reason why the government would have listened had he said anything, because he wasn't a high enough authority to be taken seriously. His way of coping with the regime was more or less the way most people in Argentina handled it, which is they still went to work and tried to get on with their lives."

During his term as provincial superior, Bergoglio was alarmed by certain progressive energies pushing the order toward aggressive confrontation with the country's ruling elites. Yet Bosca insists the future pope was never opposed to Latin America's liberation theology, which emphasized solidarity with the poor. Bergoglio accepted the premise of liberation theology but in a non–ideological fashion. His insistence on moving talented young priests into the *villas miserias* reflected that instinct.

If Bergoglio was opposed to anything in that era, Bosca said, it was giving a Catholic blessing to any possible armed Marxist insurgency. That was more than just a theoretical possibility in Argentina, in light of the Montoneros, a left-wing guerrilla movement that drew support from sectors of Catholic opinion most influenced by liberation theology. "There were a few priests in Argentina who joined the Montoneros and became guerrilla priests like Camilo Torres in Colombia," Bosca said. (Torres was a radical priest who joined Colombia's National Liberation Army and was killed in an ambush on a military patrol in 1966. He inspired a number of other progressive Latin American priests to align themselves with armed leftist movements.)

As the military regime in Argentina wore on, the Montoneros

became less a resistance movement and more a leftist urban terror group, akin to the Red Brigades in Europe. One mid-1980s estimate held the Montoneros responsible for approximately 6,000 deaths spread among the military, police and civilian populations during the previous decade.

"[Bergoglio] was in opposition to the Montoneros," Bosca said. "It wasn't opposition to liberation theology in itself, or the option for the poor," he explained.

POPE JOHN PAUL II CLEARLY LIKED what he saw in Bergoglio, whom he'd made an auxiliary bishop of Buenos Aires and later its coadjutor bishop. John Paul also elevated Bergoglio to the College of Cardinals in 2001, and in a further display of esteem awarded him the Roman church of St. Robert Bellarmine as his titular parish, named for the great 16th- and 17th-century Jesuit saint. John Paul was not the monochromatic conservative he was sometimes portrayed as during the course of his almost 27-year papacy, and his patronage of Bergoglio is a clear example of his more nuanced position. The Argentine prelate was not a stereotypical "John Paul bishop" either, meaning a conservative primarily interested in imposing discipline and holding the line on doctrinal questions.

After Francis's election, one of the first journalists to debunk the myth of the ideologically conservative new pontiff was Elisabetta Piqué. A longtime Rome correspondent for Argentina's *La Nacion*, Piqué was well positioned to have a read on Bergoglio as a moderate, not only through her reporting but also her personal life. When she and a fellow member of the Roman press corps got married and had a child, it was a second marriage for each, so the Church officially viewed their relationship as an "irregular union." Despite this, Bergoglio happily agreed to baptize their child. (His name, by the way, is Juan Pablo, in honor of Pope John Paul II.)

Piqué's situation may have been one that Bergoglio had in mind in 2012 when he angrily denounced priests who refuse to baptize children born out of wedlock, accusing those clergy of "hijacking" the sacrament and using rigid rules to preserve their own control over people's lives. Such priests, Bergoglio said, are likely to "drive God's people away from salvation." He likened them to the Pharisees, reminding these priests that Jesus regularly condemned the Pharisees while spending his time with those they regarded as sinners.

There were other ways that Bergoglio showed his non-conservative side. Devotees of the old Latin mass, usually reliable bellwethers of traditionalist sentiment in Catholicism, didn't feel they had any friend in the Jesuit cardinal of Buenos Aires. One Argentine writer described Bergoglio as a "a sworn enemy of the Traditional Mass," claiming that the future pope had willfully "blocked" implementation of a 2007 edict from Benedict XVI that gave expanded permission for use of the old Latin liturgy. Traditionalists were also scandalized by Bergoglio's 2006 decision to accept a public blessing from a cohort of Evangelical and Protestant pastors, with some deeply conservative voices actually declaring that the archdiocese of Buenos Aires had no valid government because the occupant of the See was a heretic.

Bergoglio and John Paul II were in sync on many matters: the need to reach out to the poor, the importance of ecumenical and interfaith dialogue, and a desire for a more missionary and dynamic Church. But there were also significant differences between Bergoglio's application of the John Paul II impulse and the shape it was taking in Europe and North America. For Bergoglio, the John Paul II revolution was about engagement with the world, especially the marginalized, and not holding the line in an ideological struggle with secularism. That nuance may have been lost on some of the most enthusiastic partisans of John Paul II at the time, but it certainly hasn't been lost since Francis became pope.

WHEN THE NAME JORGE MARIO BERGOGLIO was announced to the world as the new pope, there wasn't a great deal of information readily available about him in English. What was easily findable was an incendiary comment from Bergoglio during Argentina's vexed debate over gay marriage in 2010. At the time, Bergoglio had written to monasteries in Buenos Aires to issue a call to arms against the bill to legalize gay marriage. In stark language, Bergoglio made his opposition clear. "Let's not be naive," Bergoglio wrote in a June 2010 letter to the Carmelite nuns of Buenos Aires, "we're not talking about a simple political battle. It is a destructive pretension against the plan of God. We are not talking about a mere bill, but rather a machination of the Father of Lies that seeks to confuse and deceive the children of God."

President Cristina Fernández de Kirchner, a woman with whom Bergoglio had a notoriously frosty relationship, fired back that Bergoglio's rhetoric was reminiscent of "medieval times and the Inquisition."

In fact, Argentine sources confirmed that Bergoglio wanted a face-saving compromise that would have avoided the nasty public fireworks. That version of events was verified by two senior Church officials in Argentina, both of whom worked with Bergoglio and took part in confidential discussions as the country's conference of bishops tried to shape its position. "Bergoglio supported civil unions," one of those officials said.

Guillermo Villarreal, a Catholic journalist in Argentina, said it was well known at the time that Bergoglio's moderate position was opposed by Archbishop Héctor Rubén Aguer of La Plata, the leader of the hawks. The difference was not over whether to oppose gay marriage but how ferociously to do so and whether there was room for a compromise on civil unions.

Villareal described the standoff over gay marriage as the only vote Bergoglio ever lost during his six years as president of the conference.

Behind the scenes, sources say, Bergoglio tried to avoid confrontation. One young Catholic had wanted to organize a public recitation of the rosary on the eve of the vote outside the legislature, knowing that supporters of gay marriage would also be there and that the prayer would be a provocation. He wrote to Bergoglio seeking advice, he said, and Bergoglio called him directly, suggesting they pray at home instead.

Fr. Jorge Oesterheld, who served as the spokesperson for the bishops' conference in Argentina for the six years Bergoglio was its president, suggested that Bergoglio went along with the harder line espoused by the majority of the bishops, regardless of his own instinct. "At that time, there were different views within the bishops' conference on how open the Church should be [to compromise]," Oesterheld said. "The cardinal went along with what the majority wanted. He didn't impose his own views. He never publicly expressed his own feelings on the matter, because he didn't want to seem to be undercutting the common position of the bishops."

In other words, the pattern held here too: beneath Bergoglio's seemingly hard-line conservative exterior was actually a strikingly moderate churchman, not only in regard to gay relationships but also in relation to how deferential he felt compelled to be to his fellow bishops.

POLITICAL LABELS are often an inexact fit for religion, and it's true for the Catholic Church. Whereas politics is generally a zero-sum game, in which one side wins and the other loses, in Catholicism seemingly disparate impulses are often blended together. As one example, is it true to say that the late Pope John Paul II was a conservative or a liberal? Simply put, there's no easy answer. John Paul was ferociously anti-communist and pro-life, framing his papacy as a contest against a "culture of death," and he insisted on reaffirming traditional doctrines such as the ban on women's ordination to the priesthood. Yet John Paul was also a passionate advocate of ecumenism and dialogue with other religions, often scandalizing the traditionalists in his own fold; he had positions on social justice issues such as income inequality, the environment and war and peace that placed him to the left not just of Republicans in the U.S. but most Democrats too. He clashed with both the Clinton administration over U.N. conferences on population control and the Bush administration over the war in Iraq. Truth be told, John Paul II was both conservative and liberal at the same time, depending on the issue at hand.

It's even more difficult to pin Francis down. Early on, liberals were cheered by much of his rhetoric, such as his famous "Who am I to judge?" comment about homosexuality, his rejection of imperial pomp and his insistence that "thinking with the Church" cannot simply mean parroting the positions of the hierarchy. For many liberals, the simple fact that conservatives seemed alarmed by Francis was enough to make them embrace him. At some point, however, those liberals will demand movement from rhetoric to policy, and on that front, many may be disappointed. He is hardly Che Guevara in a cassock—a pope who intends to make sweeping changes in Church teachings, such as the bans on abortion, gay marriage and contraception. His automatic reply every time he's asked about those issues is that he will uphold the positions of the Church because "I'm a son of the Church."

Yet for many on the right, it's also clear that this is not "their" man. The headline of an early essay about Francis by conservative Catholics Mario Palmaro and Alessandro Gnocchi, published in the right-wing Italian paper *Il Foglio*, made the point bluntly: "Why we don't like this pope."

Aside from his incendiary rhetoric on capitalism, Francis has also ruffled conservative opinion with his determination not be a cultural warrior, meaning he doesn't intend to use his bully pulpit primarily to fight political battles over sexual morality. He has little patience for a "smells and bells" approach to Catholic worship, the ornately classical rituals that utilize intense formality to conjure a sense of the otherworldliness of faith. Progressive-minded thinkers and activists in Catholicism, who not so long ago found doors closed in their faces, are suddenly back in good graces.

One example is the English priest Fr. Timothy Radcliffe, a former superior of the worldwide Dominican order. In his books and talks, Radcliffe has regularly advocated a more accepting view of homosexual relationships, arguing that sexual orientation should not disqualify anyone from the priesthood but homophobia certainly should. In recent years, though, he has had difficulty gaining entrée to some official venues; in 2011 the Vatican forced the cancellation of a talk Radcliffe was scheduled to give to the charity confederation Caritas. Shortly after Francis was elected to the papacy, however, he asked an aide to e-mail Radcliffe, addressing him as "dear brother," expressing admiration for his books and vowing that Radcliffe would be welcome on his watch. That open-door policy has not gone down well in conservative circles, where some see it as a de facto repudiation of their efforts over three decades to promote a less compromising concept of Catholic identity.

That leaves the Catholic middle as this pope's natural constituency: people who are generally content with Church teaching and tradition but tend to be generous in how it's applied. Adherents of the middle don't have a chip on their shoulder about the bishops or the pope, but they're also not inclined to shout "hosanna!" every time someone in leadership speaks; they're capable of being critical without being axiomatically hostile. They're hungry for reform but not so much for revolution. Mostly, these are people who regard Catholicism as a force for good in the world and who long for thoughtful, inspirational leaders who can lift up the whole gamut of Catholic thought and life rather than a selective version of Church teaching tailored to advance a specific political or theological agenda.

Rodríguez Maradiaga may be the most compelling example of the revival of the Church's moderate wing. Once ostracized, he is now a regular commentator in the media and on the lecture circuit, saying things publicly that he and others like him said only in private before. In an October 2013 speech in Miami, Rodríguez essentially called for a halt to what he saw as an over-emphasis on discipline and control from the top of the Church, a control that had been paramount before the Francis era. "Too many times [the Church] gives the impression of having too much certitude and too little doubt, freedom, dissension or dialogue," Rodríguez said. "No more excommunicating the world, then, or trying to solve the world's problems by returning to authoritarianism, rigidity and moralism, but instead keeping always the message of Jesus as her sole source of inspiration."

At a more concrete level, Rodríguez felt emboldened to say in an interview on the PBS program *Frontline* in February 2014 that he has no problem with gay priests, as long as they observe the rules of celibacy. "OK, if you want to live your vocation, if you believe that [and] you are not active sexually, you can continue, of course," Rodríguez said.

However natural Rodríguez may have tried to make his position sound, it contradicts official Vatican policy. In 2005 the Vatican's Congregation for Catholic Education issued a document addressed to Catholic seminaries. It held that men with "deep-seated homosexual tendencies" are ineligible for ordination to the priesthood, making it seem as though gays were about to be flushed out of the Catholic priesthood. In reality, no such thing happened, because moderates who run Catholic dioceses and religious orders spun the document to suit their circumstances, as Rodríguez later implied. They took "deep-seated tendencies" to mean sexual activity, not just orientation. Prior to Bergoglio's election, few people were willing to admit to such an interpretation; whereas under Francis, it has become easier to justify instances of what might be called casuistry: a subtle application of seemingly rigid norms.

Since beginning his papacy, Francis has made it clear that the moderates are back in business. In September 2013, just six months after his election, Francis removed Italian cardinal Mauro Piacenza from his position as prefect of the Vatican's Congregation for Clergy, a powerful department that oversees priestly life. Named to the position by Pope Benedict XVI in 2010, Piacenza is a disciple of the legendary Cardinal Giuseppe Siri of Genoa, a strong conservative candidate for pope in four conclaves (1958, 1963 and twice in 1978) who was famously dubbed "the pope never elected" by Italian journalist Benny Lai. Piacenza is cut in Siri's image, and when Francis took over the papacy, Piacenza was the strongest traditionalist holding a senior Vatican position. Francis's decision to move him to a much less politically powerful post at the Apostolic Penitentiary sent a clear signal.

That impression was compounded when Francis named Beniamino Stella as Piacenza's replacement. Seventy-two-year-old Stella's previous job had been running the Pontifical Ecclesiastical Academy, the Vatican's elite school for diplomats. Stella is seen as a classic product of the Vatican's diplomatic corps, an instinctive moderate who abhors ideological extremes and a churchman to whom dialogue with the outside world is a keen priority.

As it became clear to Italians that conservative hard-liners are out of favor under Francis, the removal of American cardinal Raymond Burke three months later made the same point to Americans. In December 2013 Francis removed the legendary traditionalist from the powerful Congregation for Bishops, replacing him with Cardinal Donald Wuerl of Washington, D.C., who sits in the political dead center of the American bishops' conference. The decision not only reinforced impressions of the political cast of Francis's papacy, it also permanently soured his relations with some sectors of the American Catholic right.

On the policy front, nowhere are the moderate energies Francis has let loose more clear than in the debate over divorced and remarried Catholics. Officially, the Catholic Church teaches that marriage is indissoluble, in keeping with Christ's injunction in scripture that "what God has joined together, let no one separate." The only way for a Catholic whose marriage has broken down to enter into another union in the eyes of the Church is to obtain an annulment, which is a declaration from a Church court that the first marriage never existed because it failed to meet one of the traditional tests of validity. (Those tests include "lack of canonical form," which usually means that the couple got married outside the Church; "insufficient use of reason," meaning that one of the parties didn't understand what was happening at the time because of illness or insanity; and psychological incapacity to consent to the obligations of marriage.)

Few Catholics pursue an annulment, because the procedure can be expensive and time-consuming, and sometimes because one of the partners refuses to go along. Some believe the whole thing is a sham, a legal fiction intended to provide cover for what amounts to "Catholic divorce."

Sheila Rauch Kennedy is the most celebrated example of that latter camp in the U.S. In 1979 she married Joseph Patrick Kennedy II, the eldest son of the late U.S. senator Robert F. Kennedy, and the couple had twin sons. They divorced in 1991, and Joseph Kennedy sought an annulment through the archdiocese of Boston in order to marry a former aide, Beth Kelly. (In the meantime, Kennedy and Kelly were married by civil authorities in 1993 while they waited for the Church's decision.) Kennedy eventually got his annulment, something Rauch found out only after the fact in 1996. She was outraged, convinced their marriage had been fully legitimate and that it was only Kennedy money and influence that had cajoled the Church into unilaterally declaring that their 12-year union never existed. An Episcopalian, Rauch wrote an incendiary book called *Shattered Faith: A Woman's Struggle to Stop the Catholic Church from Annulling Her Marriage* about her experience. She appealed to the Vatican directly and won in 2005, meaning that in the eyes of the Church her marriage is still legitimate, creating problems for Kennedy's Catholic practice.

Under Church rules, a Catholic who divorces and remarries without an annulment is barred from taking communion at mass and the other sacraments. With divorce still prevalent, the ranks of such Catholics have grown. This exclusion from the sacraments can be a source of anguish at the grass roots, and everyone knows that many pastors quietly counsel these folks to come forward for communion despite the rules. Periodically, pastors and bishops in various parts of the world have floated the idea of formally relaxing the ban, but before the election of Francis that hypothesis had always been firmly rejected in Rome.

On multiple occasions, Francis has signaled his personal openness to rethinking the rules. Asked about his views on divorced and remarried Catholics in July 2013, Francis said that the question needs study but that he personally believes that the present is a "kairos" for mercy, using an evocative Greek New Testament term that means a specially chosen moment in God's plan of salvation. He also invoked the example of the Eastern Orthodox churches, which sanction a second marriage under some circumstances. He convened a synod of bishops in fall 2014, and will do so again in 2015, to tackle the issue head-on.

The prospect of a change to the Catholic discipline on marriage has aroused widespread opposition. In the West, many bishops believe it is the wrong time to alter the stance on marriage, the idea being that if the Church appears to open the door to divorce, then it may face even more pressure to recognize same-sex unions. In Africa, many bishops believe that a change might weaken their efforts to break the grip of polygamy in their societies. Even cardinals are publicly arguing over the issue. In October 2013 then-archbishop Gerhard Müller, the Vatican's doctrinal czar, published a lengthy essay in *L'Osservatore Romano* arguing that no change is possible because Church teaching on the permanency of marriage is not open to question. In reply, Rodríguez Maradiaga shot back in a newspaper interview that Müller, who later became a cardinal, "is a German, and above all he's a German theology professor, so in his mentality there's only truth and falsehood. But I say, my brother, the world isn't like this, and you should be a little flexible when you hear other voices. That means not just listening and then saying no."

But it may not matter what these synods formally conclude. Francis may have already achieved the breakthrough he had in mind: to signal to pastors and other Church leaders around the world that he supports generosity and flexibility in how the teaching on marriage is applied. The broad trend in Catholicism will be to weave the divorced and remarried back into the Church's sacramental life, regardless of whether there's a formal policy change in Rome.

POPE FRANCIS IS PERHAPS BEST described as a moderate realist. He's obviously committed to classic Christian orthodoxy—for instance, defending the idea of the devil as a personal force of evil and often invoking Satan in his public rhetoric—yet those beliefs are always expressed in a balanced fashion and with a special emphasis on the poor and those at the margins of society.

In his 2010 book, *On Heaven and Earth,* presented as a dialogue between him and Argentine Rabbi Abraham Skorka, Bergoglio warned of the dangers of what he called "fundamentalism."

"This type of rigid religiosity is disguised with doctrines that claim to give justifications, but in reality deprive people of their freedom and do not allow them to grow as persons," Bergoglio wrote. "A large number end up living a double life." On that front, he had a simple message for clergy: "Better to be a good Christian than a bad priest."

In the same vein, the future pope expressed a healthy skepticism about claims of healings, revelations and visions, saying that God is not like FedEx, sending messages all the time. The real tests of supernatural phenomena, he believes, are "simplicity, humility and the absence of a spectacle"—otherwise we may be dealing with a business rather than the presence of the divine.

Perhaps the most compelling proof of his commitment to balance was the revelation in *On Heaven and Earth* that Bergoglio hadn't actually voted in elections in Argentina since the early 1960s, mostly as an expression of how important he thinks it is for the clergy to remain impartial. "I am father of all and I cannot be wrapped in a political flag," he wrote. (Voting is compulsory under Argentine law and refusal to vote can result in a fine, though that obligation ceases at age 70.)

By bringing this spirit of moderate realism to the papacy, Francis has given centrists in the Church a new lease on life. One good example is Cardinal Luis Antonio Tagle of Manila in the Philippines, who has quickly become known as the "Asian Francis." Only 57 years old, Tagle rejects ostentatious dress and manner, preferring to be called by his nickname, "Chito," rather than formal titles. He emphasizes the need for the Church to listen as much as it talks, and he exudes a slow-burn charisma. Before taking over in Manila in 2011, Tagle served as bishop of the smaller Philippine diocese of Imus, where he was famous for not owning a car, preferring to either walk or hop on one of the cheap minibuses known as jeepneys that working-class Filipinos use to get around. He was also renowned for inviting beggars in the square outside his cathedral to eat with him.

Like Francis, Tagle is a moderate who prefers compromise to fire and brimstone. "Many people have told me in the past that I'm not strong enough, that I don't condemn enough," Tagle said in a March 2014 interview with the *Boston Globe*. He added that the new pope's example has helped resolve any doubts he once felt. "Now I hear the pope saying, I'm a son of the Church, I know the teachings of the Church, but why should I condemn anyone?" Tagle said.

In the Philippines, the bitterly debated Reproductive Health Law, which requires the government to make contraception widely available, was passed last year despite the Church's vigorous opposition. Although Tagle took a clear stand against the bill, he was criticized by some for not pushing harder. When a Philippine bishop threatened the country's president with excommunication, Tagle didn't join the fray. When Catholic activists labeled backers of the law "Team Death," Tagle declined to put up attack-ad posters in Manila churches.

Tagle's moderate position on internal Church questions is also clear.

He has said that he's open to allowing Catholics who divorce and remarry without an annulment to receive communion and the other sacraments. "We have a principle we have to believe in," Tagle said, referring to the idea that marriage is for life. "But the openness comes on pastoral judgments you have to make in concrete situations, because no two cases are alike."

While evangelical Catholicism was the watchword of the John Paul II and Benedict XVI eras, moderate realism seems to be the new direction under Francis. It may not make for sweeping revolutions in doctrine, but at the level of application and tone, it has the potential to shape a very different kind of Catholic Church.

3

Dialogue
and Peace

MANY PEOPLE HAVE LEFT AN IMPRINT on the life of Jorge Mario Bergoglio, including his family members, his fellow Jesuits and other churchmen around the world. Perhaps the most consequential, however, is someone the pope has never even met. Giovanni di Pietro di Bernardone, better known as St. Francis, died more than 700 years before Bergoglio was born, but he is the most celebrated of all Christian saints, beloved for his hymns to "brother sun and sister moon," his preaching to the birds and his lifelong romance with "Lady Poverty." Bergoglio may be a Jesuit—St. Ignatius Loyola, the order's founder, is also a huge influence on the pontiff—but it's significant that we now have a Pope Francis, rather than a Pope Ignatius.

During a papal election, as a soon as a contender crosses the threshold of two thirds of the vote, the most senior cardinal under the age of 80 in the order of the bishops approaches the candidate and poses two questions. The first is "Do you accept your election?" From the moment the winner says yes, he becomes the pope. The next is "By what name will you be known?" The choice of a name is therefore the first act of any papacy, and in the case of Pope Francis it was a way of making a statement about the kind of leader he wanted to be.

Francis's commitment to the poor, his environmental streak and his emphasis on a Church that finds its home in the streets are values shared by the saint whose legacy he has embraced. The new pontiff's emergence as a "peace pope" should come as no surprise, because St. Francis has always been Christianity's premier apostle of peace.

Nothing captures that aspect of the saint's legacy better than the story of Francis and the sultan. In 1219, while the Fifth Crusade raged in the Middle East, Francis and his traveling companion, Brother Illuminato, headed for the Egyptian city of Damietta, which served as a gateway to the Holy Land and formed the front lines of the battle between the Christian crusaders and the armies of Muslim sultan Malik al-Kamil. Initially, Francis tried to persuade the Christian armies not to launch an assault on Damietta, predicting—correctly, as it turned out—that it would fail. When the Christians attacked anyway, Francis boldly walked across the battle lines unarmed and asked to be admitted to the sultan. His aim was to convert the Muslim leader to Christianity, and some sources suggest Francis expected to die as a martyr.

As the saint and the sultan conversed, however, they became impressed with each other and genuinely curious about the other's convictions. (Today their conversations are regarded as history's first Christian-Muslim dialogue.) Francis remained in the sultan's camp for more than 20 days, and when he left, al-Kamil gave him an ivory trumpet as a memento of their dialogue (it rests still in the crypt of the Basilica of San Francesco in Assisi, Italy). The "little brothers," as Francis called his followers, went on to serve as the custodians of the Christian sites in the region, having been directed by Francis to live peacefully among the Muslims and to respect their faith.

Although the dialogue between Francis and al-Kamil did not bring the Fifth Crusade to a halt, it became a symbol of the positive nature of interfaith encounters and the possibilities of peace. When the new pontiff presented himself to the world in March 2013 as Francis, it signaled his intent to walk the same path. Since coming to power, Pope Francis has pursued bold and often controversial peace initiatives at three distinct levels: within the divided Christian family; among the world's great religions; and in some of the bloodiest conflict zones on the planet.

IF ANYONE WERE SEEKING a natural partner for Pope Francis in the quest for peace among Christians, American televangelist Kenneth Copeland wouldn't be the first to come to mind. Usually seen in expensive tailored suits, with his hair slicked and coiffed, Copeland is an exponent of the Pentecostal "prosperity gospel," the idea that God rewards his faithful with riches—a position that seems at odds with Francis's vision of a "poor Church for the poor." Copeland has boasted of being a billionaire, and his Kenneth Copeland Ministries owns two private jets. A larger-than-life Texan, Copeland is one of those TV preachers given to bombast, shouting "hallelujah!" and thumping his Bible with relish. Although he's friendly to Catholics, many of his fellow Pentecostals see the "Church of Rome" as representative of everything that went wrong in Christianity once it abandoned the idea of *sola scriptura* ("the Bible alone") as the only reliable guide to belief.

Imagine the astonishment when in January 2014 Copeland presented a video message from Pope Francis to a massive annual minister's conference at the Pentecostal Eagle Mountain International Church in Fort Worth, Texas. The video had been recorded a week earlier, when an Anglican Evangelical bishop named Tony Palmer, who had become friends with Bergoglio in Argentina, visited the pontiff in Rome.

Speaking in Italian with subtitles, Francis told the Pentecostals that he wanted to send them a "spiritual hug." He conceded that divisions in Christianity are the result of "sins on everyone's part," and invited them to join him in a quest for unity. "God has begun the miracle of unity," Francis said, quoting Italian novelist Alessandro Manzoni.

The audience, which had seemed stunned at the beginning, rose at the end in a standing ovation. Because Francis had closed with his trademark request that his listeners pray for him, Copeland led the crowd in a round of Pentecostal-style praying in tongues, a sort of incomprehensible murmuring believed to be the language of the angels, with the babble of thousands of voices rising up throughout the hall. After the video became public, some Pentecostal and Evangelical bloggers derided the pope's rhetoric and blasted Copeland as a heretic. Many mainstream Christian leaders, however, described the outreach as stunning, especially given the suspicion some Pentecostals have long harbored that Catholicism might be the biblical "Whore of Babylon."

As a coda to the story, Copeland and a delegation of other Evangelical and Pentecostal leaders—including James and Betty Robison, co-hosts of the *Life Today* television program, and Bishop Tony Palmer—later traveled to Rome in June 2014 for a tête-à-tête with the pope, joining him for lunch at his residence, the Santa Marta, and talking about the prospects for closer relations. The exuberant mood was best captured when James Robison asked Pope Francis for a "high five" about the need for all Christians to develop a personal relationship with Jesus. Although the Pope didn't know what a high five was, once Palmer explained it, the pontiff willingly indulged. The symbolic picture of that moment of Catholic-Evangelical détente went viral.

For the first pope named Francis, it's no accident that his peace effort begins with trying to heal the historic divisions within Christianity, because Christians can hardly be agents of unity if they aren't seen to practice what they preach. It's not a policy Francis adopted after his election, but rather a natural instinct that reflects his life experience.

At first, the election of a Latin American pope was not greeted with enthusiasm among experts in ecumenism, as the push for a Christian reunion is called. Unlike their fellow prelates in Europe or North America, Catholic bishops in Latin America generally don't have much experience working with other Christians, because until recently the continent has been almost homogeneously Catholic. What experience they do have often isn't very positive. The rapid expansion of Evangelical and Pentecostal Christianity in Latin America during the last quarter of the 20th century resulted in the conversion of more people to Protestantism than in the century following the Protestant Reformation in Europe, with one study in the 1990s concluding that Catholicism was losing 8,000 people every day. Latin American bishops often came to see other Christians as a threat, derisively referring to them as followers of "sects."

Bergoglio, however, was always the exception to that rule, beginning with his enthusiasm for the great traditions of Eastern Christianity that developed within Orthodoxy. The future pope developed an affection for Eastern spirituality early in life, beginning at the age of 12 when he attended the Wilfrid Baron School of the Holy Angels in Buenos Aires. There, he fell under the spell of Fr. Stepan Chmil, a priest of the Ukrainian Greek Catholic Church, the largest of the 22 Eastern churches in full communion with Rome. (These churches originate in Eastern Orthodoxy and still follow Orthodox rituals and spirituality but recognize the pope as their leader.) While at the Baron school, Bergoglio rose hours before his classmates so he could attend mass with Chmil, who taught him how to worship in the elaborate Eastern style. Later, as the archbishop of Buenos Aires, Bergoglio petitioned the Vatican to have himself named the "ordinary," meaning the spiritual guide, of all the Eastern-rite Catholics in Argentina, since they had no local hierarchy of their own.

As archbishop, Bergoglio cultivated close ties with the Orthodox churches, attending Christmas mass every year at the Russian Orthodox

Annunciation Cathedral in Buenos Aires. (Because the Orthodox follow the Julian rather than the Gregorian calendar, their Christmas service is generally a week after the Catholic observance.) When Bergoglio organized a prayer for peace in the Middle East in his Buenos Aires cathedral in 2012, he not only invited Muslim and Jewish leaders but local Orthodox clergy too, insisting he had no right to present himself as the lone representative of the Christian world. (In a small gesture that spoke volumes to Orthodox leaders, when Francis celebrated his installation mass as pope, he distributed hosts dipped in the communion wine, an Orthodox practice generally not followed in Catholic liturgies.)

Bergoglio also changed the way Catholics and Protestants interacted in Latin America, developing a network of contacts in the Evangelical and Pentecostal worlds. One such close colleague is Luis Palau, Argentina's most famous Evangelical preacher, a man often described as "the Latin Billy Graham." At the time of Francis's election, Palau said, "I've met him several times, gone to his place, we've talked, we've prayed together. He builds bridges to other Christian groups, like Evangelical Christians, which is a high percentage in Latin America. He's a real friend."

One of the most notable moments of Bergoglio's 15-year run as archbishop came in June 2006, when he took part in a joint Evangelical and Catholic prayer service that drew 7,000 people to Buenos Aires's Luna Park stadium, a venue normally used for boxing matches. There, Bergoglio was joined by Italian Capuchin priest Fr. Raniero Cantalamessa, who served as preacher of the papal household under both popes John Paul II and Benedict XVI, as well as a constellation of Protestant clergy. (The preacher of the papal household is a cleric who leads the pope and other Vatican officials in a retreat each year for lent and preaches on certain special occasions, such as the pope's annual Good Friday liturgy.) During the service, Bergoglio knelt on the stage and allowed himself to be prayed over by some 20 Protestant clergy, including the president of the country's Evangelical federation and the head of the Pentecostal church in Argentina. The act led a handful of traditionalist Catholics in Argentina to protest on the grounds that Bergoglio was promoting religious relativism, the idea that one religion or brand of Christianity is just as good as another. Despite such criticisms, Francis's affection for Christians outside the Catholic fold remained undimmed.

FOR A SENSE OF THE OBSTACLES Francis faces in trying to put Christianity back together again, there's no better setting than the Basilica of the Holy Sepulchre in Jerusalem, considered by Christians to be the spot where Christ was buried after his crucifixion and where he rose from the dead. It's a beautiful, haunting place, originally constructed in the 4th century and rebuilt and renovated multiple times since then. Situated in the heart of Jerusalem's Old City, the basilica rises above a shabby square and its simple white-and-beige stone exterior doesn't exactly exude magnificence. Inside, however, is a gorgeous memorial surrounding what tradition regards as the tomb of Christ, with the way toward it marked by massive candles and the interior dominated by a silver altarpiece before which monks from various Christian rites are constantly at prayer. It is one of the holiest sites on the Christian map and also one of the most bitterly contested. Six Christian denominations claim some form of jurisdiction over it, and their clergy guard those prerogatives with a ferocity that sometimes shades off into soccer hooligan-style brutishness.

The Coptic Orthodox Christians of Egypt, for instance, always have at least one monk on the roof of the basilica to guard their interests. On a warm summer day in 2002, the Copt on duty became weary of sitting in direct sunlight and moved his chair a foot to the right to be in the shade. The Ethiopian Orthodox also have a monk on duty on the roof, who took the Copt's move as a provocation and demanded that he go back. When the Egyptian refused, the Ethiopian grabbed him and tried to shove him back to his side. The Copt picked up his chair and whipped it at his assailant, who yelped in pain, thereby summoning clergy on both sides to the rooftop, some carrying iron bars they kept on hand for such emergencies. The resulting brawl left seven Ethiopians and four Copts injured before Israeli police finally pulled them apart. The monks were temporarily taken to jail to cool off, then released.

It wasn't the only such fracas. In 2004 a door to the Catholic chapel in the basilica was left open during a Greek Orthodox procession. The Orthodox community took it as an insult, suspecting the Catholics were trying to lure Orthodox worshipers, leading to a nasty fistfight. On Palm Sunday in 2008, a Greek monk was kicked out of the church by several Armenian rivals, triggering another fight and resulting in dozens of arrests. Seven months later, the Greeks and Armenians went at it again during a procession intended to honor the holy cross. Those who know the fractious reality sometimes joke that the Holy Sepulchre is not only where Christ was buried but where hopes for Christian unity go to die.

In that context, what Pope Francis did at the Basilica of the Holy Sepulchre in May 2014 was a remarkable inversion of the usual order of things. Francis joined Greek Orthodox Patriarch Bartholomew I of Constantinople for a joint prayer service. The patriarch is generally considered the "first among equals" in the Orthodox world, meaning that although the Orthodox don't have a pope with real authority over other bishops, Constantinople has an informal primacy in the pecking order. That night, the pope and the patriarch sat next to each other on the altar, embraced at the beginning and the end, extolled the other's commitment to unity and recited the Lord's Prayer together. The mutual affection was clear, including a moment when Bartholomew returned to his seat after speaking and Francis bent down to kiss his hand. While such encounters had been staged between popes and patriarchs before, they had never taken place in such a preeminent symbol of Christian division.

"We know that much distance still needs to be traveled before we attain that fullness of communion . . . we ardently desire," Francis said during the service. "Yet our disagreements must not frighten us and paralyze our progress. We need to believe that, just as the stone before the tomb was cast aside, so too every obstacle to our full communion will also be removed."

That night was the culmination of a policy of outreach to the Orthodox that has become a cornerstone of Francis's papacy. Bartholomew attended the new pope's 2013 inaugural mass, marking the first time an Orthodox leader had done so. During a lunch afterward, Francis presented Bartholomew to his cardinals as "my dear brother Andrew," a reference to the Orthodox tradition that the patriarch of Constantinople is the successor of St. Andrew, just as Catholics regard the pope as the successor of St. Peter. The two men now seem almost joined at the hip. The official purpose of Francis's 2014 trip to the Holy Land was to meet Bartholomew, in homage to a famous meeting between Pope Paul VI and another patriarch of Constantinople 50 years earlier, a meeting that led to the lifting of mutual excommunications between East and West that dated all the way back to 1054.

Francis's pursuit of Christian unity begins with the Orthodox in part because the rupture between East and West is the primordial schism, predating the Protestant Reformation by five centuries. There are also fewer doctrinal obstacles to reunion, since the Orthodox generally share Catholicism's traditional stance on matters of faith and morals. The more humble conception of papal power embodied by Francis is also appealing to many Orthodox, who have long feared that reunion with Catholicism in practice would mean being swallowed up by an imperial papacy.

Francis has been just as vigorous about reaching out to the Protestant world. A month into his papacy, he welcomed Nikolaus Schneider, president of Germany's Evangelical church, to the Vatican, where the two spoke about how Catholics and Protestants can put the divisions of the Reformation behind them and focus on building partnerships. In the months since, Francis has sat down with Evangelical leaders from around the world, including Joel Osteen, the Houston-based Protestant megachurch leader. Osteen was part of a delegation of the Fellowship Foundation, an Evangelical body that organizes the National Prayer Breakfast in Washington, D.C., that met with the pope in June 2014. Afterward, Osteen declared himself "very honored and very humbled" and said of Francis, "I love the fact that he has made the Church more inclusive.... Not trying to make it smaller, but [trying] to make it larger, to take everybody in. So that just resonates with me." The following month, the pope headed to the southern Italian region of Campania in order to see an Evangelical pastor and old friend, Giovanni Traettino. While there, he prayed with both Evangelicals and Catholics in Traettino's Evangelical Church of Reconciliation, one of just a handful of times when a pope has entered a Protestant church to pray.

Despite these signs of momentum, serious obstacles remain before achieving a full reunion among Christians. In recent years, it has become common for experts to talk about an "ecumenical winter," referring to the reality that hopes for a swift reunion have been dashed by hard experience. Decisions within the Anglican Communion to ordain women as both priests and bishops, for instance, have made structural détente with Catholicism problematic, while liberalizing trends in sexual ethics have had the same affect within mainline Protestantism. Francis has no magic formula for dissolving these obstacles. He has signaled that he will continue the effort, quietly laying the groundwork for a wider swath of Protestant churches to sign the joint declaration issued by Catholics and Lutherans in 1999, expressing a consensus that salvation is through faith alone and cannot be earned, as Protestants insist, and that good works are an essential duty for all Christians, as Catholics believe. A friend of the pontiff's proposed that the world's other great Protestant churches ratify the agreement in 2017, the year that marks the 500-year anniversary of Martin Luther's uprising that led to the Reformation, and Francis has given his support.

Yet the distinctive Francis touch is less about doctrinal breakthroughs or structural realignments and more about a new spirit in which friendship between Catholics and their fellow Christians becomes progressively normalized, thereby opening vistas for partnership on a wide range of social, cultural and humanitarian concerns. A case in point was when Francis invited the Palestinian and Israeli presidents to Rome for a peace prayer in June 2014. Francis asked Bartholomew I to join him in hosting the gathering, so it was both the Orthodox and Catholic leaders who officially brought together Shimon Peres and Mahmoud Abbas. In so doing, Francis created the expectation that in the future, whenever he wants to act as a peacemaker in a global conflict, Bartholomew will be at his side. Aides said the pope was conscious of training people to think in those terms.

Francis's plan for Christian peace seems to encompass growth, via friendship and common cause, into a new spiritual space where progress on doctrinal and structural fronts may become more thinkable. In that regard, the work of his friend Tony Palmer was emblematic. Palmer once worked for Copeland's Pentecostal ministry and raised his kids as charismatic Catholics (a charismatic practices Pentecostal-style spirituality within one of the mainstream Christian churches) to reflect his wife Emiliana's Italian heritage. Palmer saw his mission as bringing Christians together, using the charismatic movement as a bridge. His passion was reflected in his deliberately provocative accusation that many Christians suffer from "spiritual racism," the conviction that their church is superior to others. Palmer believed that if you stop acting as if denominational boundaries have to keep Christians apart, then they don't.

"You can be Catholic and Charismatic and Evangelical and Pentecostal, all at the same time," Palmer said as he presented the pope's message to Kenneth Copeland in January 2014, insisting that "Jesus was all of those things."

"How much of Jesus do you want?" Palmer joked. "Do you only want one denomination of Jesus? Jump in, get it all!"

Sadly, Palmer died in a motorcycle accident near his home in Bath, England, in July 2014. (At his funeral, a message from Pope Francis was read aloud by Emiliana.) But Palmer's vision of living in a "post-Reformation" Church, one in which difference does not mean division, lives on in Francis's papacy.

FRIENDSHIP IS A CORNERSTONE of Francis's papacy at all levels. During the Clinton presidency, the acronym FOB, "friend of Bill," came to indicate an intimate of the president who had access to the corridors of power and who helped shape his agenda. Today, Catholicism has its own FOB class. Bergoglio tends to rely on people he has known and trusted for years, such as Rabbi Abraham Skorka, rector of a Latin American Jewish seminary in Buenos Aires, with whom he co-authored the 2010 book *On Heaven and Earth.* The two men also did a TV talk show together, producing 30 episodes in which they conversed about a wide range of subjects. In a sign of how much those Argentine ties matter, when Francis traveled to Israel and Palestine in May 2014 he wanted two people by his side: Skorka and Omar Abboud, head of a council of Islamic leaders in Argentina. It was the first time a pope had ever asked followers of non-Christian religions to be members of his entourage for an overseas trip.

Francis's outreach to other religions begins with Judaism, anchored in relationships he has built up over a lifetime. An estimated 200,000 Jews live in Argentina, making it the sixth largest Jewish community outside Israel. Bergoglio made a point of attending services each year for the prayers of Selichot on the Saturday night before the High Holy Days of Rosh Hashanah and Yom Kippur. When the largest Jewish community center in Buenos Aires was bombed in 1994, Bergoglio played a key role in the national response, mobilizing the Church to provide immediate relief and also pressing the government for an aggressive investigation of the attack. Although some have accused Iran of orchestrating the bombing through Hezbollah, no suspects have ever been convicted, and investigations have been marked by incompetence and accusations of cover-ups. Francis stayed on the case, becoming the first public personality to sign a petition for justice in 2005, and was also a signatory to a document called "85 victims, 85 signatures" as part of the bombing's 11th anniversary. In June 2010 he visited the rebuilt center to express solidarity with the Jewish community.

Abraham Foxman, the longtime national director of the Anti-Defamation League—and an occasional critic of the Vatican—said in a 2013 interview that Jews "couldn't have wished or hoped for a better pope" in Francis. "We woke up to a pope who didn't wait to become pope before going to a synagogue, because he went to the synagogue as the cardinal of Buenos Aires and had a great relationship with the Jewish community," Foxman said. "We're comfortable that he understands us, that he has a sensitivity to the issues and that he'll be a voice to continue to make the relationship more open."

Since arriving in Rome, Francis has worked hard to keep those friendships warm. In January 2014 he welcomed a delegation of Jewish leaders from Argentina, led by Skorka, to the Vatican, sitting down with them over lunch at the Santa Marta. The pontiff arranged for the meal to be catered by a famous kosher restaurant from Rome's historic Jewish enclave, Ba' Ghetto. (For the record, the restaurant's owner said Francis was particularly impressed with the pistachio mousse.) While in Rome, the delegation met with the Vatican's top official for relations with Judaism, Swiss cardinal Kurt Koch, who stressed that Francis had told him that improving Catholic-Jewish relations would be a priority of his papacy.

It's not just the Jews with whom Francis has a history. In Buenos Aires, the future pope visited both the At-Tauhid Mosque located in the city's Floresta neighborhood and the Arab-Argentine Ali Ibn Abi Talib School. He invited local Muslim leaders to visit him, once receiving two clergymen at the headquarters of Argentina's bishops' conference during the time he served as president. Sheikh Mohsen Ali recalled that he and Bergoglio met there in 2006 to discuss the Lebanese War between Israel and Hezbollah, with Bergoglio expressing concern not just over the conflict itself but also the way it was creating a new rupture between his Jewish and Muslim friends in Argentina.

Bergoglio sympathized with the anger Muslims felt over a September 2006 speech by Pope Benedict XVI, in which he quoted a Byzantine emperor linking Muhammad with violence. At the time, a Bergoglio spokesman said the speech risked destroying in "20 seconds the careful construction of a relationship with Islam that Pope John Paul II built over the last 20 years." Benedict was not amused, and Bergoglio's spokesman was compelled to resign.

Besides his one-on-one relationships, Bergoglio tries to bring leaders of different creeds together. In 2000 he organized the planting of an olive tree for peace in the Plaza de Mayo in Buenos Aires, flanked by Muslims, Jews and leaders of other Christian churches. A picture of that gesture now occupies a place of honor in the Vatican's Pontifical Council for Promoting Christian Unity. The soccer-loving Francis later received a branch of the tree from star players Lionel Messi of Argentina and Gianluigi Buffon of Italy, who jointly founded a peace movement for young students called *Scholas Occurrentes*, formally known as the Worldwide Network of Schools Getting Together. The organization staged a gala soccer exhibition at Rome's Olympic Stadium in September 2014 featuring Diego Maradona, Roberto Baggio and others.

BERGOGLIO'S BACKGROUND as the first pope from the developing world lends him a unique perspective on relations with other faiths. This point was made by Skorka in a 2014 interview in Rome. While Jewish-Catholic exchanges in the West often pivot on the past— the history of anti-Semitism, the Holocaust and so on—the focus in Latin America is more on the present, Skorka explained. After a 2004 meeting of the International Jewish Catholic Liaison Committee in Buenos Aires, German Cardinal Walter Kasper, who was the Vatican's top official for relations with Judaism, said it had been "the first meeting not to focus on past issues but rather how to join forces to face the dramatic needs of the present and future." Skorka suggested that this focus partly reflected the climate in Argentina created by the economic crisis that erupted in the late 1990s and caused widespread unemployment, riots and the collapse of the government, leaving half of the country's population and 70 percent of its children in poverty. "The crisis created a situation in which religious institutions were called upon to work together in a very deep way," Skorka said. "There was [a lot] of coordinated work to help people in dire need."

One example of that principle in action was the Solidarity Network (Red Solidaria), founded by social entrepreneur and Catholic layman Juan Carr, which functions like a humanitarian exchange broker, connecting people who want to serve with people in need. During the crisis, the network provided food aid, access to shelter, job placement services for the unemployed and other forms of relief. It has grown to 800 volunteers and 38 offices up and down the country, and Carr was nominated for the Nobel Peace Prize in 2012. Carr said that Bergoglio was a major patron of the network, promoting the idea that "the spiritual and the social components of the Church have to go together."

"That was something new," Carr said, "because in Latin American Catholicism, people tend to emphasize one or the other."

According to Skorka, something interesting happened in the middle of the economic meltdown. "Society started to ask who can we really trust, and religious institutions came to the fore," he said, adding that the situation induced religious leaders to develop "a tremendously pragmatic" form of dialogue—one that's not focused on old theological or spiritual divisions but on what different faiths can do together right now to serve people at society's edges and to build a better world.

Skorka's insight suggests that a pragmatic focus on the here and now is at the heart of interfaith cooperation, such as the initiative Francis launched in 2014 with the archbishop of Canterbury and the Grand Imam of Egypt's prestigious Al-Azhar University and Mosque, sometimes considered the Vatican of the Sunni Muslim world, to combat human trafficking by training adherents of different faiths to spot and denounce such abuses.

The core of the pope's vision is not him and the Dalai Lama praying together, nor is it sitting across a table from a Zoroastrian priest debating different understandings of the devil. Rather, it's standing together in a conflict zone offering to serve as mediators, or working together in a breadline feeding the poor. Peace is a natural by-product of such partnerships, as Francis seems to believe.

NOWHERE IS THE CONTRAST between Benedict XVI and Francis more tangible than in the degree to which the papacy seems to have recovered its diplomatic and geopolitical swagger. The normalization of relations between the U.S. and Cuba in December 2014 came about in part thanks to Francis, who wrote private letters to President Obama and Cuban president Raúl Castro that reportedly helped break the ice between the two leaders.

Massimo Franco is one of Italy's most respected journalists, a veteran reporter who has covered all of Italy's political figures of the late 20th century, a crop that includes several Vatican heavyweights who left a mark on their times. Under Benedict XVI, however, Franco says he watched the Vatican's relevance on the global stage diminish. When the Arab Spring began to unfold in late 2010, one normally would have expected the Vatican to have something to say, especially about the persecution of Christian minorities in Arab nations. By that stage, however, lingering resentment among Muslims over Benedict's controversial 2006 speech linking Muhammad with violence, combined with a perceived loss of moral authority because of sexual abuse scandals, had left the Vatican in Franco's eyes all but irrelevant.

In 2010 a wistful Franco published a book titled *Once Upon a Time, There Was a Vatican*, documenting what he believed to be a slow slide toward diplomatic extinction. The book opens with a scene at a reception held at one of Rome's pontifical colleges, attended by a number of diplomats. Franco quotes an ambassador to the Holy See comparing the mood to what it must have been like under the dying Republic of Venice in the late 18th century, which was soon to be swallowed up in the conquests of Napoleon Bonaparte. "How many of us will even still be here in 10 years?" the man said.

Franco has acknowledged in a series of essays and interviews that nobody has the Republic of Venice on their minds today. The more natural comparison is to the early days of the papacy of John Paul II, when the Polish pope mobilized the solidarity movement and set the dominoes in motion that led to the collapse of communism in Central and Eastern Europe. In a sign of the times, Ireland reopened its embassy in the Vatican in November 2014 after closing it for three years, a move justified as a cost-saving measure but also thought to be due to a standoff over the Vatican's handling of sexual abuse cases. Other nations are also talking about expansion rather than retrenchment. It has become a running joke in Rome that ambassadors who arrived during the Benedict years expecting a quiet assignment to wind down their careers have suddenly found themselves at the center of a whirlwind.

"Francis is not resigned to a passive vision of world affairs," said Marco Impagliazzo, president of the Rome-based Community of Sant'Egidio, a Catholic organization active in conflict resolution and peace brokering, in a 2014 interview. "We must prepare for a new age of political audacity for the Holy See."

For his part, Franco believes Francis is potentially even more crucial a political actor than John Paul II. "By virtue of being Polish, John Paul was hugely important for the fate of communism and for the reunification of Europe," Franco said in 2014. "As the first pope from the developing world, Francis is important for every major issue facing the world today: poverty, the environment, immigration and war."

WHILE FRANCIS CLEARLY WANTS to deploy whatever influence he can to promote peace, the pontiff is selective about how, and how often, he wades into conflicts.

His first real test came over Syria. In August 2013, after President Bashar al-Assad's regime was believed to have carried out a sarin chemical attack on opposition areas near the capital, Damascus, Western leaders began trying to foster public support for the use of military force. U.S. Secretary of State John Kerry said, "History would judge us all extraordinarily harshly if we turned a blind eye," while President Barack Obama put Congress on notice that he was weighing a "limited, narrow" attack.

As the first pope from the developing world, Francis feels a special responsibility to listen carefully to what he calls the "peripheries," the places outside the usual Western centers of power. That summer, he was therefore determined to consult Syria's Christian leadership before reacting. Christians are an important minority in Syria, composing about 10 percent of the population of 22.5 million. The majority is Greek Orthodox, followed by Catholics, the Assyrian Church of the East and various kinds of Protestants. The leaders of those churches told the pope, both in writing and during face-to-face encounters in Rome, that forcing Assad from power was a recipe for disaster.

As they saw it, if Assad fell, Islamic radicals would most likely fill the void—the choice for Syria is not between a police state and a democracy, but between a police state and annihilation. That's not just the position of the bishops, but a sentiment widely shared by Christians. When Russia and China blocked a U.N. resolution condemning Assad in February 2012, Western reporters found a Christian bar in Damascus offering an impromptu two-for-one happy hour special on drinks to celebrate the decision. Most Syrian Christians recognize that Assad is a thug but believe that the alternative is even worse. That judgment was confirmed in the summer of 2014, when forces of the Islamic State of Iraq and the Levant proclaimed a caliphate in northern Iraq, driving tens of thousands of Christians and minority Yazidis from their homes and beheading a pair of American journalists and a British aid worker.

Francis has made clear that the crisis in Syria is a deep concern. He used his first *Urbi et Orbi* ("to the city and the world") message on Easter Sunday 2013 to invoke prayer "for dear Syria . . . for its people torn by conflict and for the many refugees who await help and comfort."

"How much blood has been shed!" Francis said that day. "How much suffering must there still be before a political solution to the crisis will be found?"

In private, Francis stressed during meetings with the Vatican's diplomatic team that he wanted updates from religious orders and other Catholic groups on the situation on the ground in Syria and told his brain trust that he planned to oppose expanding the conflict in Syria in every way he could. The Vatican swung into action, even dispatching anti-war messages through the pope's Twitter account.

In substance, Francis steered the Vatican closer to Russia's and China's position than to the Western powers'. It was a clear signal that he wanted the Catholic Church to act on the global stage as something more than the chaplain to NATO, which is what critics of Vatican foreign policy in the Soviet bloc used to charge.

Although Syria was not the only crisis percolating, Francis felt a special urgency about getting involved because of the precedent of Iraq.

At the time of the first U.S.-led Gulf War there were an estimated 1.5 to 2 million Christians in Iraq. Although they were second-class citizens under Saddam Hussein, they were basically secure. Hussein's most visible international mouthpiece, former foreign minister and deputy prime minister Tariq Aziz, was himself a Chaldean Catholic. Today, up to 400,000 Christians are thought to be remaining in the country, but many believe the real number is lower, as Islamic radicals have had a free hand in targeting the Christian minority. Francis was determined not to stand by while another Christian community in the Middle East suffered the same fate.

Looking back at John Paul II's vain efforts to stop the Iraq offensive in 2003, which included dispatching personal envoys to both Sadaam Hussein and President George W. Bush in February and March of that year, Francis felt the intervention had been too political. It failed, in Francis's eyes, to draw on what's most distinctive about the papacy as a global force: its spiritual capacity. So Francis opted to do something only a religious leader could do: he called a global day of prayer and fasting for peace in Syria on Sept. 7, 2013, inviting the world's 1.2 billion Catholics, as well as all women and men of goodwill, to help him storm heaven with prayer.

When darkness fell in Rome that evening, Pope Francis stepped out into St. Peter's Square to preside over a five-hour prayer service designed specifically for the Syria campaign. For those who had been accustomed to the high school pep rally feel of most of Francis's public appearances up to that point, the night had a completely different vibe. The pontiff was somber and there was no chanting of his name, no exuberant waves during swings around the square. The service began when four Swiss guards proceeded through the square with the icon *Salus Populi Romani* (Mary, the Queen of Peace and protector of the Roman people). The pope led a rosary recitation, a meditation and a Eucharist ceremony. Bible readings from the Gospel of Luke focused on Mary, and the crowd followed along with a 51-page booklet produced by the Vatican. Priests heard confessions under the colonnades, emphasizing Francis's desire for a penitential spirit that night, one that made clear he sees war and violence as sin.

"How many conflicts, how many wars have mocked our history?" Francis asked. "Even today we raise our hand against our brother. . . . We have perfected our weapons, our conscience has fallen asleep, and we have sharpened our ideas to justify ourselves as if it were normal [that] we continue to sow destruction, pain, death. Violence and war lead only to death."

The Vatican estimated the global television audience for the service to be in the hundreds of millions. Thousands of Catholic parishes and other venues staged their own prayer services that day too.

It's not clear how much credit Francis can claim for halting the initial rush to declare war against Assad. Before Francis stepped out into the square that evening, support for Western strikes in Syria was already beginning to erode. U.K. prime minister David Cameron had already lost a vote in the House of Commons seeking support to join the U.S. in military action, and French president François Hollande was softening his earlier bellicose rhetoric. Nonetheless, the pope's stance was given wide play in the Arab media, and when he visited the Middle East in May 2014, Syrian Christian refugees in Jordan brandished signs thanking the pontiff for "saving our country."

IN JUNE 2014 FRANCIS MADE an even riskier and more audacious diplomatic foray: an invitation to the presidents of Israel and Palestine to pray for peace in the Vatican, in an effort to revive the stalled peace process.

The invitation was a result of Francis's May 2014 trip to Jordan, Israel and the Palestinian territories, the region known to Christians as the Holy Land. The visit crystallized Francis's reputation as a pope of surprises, because it was punctuated by moments that veered off script and left the pope's advisers scrambling to keep up.

The shocks began on May 25 when Francis called on Palestinian president Mahmoud Abbas in Bethlehem. Afterward, the pontiff was scheduled to proceed to Bethlehem's Manger Square to celebrate mass for the city's dwindling Christian population. His route for the short drive took him immediately next to the massive 26-foot-high barrier separating Israel from the West Bank, known as the "security fence" by Israelis and the "apartheid wall" by Palestinians. At a certain point, and with no advance warning to anyone, Francis asked his driver to stop and pull over. There was a moment's delay as his security team scrambled to get into position and then the pope got out, walked over to a portion of the wall where "Free Palestine!" had been graffitied, and paused for about five minutes of silent prayer. At the end, Francis placed his hands on the wall and leaned in until his forehead came to rest, then made the sign of the cross. It became the most powerful visual of the trip and was almost universally taken as a gesture of solidarity with Palestinian suffering.

While it was happening, a visibly flustered Vatican spokesman, an Italian Jesuit named Fr. Federico Lombardi, was madly thumbing his BlackBerry. Lombardi knew that the stop at the wall was political dynamite and was desperately trying to invent a nonpartisan way to frame it. Later that day, Lombardi told reporters that Francis wasn't taking sides but was simply expressing a biblical lament. "The pope thinks like a prophet," Lombardi said. "He imagines a day when a wall won't be necessary to keep these two peoples apart. This was not a statement about the present political situation."

It wasn't clear at the time if even Lombardi quite bought the line. The Palestinians certainly didn't, immediately announcing plans to issue a postage stamp commemorating the pontiff's stop (Abbas informed Francis of the proposed stamp at the mass in Manger Square, less than an hour later). The Israelis didn't swallow it either, with a foreign ministry spokesperson describing it as a "cheap propaganda stunt," and a testy

Prime Minister Benjamin Netanyahu demanding the pope add a stop the next day at a memorial for Israeli victims of Palestinian terrorism.

In a sense, Lombardi and other Vatican officials trying to spin the stop at the wall lucked out, because two hours later the pope supplied an even more startling storyline when he announced that he had invited both Abbas and Israeli president Shimon Peres to join him for a prayer for peace "in my house." Both leaders swiftly accepted the invitation, and the date was set for June 8.

In the run-up, the Vatican did everything it could to lower expectations. "Anybody who has even a minimum understanding of the situation would never think that as of Monday, peace will break out," said Fr. Pierbattista Pizzaballa, a Franciscan priest based in the Middle East who organized the event. The pope's lone ambition, he said, was to "open a path" that was previously closed.

Pizzaballa, who runs a Franciscan outfit responsible for taking care of holy sites in the region, is well versed in the delicate balancing act that is Middle Eastern diplomacy and carefully scripted every detail of the June prayer meeting. Peres and Abbas arrived separately at the pope's residence at the Domus Santa Marta, where each had a brief private moment with the pontiff. Francis and his guests were then joined by Patriarch Bartholomew I of Constantinople, with TV cameras capturing the four men exchanging embraces and kisses. They proceeded to the Vatican gardens, chosen as the setting because they contain no obvious Christian symbolism, and took part in a service that featured scriptural readings and prayers for peace from Judaism, Islam and Christianity.

Francis's message was brief but forceful. "Peacemaking calls for courage, much more so than warfare," he said. Only the tenacious, he argued, "say yes to encounter and no to conflict; yes to negotiations and no to hostilities; yes to respect for agreements and no to acts of provocation."

With the benefit of hindsight, the peace prayer seemed to carry three layers of significance. First, it pioneered a new channel of back-door diplomacy under the cover of religious piety. Second, it solidified a Vatican recipe for making prayer with followers of other religions theologically acceptable. Whenever popes staged such events in the past, there was always blowback from traditionalists who grumbled that such exercises promote the idea that all religions are equal, amounting to a sort of New Age sacrilege. This time, there was no single moment of joint prayer but rather separate prayers for Jews, Muslims and Christians. Organizers insisted that the leaders were not "praying together" but instead "coming together to pray." Third, the fact that Francis invited Patriarch Bartholomew I of Constantinople to join the summit has ecumenical importance, because it signifies that it wasn't just a papal undertaking but a broader Christian project. It also suggests that in the future the pope will look to build ecumenical coalitions behind his peace initiatives.

In one night of prayer, Francis put the Vatican back on the geopolitical map, avoiding a potential quagmire in interreligious relations and giving Christian unity a shot in the arm. Even without a peace deal, it wasn't bad for a night's work.

Exactly one month later, after aerial and seaborne bombardments failed to stop missile attacks by Hamas on Israeli territory, Israel launched Operation Protective Edge, an offensive in the Gaza Strip that left hundreds dead, mainly civilians. The fighting capped a sharp deterioration in relations since the Palestinians had installed a new unity government featuring Hamas and also reflected the Israeli public's anger over the abduction and killing of three Israeli teenagers in the West Bank.

Despite the failure of the peace summit to stop conflict from breaking out in Gaza, the night of prayer still seemed a watershed, signaling Pope Francis's importance in the popular imagination.

In August, flying back from a week-long trip to South Korea, Francis defended the peace initiative. "That prayer for peace, absolutely, was not a failure!" he said. "Now the smoke of the bombs of the wars don't allow us to see the door, but the door is still open from that moment. As I believe in God, I believe that God is watching that door and all who pray and ask that he help us."

Peres seemed to concur. In early September 2014, not long after he stepped down as Israeli president, he traveled to Rome to propose that Pope Francis launch a United Nations of world religions, telling an Italian newsmagazine, "For the first time in history, the Holy Father is a respected leader, valued as such by the diverse faiths and their exponents." He added that "he's truly the only one who can lead this project." The Vatican said at the time that Francis had listened to the pitch carefully but hadn't made any commitment.

To be clear, Francis is not an absolute pacifist. During that same flight back from South Korea, he also issued a cautious yellow light for an anti-ISIS bombing campaign by the U.S. in Iraq, saying that "it is legitimate to stop an unjust aggressor." He immediately added several qualifications, including that stopping someone does not always have to mean dropping bombs and that it would be better to have U.N. authorization for any use of force. That said, the clear thrust of the pope's words was that something had to be done. Francis's clear preference is for nonviolent solutions to conflicts, but his view of the world cannot be reduced to a simplistic version of "give peace a chance."

BY NOW, FRANCIS HAS DEMONSTRATED how he wants to engage the world as a peace pope. He approaches conflicts in a uniquely spiritual fashion. He doesn't become absorbed in the nitty-gritty of tactics and strategy like Pope John Paul II, who during the Reagan years used to meet in secret with CIA director William Casey to go over satellite telemetry regarding Soviet troop movements near the Polish border. Instead, he wants to rely on the resources of faith—prayer and fasting, invocations of the sacred texts of the world's great religions, and popular devotions and religious observances. In his eyes, it's not only the appropriate way for a pope to exert his influence, it's also good politics. Many of the world's bloodiest conflicts have a clear religious subtext, which means that a spiritual leader can engage them in a fashion that no secular diplomat could.

As he considers where to get involved, Francis is willing to roll the dice when caution might counsel restraint. In an interview with the Barcelona newspaper *La Vanguardia* shortly after the peace prayer with Abbas and Peres, Francis disclosed that 99 percent of his aides in the Vatican were opposed to the idea when he first discussed his plans. Not only did they object to the novelty of it, but they advised him that it wasn't smart to risk his credibility on an initiative doomed to fail.

American cardinal Theodore McCarrick, himself a veteran diplomatic troubleshooter, seemed to capture Francis's spirit best in an interview in Jerusalem with the *Boston Globe* shortly after the prayer summit was announced. "He's not putting himself out on a limb," McCarrick said of the peace initiative. "He's putting himself up on the cross, and that's what he's called to do."

The Francis brand of diplomacy is premised on personal relationships. American Catholic writer David Gibson refers to this one-on-one style as the "Francis doctrine," citing the pope's remarks immediately after his return from the Holy Land that peace is not mass-produced but "handcrafted" every day by individuals.

This artisanal approach runs through the pope's peace efforts. Francis felt emboldened to invite Peres and Abbas because he had established a personal rapport with both leaders during previous encounters in the Vatican. He brought Skorka and Abboud along to the Middle East not just because they're well-established points of reference in interfaith dialogue but because they're old friends. He has set up Bartholomew I of Constantinople as his geopolitical partner not just because he's a prominent Orthodox leader but because the two men clearly like and respect each other. In the future, it's reasonable to expect that Francis will pick where to deploy his political capital in part based on where he has developed personal ties.

No one knows yet whether this personal brand of diplomacy will succeed or fail at the level of realpolitik, but Francis seems comfortable letting things shake out as they will. The pontiff's sangfroid was crystallized in January 2014 when he invited two Italian children to join him at the window of the papal apartment for his regular Sunday address, and at the end they released two white doves. However touching the image was intended to be, it quickly took a sour twist when a seagull and a crow attacked the doves, with only one escaping. The outcome struck many observers as an apt metaphor for the pope's peace efforts, given that some have seemed to take flight while others have been devoured by hostile forces.

A visiting monsignor who was at the dinner table with the pontiff at the Santa Marta that night said he brought the incident up with Francis. When asked if he'd been embarrassed by snide commentary in the press about what had happened, the pope appeared unperturbed.

"What's to be embarrassed about?" Francis was said to have replied. "One out of two is a success, right?"

4

God and Mammon: Reforming the Vatican's Finances

IT WAS THE CHURCH'S FORAY into the pornography business that first alerted the Vatican that something was amiss in the picturesque Slovenian archdiocese of Maribor.

A sleepy Alpine hamlet best known for its world-class ski trails, Maribor came to the attention of Roman officials in 2007 when they began receiving letters from Slovenian Catholics who had invested their life savings in a couple of Church-owned funds. The investors were surprised to learn from local newspapers that their money was being used to finance a new 120-channel package for a national media company called T2 that featured, in the words of a banker, "the finest pornography in Slovenia."

The affair raised serious questions about the financial judgments being made by leaders of the local Church. Italian newsmagazine *l'Espresso* reported that the Vatican Bank had given a large loan to cover

Maribor's debts, but in an October 2013 statement the director of the Vatican press office, the Rev. Federico Lombardi, said, "No loan to the Maribor archdiocese was meant to be or will be granted" by the Vatican.

Under Pope Benedict XVI, the Vatican dispatched Gianluca Piredda, an Italian financier and founding partner of a multinational consulting firm, to get to the bottom of things. Piredda arrived in Slovenia as an apostolic visitor, meaning he carried the pope's personal authority, and the news he brought back was not good. Beyond the dubious choice to put Church money into sexually explicit programming, Piredda unearthed a much bigger problem. He discovered that two investment funds operated by the archdiocese were badly overextended in specu- lative enterprises and that when the inevitable collapse came, ordinary Slovenians would face a disaster of "Biblical proportions." Piredda's report led to a stern meeting between Benedict XVI and the Catholic bishops of Slovenia in Rome in 2008. The German pontiff demanded that the Slovenians show "greater fidelity to the Gospel in the adminis- tration of Church property." But it was too little, too late. The story of what went wrong in Maribor reads like a scriptural injunction against serving both God and mammon.

After the collapse of communism, Slovenia launched a sweeping privatization campaign that included issuing certificates worth up to 3,000 euros to all Slovenians so they could invest in stock options and develop a portfolio that would provide income in retirement. Slove- nians were free to hand those certificates over to anyone they wanted to manage them on their behalf. The Maribor archdiocese jumped into the game. More than 65,000 Slovenian Catholics eventually invested their share certificates in two investment funds created by the archdiocese. At its peak, the funds had more than 100 million euros under management. The Church put its moral authority behind the investment funds, encouraging rank-and-file faithful to participate. Slovenia's top Catholic education institute, St. Stanislaus Institute, launched a PR campaign asserting that investing with the Church "out of love" would bring "inner joy, now and in eternity."

After some early success investing in small local enterprises, the Church began branching out, investing in chemical, paper and tele-communications firms. Money also went into large infrastructure and real estate projects beyond Slovenia, including some that could only be described as highly risky. There was a petroleum concern, a tita-nium firm and even a slaughterhouse in the future pope's Argentina. The most expensive investment was in T2, the Slovenia-based media company with the first-class porn. Over time, the companies in which the funds were invested became increasingly burdened by debt, and when the Eurozone crisis hit in 2009 the house of cards collapsed. The two funds went belly-up, with debts estimated at a minimum of $700 million, leaving the Maribor archdiocese bankrupt and wiping out the savings of thousands of devout Slovenians.

"I think the incompetence of highly ranked Church officials can definitely be a partial explanation of why this happened," said Slove-nian economist Igor Masten in a 2014 interview. "Basically, they took a very long-term investment but financed it with mostly short-term bank loans." Masten sat on the supervisory board of Slovenia's largest commer-cial bank, where he saw firsthand how the Church's financial team did business. "It's incredible how they obtained this quantity of loans. My impression was that personal connections, combined with political influ-ence, were used to obtain funds on a large scale," Masten said.

By the time the scale of the problem became clear, Benedict XVI was already privately getting ready for his resignation. Cleaning it up would await a new pope, and under Francis heads began to roll. The cleric in charge of overseeing the funds, Fr. Mirko Krasovec, was exiled to an Austrian monastery in April 2013. By August, Pope Francis requested the resignations of the archbishops of Maribor and the national capital of Ljubljana, both of whom stepped down and apologized. A Slovenian prelate in Rome, Cardinal Franc Rodè, said that the new pope "wanted to use Slovenia as an example for the entire Church, to demonstrate that there won't be compromises regarding financial problems." In the meantime, many of the Catholics who saw their life savings evaporate say they're having a hard time reconciling their faith with the experience of being bilked. One, who asked not to be identified, said, "I still try to go to church on Sunday, but most of the time I'm so angry I could scream."

Sorting through the debris, some analysts are inclined to ascribe what happened in Maribor primarily to naïveté and the overheated boom mentality of the immediate post-communist years, while others charge explicit corruption. Krasovec was not only exiled to Austria but has since been convicted of embezzling European Union grants (he appealed at a hearing in October 2014, but at press time a verdict had not yet been announced). Whatever the outcome, Maribor now stands as a metaphor for the risks to the Church's moral authority, not to mention its pocketbook, when financial supervision is either weak or nonexistent.

A Franciscan friar named Bogdan Knavs, who has spent time counseling those who lost their nest eggs and who has followed the affair closely, says that apologies and resignations go only part of the way to repairing the damage. At some point, he believes, the Church must make restitution to those it encouraged to invest. "If this injustice is not settled," Knavs warned in a 2013 essay, "the stain will blight the Church for decades."

The financial implosion in Maribor was extraordinary. As *l'Espresso* put it, "[It is] one of the most devastating financial disasters in the history of the Church." Yet the rotten mix of forces—clerics who lacked training in business or finance and who relied on personal connections and political benefit instead of good business practice; and the temptation of ready money with no oversight or accountability—is hardly unique to Slovenia. A 2006 study by Villanova University found that 85 percent of Catholic dioceses in the U.S. had experienced some form of embezzlement within the previous five years, mostly at the parish level.

Financial scandals are a special source of anguish for the reforming

Pope Francis, because they bring together the three vices that distress him more than anything else: corruption, exaggerated clerical privilege and indifference to the poor.

No one questions that the Catholic Church needs financial resources to fulfill its mission. As the late American archbishop Paul Marcinkus, the former head of the Vatican Bank, once said, "You can't run the Church on Hail Marys." It costs money to deliver many of the services the Church offers, and it has to come from somewhere. In spring 2014, a mini-scandal broke out in the small Italian town of Villa di Baggio when the local pastor, Fr. Valerio Mazzola, published a price card listing the going rates for certain services. A wedding in the parish cost $260, while a funeral ran to $120. When people protested at the idea of charging for sacraments, Mazzola insisted that the amounts were merely a suggestion for what people might voluntarily offer. "How am I supposed to pay the bills if people don't know what this stuff costs?" he said.

But the Catholic Church has a long and somewhat dubious history with money. Today, perhaps the most audacious of all Pope Francis's plans is to make the Vatican into a global model of best practices in financial administration—not just as an end in itself but as a way of leading the Church at all levels to clean up its act.

FRANCIS HAS MADE the Vatican's financial operation a focus of his reform agenda. And the man he has tapped to lead the charge is a larger-than-life figure: a 6-foot-3 bruiser who looks like he might have been a bare-knuckle street fighter and who in reality is a former Australian Rules football player. Australian cardinal George Pell, the first-ever secretary of the economy—basically, Francis's financial czar—has been tapped to impose transparency and accountability on a system historically allergic to both.

Although George Pell and Pope Francis are both devout churchmen, as personality types they could hardly be more different. Where Pell is an archconservative who relishes the wars of culture, Francis is the pope of "Who am I to judge?" fame; where Pell is a blunt Anglo-Saxon, Francis is a warm Latin American; where Pell is attracted to uncompromising doctrinal positions, Francis is a unifier desperate to bring the Church's divergent camps together. Francis is also probably the last person you'd fear meeting in a dark alley, while Pell may be the one member of the College of Cardinals you'd want by your side if a fight broke out in a Roman wine bar.

Pell is known in Catholic circles in Australia and across the English-speaking world as a robustly conservative bishop. He rose to prominence in the John Paul II and Benedict XVI years but is not the kind of prelate one would expect to flourish under Francis. Pell was an early and enthusiastic supporter of the Vatican's former doctrinal czar, Cardinal Joseph Ratzinger, for the papacy in 2005, and his influence in moving the Church in a conservative direction has been considerable. Pell was the chair of a special papal commission, Vox Clara ("clear voice"), a body that argued that the mass translation adopted after the Second Vatican Council was full of mushy, imprecise language that didn't adequately capture either the tone or content of Catholic worship. Over the objections of more progressive liturgical experts—not to mention many regular, churchgoing Catholics—Pell pushed through a new text full of more traditional-sounding flourishes, which critics have derided as both archaic and sexist. "One in being" became "consubstantial," while "man," "men" and "brothers" are routinely used to mean "people."

In the immediate wake of the papal election in March 2013, close friends of Pell reported that he seemed dispirited, perhaps sensing that the new boss was going to take the Church in a different direction. Privately, many Pell allies were saying he may have gotten lucky in 2010 when he was rumored to be on the brink of being named head of the Vatican's powerful Congregation for Bishops (responsible for recommending new bishops around the world to the pope) but was passed over in favor of Canadian cardinal Marc Ouellet. Had Pell been appointed instead, it's likely Francis would today be looking for ways to get rid of him, given that the new pontiff has already removed a couple of traditionalists from the bishops' body and replaced them with moderates.

Neither Pell nor anyone else realized, however, that Francis had another set of plans for this linebacker in a cassock. What Francis grasped is that Pell's doctrinal conservatism by no means made him an apologist for the Vatican's old guard. On the contrary, few prelates have been more acerbically critical of what Pell sees as outdated, dysfunctional and stereotypically Italian ways of doing business. In the run-up to the conclave of 2013, Pell was the first cardinal in the world to put governance on the table as a voting issue. In an interview shortly after Benedict XVI announced his resignation, Pell said that Benedict had been a "magnificent teacher" but a poor administrator. "Governance is done by people around the pope," Pell said, adding that during the Benedict years "it wasn't always done brilliantly."

In private, Pell was more forceful. In pre-conclave meetings, Pell used different metaphors to press the case, insisting that the next pope should be a reformer who could "clean out the stables," as well as a tested administrator with "mud on his boots" from spending time in the trenches. Other cardinals said Pell was virtually leading a guerrilla insurrection against a Vatican establishment that he believed had broken down.

The newly elected Pope Francis had Pell in his sights to fix the Vatican's financial problems. For a start, Francis had heard Pell rage against the Vatican's financial administration, and Bergoglio also understood that previous attempts at financial reform had failed, in part because the people in charge had made the strategic decision to try to adjust themselves to the existing culture of the place rather than to bulldoze through it. In the 1980s a no-nonsense American named Cardinal Edmund Szoka was brought in to try to right the ship, and while he did succeed in ending 23 consecutive years of deficit spending, his larger reform program essentially went nowhere. For example, Szoka wanted to implement a five-day, 40-hour workweek from Monday to Friday as a way of increasing productivity, but Vatican personnel still work mornings from Monday through Saturday and a couple of afternoons each week. (The 35-hour schedule is a source of wry humor—Pope John XXIII supposedly once quipped, "It's the mornings when [the staff] don't work. In the afternoons they don't even show up!")

In April 2013 Pope Francis named Pell as a member of his new "G8" Council of Cardinal Advisers, signifying his status as a key intimate of the new pontiff. Francis made a habit of reaching out to Pell to talk privately about his plans for Vatican reform, relying on the notoriously blunt Australian to help him identify whom he could trust.

In March 2014 Francis asked Pell to drop by the Domus Santa Marta for a chat. The two men spent more than an hour together, speaking largely in Italian since Pell doesn't speak Spanish well and Francis is uncomfortable in English. They covered a lot of ground, ranging from looming personnel moves in the Vatican to upcoming business facing the G8, but Francis kept bringing the conversation back to the need for rapid movement on the financial front. The pope told Pell that he was in earnest about wanting greater transparency and about freeing up resources to help the poor. He also voiced personal pain at the idea that impoverished Catholics around the world were turning over their hard-earned money every Sunday in the collection plate, only to see the Vatican gripped by yet another episode of corruption or mismanagement. Eventually, Francis asked the 71-year-old Pell if he would be willing to make the new post of financial czar his last major job in the Catholic Church.

Pell later recalled that he didn't have much choice other than to say yes, in part because of his deeply traditional Catholic belief that the pope is the vicar of Christ on earth and hence one simply doesn't say no when he calls, and also because he'd spent so much time over the years complaining about the dysfunctional and opaque approach to business management in the Vatican that it would have been churlish to refuse. An improbable partnership between the populist pope and the polarizing cardinal was thereby forged.

Shortly afterward, Francis unveiled a sweeping overhaul of the Vatican's financial structures that had been largely worked out in conversation with the G8 members and with his two study commissions and also discussed in detail with Pell during that tête-à-tête. It features a new three-tier structure to oversee financial operations.

The first part of the overhaul was to create the Council for the Economy, a body with the power to supervise the financial structures and activities of every department of both the Holy See and the Vatican City State. The new council is made up of 15 individuals, including eight cardinals and seven laity. It is the first time a decision-making body at such a senior level in the Vatican has included laypeople with the same voting rights as cardinals. The body replaces an earlier council composed of 15 cardinals and is in part a response to criticism that in the past, financial supervision had been entrusted to clerics who often lacked training and expertise. In remarks during the council's first formal meeting in May 2014, Francis told the members they will be responsible for engineering a "change in mentality" with regard to Vatican finances in the direction of greater transparency, efficiency and service to the poor.

The second body created is a Secretariat for the Economy, led by Pell, with day-to-day responsibility for implementing the directives that come from the Council for the Economy and the pope. This group is responsible for preparing and policing an annual budget for the Vatican as a whole and for its individual departments; conducting quarterly reviews of performance; stepping in at other moments as warranted to inspect the books; and, if necessary, imposing spending controls. In an interview with the *Boston Globe* shortly after his appointment was announced, Pell said his ambition was to save "millions, if not tens of millions" of dollars each year by carrying out rational accounting measures. According to

Pell, "a poor Church doesn't mean a broke Church."

The choice to call the new body a secretariat confirmed to insiders that Francis wants it to have real authority, since the only other department with that name, the Secretariat of State, has long been considered the dominant agency on the Vatican scene, controlling both foreign policy and internal administration and acting as an overseer for other departments. After Pell was in place, Francis named a Maltese monsignor, Alfred Xuereb, as the No. 2 official in the secretariat, and a British priest, Brian Ferme, as the pope's personal prelate to the council overseeing the secretariat.

The final part of the new order was the creation of the position of auditor general, independent from both the Council and the Secretariat for the Economy and reporting directly to the pope. This figure performs separate reviews of accounts to ensure that there are "two sets of eyes" on everything, as Pell put it.

As a result of the changes, Pell is now at the top of a large and extraordinarily powerful pyramid designed to fully modernize the Vatican's financial dealings. "There has never been anything like this in the Vatican that's explicitly designed to foster a system of checks and balances," Pell said in a March 2014 interview. "There's a lot of muddle and a considerable amount of imperfection, [but] there's no reason [the changes] can't be done fairly quickly."

Pell has so far proved to be as uncompromising as Francis had hoped, as illustrated by his handling of the fate of the Institute for the Works of Religion, also known as the Vatican Bank. The bank was set up in 1942 to manage funds belonging to the Vatican and other Catholic organizations such as religious orders and lay movements. Due to a number of scandals, there was speculation that Pope Francis might abolish the bank completely. He had floated the idea shortly after his election, and a couple of his top advisers repeated that closure was on the table. As a result, the bank was paying higher transaction costs because of uncertainty about its future. It was also to convene a meeting with economic officials in several orders of nuns that are among the bank's most important customers. (Women's religious orders around the world run large education and health-care systems, and much of their income is deposited in the Vatican Bank.)

In April 2014 the president of the Vatican Bank explained to Pell that it was time to either fish or cut bait on the question of whether the bank was going to continue to exist. Pell called together the key players involved and asked for opinions on the idea of releasing a public confirmation that the bank will survive. When the meeting came to no consensus, Pell ended it abruptly by announcing that a statement was going out anyway. On April 7 the Vatican press office released a communiqué saying the bank "will continue to serve with prudence and provide specialized financial services to the Catholic Church worldwide."

In a similar vein, in July 2014 Pope Francis approved another series of measures recommended by Pell. They included tapping French businessman Jean-Baptiste de Franssu to succeed Ernst von Freyberg at the Vatican Bank, creating the new Vatican Asset Management to coordinate billions of dollars in investments previously spread across several departments, launching study panels for pensions and media operations and assigning the new Secretariat for the Economy control over purchasing and human resources. The political impact of the changes was huge, as the Secretariat for the Economy under Pell absorbed a key chunk of the Administration of the Patrimony of the Apostolic See (APSA) and the new asset-management office answers to Pell.

Yet another sign of Pell taking charge came in December 2014, when he revealed to Britain's *Catholic Herald* that his team had found "hundreds of millions of euros" tucked away in the accounts of various departments that had never been reported. Pell pointed his finger at the once-mighty Secretariat of State, saying the Vatican's old culture was to never let the "outside world" know the full story. Putting a positive spin on things, he said the discoveries meant the Vatican is in better financial shape than previously thought. At the same time, the announcement was a sign that Pell and his staff are not deferring to anyone in trying to get a handle on the fiscal situation. After these moves, there is no doubt about who's wielding the power of the purse: his name is George Pell.

EACH YEAR, THE VATICAN SPENDS about $650 million, roughly half of it to operate the Holy See, the bureaucracy that runs the Catholic Church, and another half to fund the Vatican City State, which oversees the 108-acre physical territory that includes the Vatican museums, post office and gardens. To cover those outlays, it depends on three basic revenue streams. The first is interest and dividends from its investment portfolio, a fund which has its origins in a lump-sum cash settlement paid by the Italian government back in 1929 to offset the loss of the old Papal States in central Italy. In today's money the value of that payout was about $100 million, some of which the Vatican used to build a train station and the rest of which was invested. The second stream is rental income from buildings and apartments owned by the Vatican in Italy and other parts of the world. The third revenue stream comprises contributions from Catholic dioceses and movements around the world, with the Germans and the Americans vying every year to be the largest national contributor. Generally the Vatican's annual income and annual expenditures balance each other.

In truth, the Vatican is not the financial colossus of popular mythology. Harvard University has an annual budget more than five times as large. The University of Notre Dame has an annual budget of around $1.3 billion—the Catholic university could fund the Vatican City State three times every year and have plenty of cash left over for new football uniforms.

In terms of assets, the Vatican Bank manages about $9 billion. While not chump change, it would not register on a list of the world's major financial institutions. JP Morgan Chase & Company, the largest bank in the U.S., controlled $2.14 trillion in assets in 2014. Most of the $9 billion under management in the Vatican Bank isn't the pope's money. It belongs to Catholic dioceses, religious orders, lay movements and associations and other Church-affiliated organizations around the world. Each year the Vatican Bank contributes about $50 million to the pope for use as he sees fit, but otherwise he's not in a position to draw on the bank's assets on a regular basis.

Yet despite its relatively modest financial footprint, the Vatican seems to have a genius for breeding financial scandal that is completely out of proportion to its resources.

THE GRANDDADDY OF ALL SCANDALS involved an Italian financier named Roberto Calvi, dubbed "God's Banker" for his close Vatican ties. Calvi was found hanged under London's Blackfriars Bridge on the edge of the city's financial district in 1982. Police found Calvi's pockets stuffed with bricks and the equivalent of about $15,000 in cash in three different currencies. His death has variously been ruled a suicide and a homicide by teams of English and Italian investigators, and to this day there is no consensus. Calvi was on the lam after the spectacular collapse of Banco Ambrosiano, a private Italian bank that he headed, amid a sea of bad debt, much of which had been underwritten by the Vatican Bank at the behest of its then-president, American archbishop Paul Marcinkus. The Vatican denied any legal responsibility for Banco Ambrosiano, insisting that Marcinkus had merely issued letters of "patronage" offering informal support for Calvi. Nevertheless, in 1984 the Vatican Bank entered into a gentlemen's agreement with 120 creditor banks to pay $240.9 million as a voluntary contribution to making good on the debt. At the time, the Vatican was trying to renegotiate its concordat, or treaty, with the Italian state; one minister in the Italian government had proposed that the Vatican pay a staggering sum of $1.3 billion for its role in the Ambrosiano debacle, so the quarter-billion offer seemed like a good deal.

The Calvi affair has become legend. It has been described as an occult hit carried by dark forces—with Italy's infamous P2 Masonic ring one candidate and the conservative Catholic Opus Dei movement another—and somehow connected to the death of Pope John Paul I, the "smiling pope" who reigned only 33 days in 1978. That such theories even exist illustrates how badly poor financial management has damaged the Vatican's moral authority.

The hard truth is that electing a new pope is not tantamount to flipping a switch and changing the system overnight. Shortly after Francis's election, 62-year-old cleric Nunzio Scarano was arrested by Italian authorities. Scarano had served for 22 years as an accountant in APSA, the department that handles the Vatican's real estate holdings in Italy and around the world (for instance, the Vatican once held a minority share in Washington's Watergate complex). APSA also administers the Vatican's investment portfolio.

Scarano was a smooth character in a Roman collar. Silver-haired and often clad in elegant clerical attire, he supposedly got by on a modest salary of a little more than 30,000 euros a year, yet he was known in Rome as "Monsignor 500," because he always seemed to have a wad of large euro notes in his pocket. Scarano often boasted about his ties to the rich and famous and kept company with a gaggle of Italian fat cats. He also claimed to hold a private art collection that included originals by Chagall, Van Gogh and Bernini.

Over a period of 10 years, the equivalent of almost $8 million moved in and out of Scarano's accounts at the Vatican Bank. When Scarano was arrested, prosecutors alleged he had been a key figure in a plot to smuggle $26 million in cash from Switzerland into Italy on behalf of a family of Italian shipping magnates seeking to evade tax reporting requirements. According to the arrest warrant, Scarano was conspiring with a former Italian secret service agent and was planning to use his Vatican diplomatic passport to smooth reentry into Italy (on a private Gulfstream jet). The scheme ultimately collapsed, as the various alleged culprits were arrested and promptly began pointing the finger at one another.

Scarano was placed under house arrest in Salerno while the charges made their way through the legal system. In January 2014 a second arrest warrant was issued, this time on charges of faking Church donations in order to cover a substantial money-laundering operation through his accounts at the Vatican Bank. Prosecutors say that Scarano persuaded about 60 people to write checks in his name worth about 10,000 euros each, ostensibly to cover the debts of a real estate company. Investigators say he actually paid each of these people for their checks with an equivalent amount in cash, then used the checks to create a false paper trail to explain other deposits of obscure origins.

On both charges, Scarano says his motives were innocent, that he was simply trying to help a friend. His attorney, Silverio Sica, has firmly rejected claims that the monsignor is guilty of breaking Italian law. As of December 2014, a criminal trial against Scarano and 49 other people charged with abetting his activities was ongoing.

Notes from the interrogations of Scarano, published later in the Italian newspaper *Il Fatto Quotidiano*, reveal that he saw himself as a creature of a corrupt culture. Scarano claimed that during his time at APSA, officials routinely accepted gifts from major global banks looking to capture part of the Vatican's assets, including such perks as "trips, cruises, five-star hotels, massages, etc." Scarano also asserted that officials rigged a bidding process to perform repairs on Vatican properties in favor of a well-known Italian businessman, supposedly in exchange for a share of the profits. Further, Scarano is quoted as alleging that APSA operated as a parallel bank, allowing lay Italian VIPs to put money into APSA's investment funds, in part to avoid paying taxes. Scarano even tried to paint himself as a reformer, asserting that he had tried to bring suspicious movements of money at the Congregation for the Evangelization of Peoples—the Vatican's missionary arm, also known as Propaganda Fidei—to the Vatican's attention but that no one had wanted to listen.

Most institutions will at some point attract a controversial figure like Scarano, but a close reading of the Vatican's recent record suggests that he's merely an especially brazen example of a widespread culture of corruption. For evidence, one need only visit Rome's Prati neighborhood, just north of the Vatican by the Tiber River. There, in an understated but elegant building on the tree-lined Via Monte Zebio, lies a sprawling seven-and-a-half-room apartment with an estimated market value of $1.8 million. Its current occupant, an Italian politician named Nicola Cosentino, didn't pay anything close to that amount when he bought the place in 2004 (he got it for $800,000). A former official in the center-right government of previous Italian prime minister Silvio Berlusconi—and a distant relative of an infamous mob boss in Naples—Cosentino scored the sweetheart deal from Cardinal Crescenzio Sepe, who at the time was serving as prefect at Propaganda Fidei. The congregation also happens to be one of the biggest holders of real estate in Rome.

During his term at Propaganda Fidei, from 2001 to 2006, Sepe became renowned in political circles for his alleged willingness to make properties available to VIPs at below-market prices. Antonio Corbo, a former top financial official in the city of Melfi and a onetime rising star in Italian politics said that in those years, "There wasn't a politician, government minister or member of parliament just elected who didn't go to His Eminence [Sepe] while they were in Rome to work something out."

As it happens, these deals were being cut at precisely the same moment that Sepe and Propaganda Fidei were allegedly seeking favors from the Italian government, including millions of euros in public funds allocated for remodeling projects at the department's headquarters in Rome's chic Piazza di Spagna (the remodeling was never actually completed). In 2010, Italian magistrates announced they were opening an investigation into Sepe based on suspicions of a quid pro quo, meaning that the cut-rate prices on apartments were tantamount to bribes meant to pry loose the public coffers. Although the investigation was still open at press time, Sepe has declared his innocence, insisting, "I acted solely for the good of the Church."

Eerily similar words were uttered in 2014 by another Vatican heavyweight who likewise found himself the target of corruption allegations. Italian cardinal Tarcisio Bertone, who was the secretary of state—in effect, the Vatican's prime minister—during the reign of Pope Benedict XVI was accused of having used his personal influence to direct almost $20 million in Vatican Bank funds to Italian film company Lux Vide, which made documentaries about religious figures and was on the brink of insolvency. Lux Vide was run by Ettore Bernabei, a Bertone ally and a former director general of the Italian state TV network RAI. Although the Vatican ruled out any criminal charges against Bertone, the morals governing his actions were dubious. The money was loaned at the very end of Benedict's reign, and one year later the board of supervisors for the Vatican Bank basically decided to write off the debt, acknowledging that the struggling company would never be in a position to pay it back. The obligations were transferred at no cost to a Catholic foundation, which thereby became a minority owner of Lux Vide. The impression was that Bertone took advantage of his final days in power to deliver a $20 million favor to a crony, at the expense of the dioceses, religious orders, Catholic charitable organizations and others who entrust their resources to the Vatican Bank. Bertone has denied doing anything illicit, saying he was merely acting to help a friend who had provided loyal service to the Church.

To add insult to injury, the revelations came at the same time a spacious apartment in the Vatican's Palazzo San Carlo was being renovated for

Bertone's use in retirement. Given that the renovation combined two smaller apartments into one, the former secretary of state now has a total living space estimated to be five times the size of Pope Francis's modest quarters. The contrast was too much even for some of Bertone's former foot soldiers. Fr. Paolo Farinella, a priest from Genoa, where Bertone had previously served as archbishop, said the cardinal "should be ashamed." He added, "People are dying of hunger, and we can't live like this. . . . The pope should make him resign as a cardinal." Francis didn't take that step, but Bertone was compelled to publicly defend himself. He sent a letter to the diocesan newspapers of Vercelli and Genova, where he had previously served, addressing criticisms made against him and describing the supportive phone call he'd received from Pope Francis in which Francis expressed his "solidarity and his disappointment for the attacks" on Bertone. It was a highly unusual step for a former Vatican prime minister.

The Vatican is not the only place where financial mismanagement and scandal in the Catholic Church occurs. Michael W. Ryan, a retired U.S. Postal Service inspector and lifelong Catholic, has made a personal crusade of better money management in the Church. His estimate is that Catholic parishes in the U.S. lose as much as $90 million annually due to inadequate control of the fruits of the collection plate.

Two of the worst recent offenders were in Florida. Frs. Francis Guinan and John Skehan served as pastors of the affluent parish of St. Vincent Ferrer Catholic Church in Delray Beach, until they were arrested in 2006 and charged with several counts of grand theft. It turns out that both men had been skimming from the collection plate for years, often in a remarkably brazen fashion. Skehan took the cash out of the church in his cassock and then stuffed it above the ceiling tiles of his nearby condominium—a residence he'd financed with some of the looted funds. (He also managed to buy a $250,000 coin collection, as well as a cottage and a pub in his native Ireland.) Guinan, meanwhile, was able to cover the cost of enrolling his girlfriend's son at a local Catholic high school and took frequent gambling trips to Las Vegas and the Bahamas. Investigators believe the two priests were responsible for looting more than $1 million from St. Vincent Ferrer church over several years. Although Skehan and Guinan claimed they were trying to help parishioners, they were both convicted and completed prison sentences.

When Pope Francis says the Catholic Church must always welcome sinners but should shun the corrupt, Skehan and Guinan are assuredly the sort of people he has in mind. The aim of his reform is to stop the Vatican from providing cover for such corruption and become a role model in the fight against it.

THE PURSUIT OF FINANCIAL REFORM began under Pope Benedict XVI, who in 2010 launched a financial watchdog agency within the Vatican, called the Financial Information Authority and known by its Italian acronym, AIF, to ensure that the Vatican complies with international standards in the fight against money laundering. In 2011 and 2012 Benedict also invited the first-ever evaluation of the Vatican's financial operations, turning to Moneyval, the Council of Europe's anti-money-laundering agency. Never before had the Vatican opened its financial and legal systems to this sort of external, independent review, with the results made public.

Benedict wasn't done. In his last personnel move as pope, shortly before his resignation in February 2013, Benedict brought in a new president for the Vatican Bank: a businessman and fellow German, Ernst von Freyberg. Von Freyberg denies there was any Teutonic conspiracy behind the move. "If there was, no one ever told me," he said, explaining that he met Benedict XVI exactly once before he resigned, and all the pontiff said to him was "Welcome to Rome." Von Freyberg quickly got down to work, hiring the American regulatory-compliance firm Promontory to conduct a wide-ranging review of the bank's accounts, resulting in around 1,600 of them being closed. Von Freyberg turned over the massive president's office to the Promontory team, settling instead in a small room in another wing of the bank's historic headquarters in the Tower of Nicholas V. Promontory installed banks of computer terminals tracking the movement of every euro into and out of the institution. For the first time, the Vatican knew exactly where its funds were and what they were being used for.

In a few cases, the bank didn't even have to go through the process of closing an account, because a disgruntled client was put off and chose to walk away. Cardinal Juan Luis Cipriani of Lima, Peru, announced he was pulling his money out after von Freyberg's team sent him a raft of paperwork, saying that he didn't feel like undergoing an "inquisition" and that he'd get better treatment at an ordinary commercial bank.

Benedict's efforts at reform have accelerated under Pope Francis, with a December 2013 progress report from Moneyval concluding that "much work has been done in a short time" to bring the Vatican in line with global best practices. For one thing, Francis has refused to invoke traditional claims of sovereignty to fend off investigations into personnel such as Scarano. On the contrary, during a flight from Rio de Janeiro to Rome in July 2014, he jokingly said to the traveling press corps that Scarano had so far avoided jail only "because he resembled the Blessed Imelda." (The reference was to a 14th-century Italian nun known for her piety, who also has a strong following in Argentina.)

At the same time Francis was creating new structures to oversee Vatican finances, he also authorized the release of a detailed 100-page financial statement from the Vatican Bank in October 2013, based on a review by global auditing firm KPMG, the first time the institution had published an independently certified summary of its holdings. He rubber-stamped the hiring of several other big consulting firms, including Ernst and Young and McKinsey & Company, to advise the Vatican on modernizing its financial operation. The personnel deployed by these firms became so ubiquitous that at one stage a well-known Italian writer joked that there were now more consultants inside the Vatican than priests and that the Holy See ought to consider temporarily relocating to New York to cut down on their travel costs. But Francis saw the decision to bring in outside secular professionals as another way of rejecting the myth of clerical omniscience.

Another major step toward discipline came in February 2013, in the form of a letter from the pope's new secretary of state, Italian cardinal Pietro Parolin, imposing a hiring freeze on all Vatican offices, as well as suspending pay increases and internal promotions and forbidding overtime. By the usual standards of Vatican circumspection, the letter was remarkably candid. Parolin began by admitting that the Vatican was in the red and said it had no choice but to tighten its belt. He made the hiring freeze and other measures stick, refusing to grant the one-off exceptions that were historically regularly given.

After Francis created his new centralized finance ministry and put Pell in charge, the Vatican assembled a colorful cast of characters to help carry the load. The lineup begins with Cardinal Reinhard Marx of Munich, Germany, chosen by Pope Francis as the head of the new Council for the Economy. (The irony of having a churchman named Marx in charge of money isn't lost on anyone.) Like Pell, Marx is a member of the pope's G8 council of cardinal advisers, and he has a reputation for social concern. The bearded, somewhat portly Marx is a physical contrast to the lanky Pell, and Marx is theologically more to the left, but both are impatient with what they see as an Italian-dominated, archaic way of running the Vatican.

Outside the ranks of the cardinals, the key reformer in Francis's Vatican is a Swiss lawyer and anti-money-laundering expert with movie-star good looks named René Bruelhart. He directs the AIF, whose mission is to monitor compliance with global standards regarding money laundering and the financing of terrorism, and its power has been significantly enhanced by Pope Francis to become both a financial intelligence unit and a supervisory body. Bruelhart has been aggressive about implementing that mandate, carrying out an inspection of the Vatican Bank in early 2014 and preparing to launch a similar review of operations at APSA.

Bruelhart's background gives him international credibility. As a director of Liechtenstein's financial intelligence unit, he made his mark by cleaning up the tiny nation's reputation as a fiscal pariah. In 2003, when Bruelhart helped return a Falcon 50 business jet worth several million dollars to the new Iraqi government after the fall of Saddam Hussein, it was the first case in which an asset held by Saddam outside Iraq was successfully repatriated. Since arriving in Rome in September 2013, Bruelhart has put out two annual reports listing the number of suspicious transaction reports his office received in the previous year. In 2012 the number was six, while in 2013 it leaped to 202, a spike that Bruelhart attributes not to an increase in illegal activity but rather to the fact that "the system works"—that new reporting protocols are actually being followed.

Another important figure is economist Joseph F.X. Zahra ("F.X." is for legendary Jesuit missionary Francis Xavier), the former director of Malta's Central Bank, who was named in February 2014 the senior lay member of the new Council for the Economy. A Renaissance man, Zahra is also a playwright and the author of a book of verse. A regular at the Domus Santa Marta, he often spends an hour or more of private time with the pope in his two-room residence, and the pope regularly calls him (including one time when Zahra was in the shower and he took the call). Zahra has said he isn't worried about resistance from a clerical old guard in the Vatican, because it's clear that Francis is throwing his political support behind the reform push. "What people have to understand is that holding on to the status quo is unsustainable, that they have to move with the times," Zahra told the *Boston Globe*.

Many of the key figures in Francis's reform effort are non-Italians, expressing the Argentine pontiff's calculus that one way to bring the Vatican into the 21st century is to internationalize its financial management.

Yet the pope also knows that whatever else happens, the Vatican is located in Italy, and so having a couple of Italians as part of the team is essential.

One such Italian is the new prelate at the Vatican Bank, Monsignor Battista Ricca, a veteran of the Vatican diplomatic corps with no special training in finance. Although his résumé may seem to go against Francis's push for a new way of doing business, Ricca had actually run afoul of the old power structure in the Secretariat of State and had been sent out to pasture as the head of three Vatican-owned residences in Rome, including the Domus Santa Marta (which is where he got to know the new pope). By tapping Ricca, Francis was sending a clear signal that he didn't trust the judgment of the power structure and wanted his own eyes and ears at the bank.

Blowback was not long in coming. In July 2013 a veteran Italian journalist published a steamy exposé in *l'Espresso* claiming that when Ricca was an envoy in Uruguay in the late 1990s he had been involved in various homosexual escapades. When Francis refused to remove Ricca, it communicated that the pontiff doesn't intend to allow his reform campaign to be derailed by character assassination. Insiders say the affair actually strengthened Ricca's position at the bank, making him seem bulletproof because the boss had his back.

The other Italian the pope turned to was Franco dalla Sega, a 54-year-old professor, lawyer and business consultant who was named a special consultant at APSA in April 2014. Despite the vague title, the post is important, given that the toughest nut to crack will probably be APSA. Dalla Sega has close ties to the worlds of Italian banking and finance and may well emerge as the primary interlocutor for the new-look Vatican with its counterparts in the Italian banking and financial regulatory systems. "Once upon a time, we used to say that people in northern Italy with money to hide would go to San Marino or Switzerland, people in the south would go to Sicily, while in Rome they'd go to the Vatican," dalla Sega said in May 2014. "What Pope Francis wants to do is take the Vatican off that list."

DESPITE FRANCIS'S EFFORTS, history has proved the Vatican stubbornly resistant to reform. In 1967 Pope Paul VI created a Prefecture for Economic Affairs in an effort to provide an accurate overall picture of the Vatican's financial condition. Four years later, the pontiff was presented with the first balance sheet since the loss of the pope's temporal power a century earlier but felt he couldn't make it public since no one would take it seriously. Among other things, the various departments used different methods for calculating the worth of their holdings—some relied on the purchase price, others on estimated current market value, others on what they thought they could realistically get for it, and so on. That largely remains the case today, almost 50 years after Paul VI set out to bring the Church into the modern world.

In addition to the weight of history, there are three other mammoth obstacles standing in the pope's way. First, although the Vatican is in principle a global institution akin to the U.N., it is still physically located in Rome and heavily conditioned by Italian culture. For the most part, technical administration has been done by figures in Italian business and banking. The result is that the Vatican has long reflected Italian culture when it comes to money: the most serious problem isn't occasional instances of flagrant abuse but the fact that behavior long considered taboo in modern business practice isn't even perceived as corrupt. Rigging competitive bidding procedures to steer contracts to one's relatives or friends, hiring people based on patronage rather than competence and not asking too many questions about where the money comes from are regarded as how things are done by many Italians of a certain generation. That's part of the reason why a 2014 study by the European Union concluded that half of the 120-million-euro cost of corruption in member states came from Italy alone. The same study included a poll suggesting that 97 percent of Italians believe corruption is widespread in their country and 88 percent have found that sometimes paying a bribe is the easiest way, if not the only way, to obtain public services. Italians who need a permit to remodel their homes often feel compelled to slip a few euros into the hands of a zoning official, and those who live in apartments often pay rent in cash because their landlords have no intention of reporting the income. If that's the experience Vatican personnel have outside of work, it may be unrealistic to expect them not to replicate those attitudes and practices while in the Holy See.

Second, while Francis may have lined up the generals to wage this war, it's not clear yet whether he has the foot soldiers to pull it off. In the Vatican Bank, some see the Promontory team as a band of interlopers. The fact that the Promontory operatives are physically segregated from the rest of the staff—in addition to their speaking German rather than Italian—doesn't help. At APSA, many veterans perceive the rumored overhaul as an overreaction to the private sins of Scarano. Given that Vatican labor laws (modeled on Italy's) make it virtually impossible to fire anyone, and given the moral reluctance of most Vatican officials to be seen as acting in contradiction to the Church's traditional teaching on the protection of labor rights, it's unlikely that Francis and his reform team will lead a purge.

Third, there's the thorny question of what financial reform means in the first place. For instance, is reform exclusively about maximizing income and minimizing expenses, thereby reducing the burden on dioceses around the world? That seems to be central to Pell's understanding. If so, it would be logical to adopt a different approach to the scores of apartments the Vatican owns around Rome that are currently assigned to workers at below-market rates as informal compensation for paying low salaries. In many cases, the apartments are badly in need of repairs. Over the years, consultants have advised the Vatican to kick its workers out of these apartments, invest in repairs and then sell the properties for a handsome profit. Yet is evicting blue-collar Vatican employees from their homes in the name of maximizing income really consistent with the pope's call for a "poor Church for the poor"? Those kinds of questions remain to be answered.

The situation is different from past eras when the Vatican went through a spasm of reform. That's partly because of Francis, the first pope since Paul VI to make internal governance a real priority; and because of Pell, who's nobody's idea of a milquetoast; and also because of the dynamics of the last conclave, the most anti-establishment papal election in a century.

Experts like Kerry Robinson, an American lay Catholic and founder of the National Leadership Roundtable on Church Management (an organization that aims to provide Catholic bishops with resources to promote best business practices), have warned for years that financial meltdowns could become just as damaging to the Church's moral authority and public image as the child sexual abuse scandals. "There's a real danger that the financial scandals we've seen are only the tip of the iceberg," Robinson said. "If they're not addressed, they could actually dwarf the abuse crisis, which is why what Francis is doing is so important."

When he was appointed to his new role as the pope's financial czar, Pell said the idea was to transform the Vatican from an embarrassment to a model of best practices with regard to money management, setting a tone for the Church all around the world. With Francis and Pell framing things that way, many observers agree that they are now engaged in a race against the clock to prevent debacles and restore confidence among the world's 1.2 billion Catholics that when they give money to support the pope and the Vatican, it will be responsibly managed.

5

Women and
the Church

DESPITE BEING A MEMBER of the Jesuit religious order,
Pope Francis is generally one of the least "Jesuitic" public figures around,
in the pejorative sense of the term (that is, a person who is hair-splitting
and a master of saying one thing but meaning another). He uses home-
spun pastoral imagery that ordinary people have no problem understanding—for instance, advising married couples to fight as much they
want but not to go to bed angry. Even when he's on a theological jag,
he's usually fairly straightforward. When he talks about mercy, no one
suspects him of secretly reviving the Inquisition. Yet when it comes to
the subject of women in the Catholic Church, Francis has managed to
create lively expectations without being terribly clear about how he
plans to fulfill them.

On two occasions when the pontiff has been asked about possibly
admitting women to the ranks of the clergy, he has given a firm no.

At the same time, he has said that he wants to see a "greater role" for women in Catholicism, including participation in the "important decisions . . . where the authority of the Church is exercised." He has also said that he wants a "deeper theology" about the place of women in the faith, one that will emphasize the critically important contributions they make. During his first two years in office, however, there were relatively few steps forward in either regard. No groundbreaking new roles for women were created and no new theological study was commissioned. While Francis's popularity tends to insulate him against the criticism that such a record might otherwise attract, over time his ability to reframe impressions of the Catholic Church as a boys' club, at least at the top, will be an important measure of his success—not merely because it's a question of interest to the outside world but also because Francis himself has set it as a standard. During a 2013 Vatican symposium on women, he described the recognition of women's role in the Church as a cause that's "close to my heart."

The issue of women in the Church is not an abstraction for Francis. Rather, he has a lifetime of relationships with a variety of strong, accomplished women to draw upon and envision ways in which Catholicism might evolve.

IN THE EARLY 1970s Alicia Oliveira was a single mother of three, a lawyer, judge and typical anti-clerical left-wing Peronist. Juan Perón served three times as the country's president and dominated its national life from the 1950s through the 1970s. Though almost impossible to define with precision, Peronism is said to be based on three pillars: social justice, economic independence and political sovereignty. It was regarded as a third way between communism and capitalism. Peronists asserted the dignity of the working class and ordinary people over the elites and the social dominance of the Church. By the 1970s, however, it had fractured into a right wing that supported a security state and a left wing that flirted with Marxism. Oliveira located herself in that second, leftist camp, which tended to harbor a special loathing for Catholic clerics.

It was therefore counterintuitive that one of her close friends was a Jesuit priest thought to be a right-wing Peronist—a man who was about to become his order's top official in Argentina. Although the bond between a left-wing, non-believing judge and the apparently right-wing Bergoglio seems odd, they were upside-down times in Argentina, as the country was on the brink of the Dirty War.

In 1972 Perón, who had been exiled by a military dictatorship, was about to return to Argentina. Oliveira was by then Argentina's first female criminal judge. She was also among the founders of Argentina's Center for Legal and Social Studies, a progressive human-rights and pro-democracy group that was regarded with deep suspicion by the military and security forces. Bergoglio was not yet the provincial superior of the Jesuits, but when he was asked to handle a small legal matter for the order, on the advice of a mutual friend he sought out Oliveira. As they worked on the legal issue, the unlikely couple talked about the current state of affairs in the country and found themselves to be kindred spirits. They struck up a friendship, chatting on the phone and occasionally getting together with other friends to talk about which way the winds were blowing.

Three years later, with rumors of another military coup circulating, Oliveira was concerned for her and her children's safety. Bergoglio, by then in charge of the country's Jesuits, invited her and her family to move into the order's Colegio del Salvador in Buenos Aires, but Oliveira turned him down, later admitting she had told Bergoglio, "I'd rather go to prison than live with priests!"

The coup finally came in 1976, and with it a military regime led by Jorge Rafael Videla, a senior commander in the armed forces who eventually ruled the country as a dictator from 1976 to 1981. He presided over the most intense phase of the Dirty War, when tens of thousands of political dissidents disappeared and were killed. (After Argentina returned to democracy in 1983 Videla was charged with crimes against humanity and sentenced to life in prison, dying in incarceration in 2013.) After Videla's rise to power, Oliveira was fired from her court position and forced to take refuge in the apartment of a friend, another female lawyer and left-wing Peronist named Nilda Celia Garré. (Both would go on to serve in the left-wing governments of Nestor and Cristina Kirchner in the 2000s.) When Oliveira went into hiding, an anonymous bouquet of red roses arrived for her with a note praising her work as a jurist—she recognized the handwriting as that of her friend Bergoglio. To protect her children, Oliveira left them with another friend, so they would be safe if she was arrested. But twice a week, Bergoglio picked up Oliveira and escorted her into the relatively safe confines of the Colegio del Salvador, where she and her children could spend time together. (One of her sons was attending the college at the time.) His gesture wasn't nothing: each time Bergoglio brought Oliveira out of hiding and into the college, he violated a military edict against harboring enemies of the state and risked arrest.

Many years later, when Bergoglio became Pope Francis, he faced questions about his past. The hunt focused primarily on his time as a Jesuit superior in Argentina during the Dirty War. Francis had plenty of people ready to stick up for him, but none were more forceful or effective than Alicia Oliveira. In an interview with the Argentine daily *La Nacion*, she told of a case in which Bergoglio provided his own passport and clerical clothes to a man who bore a passing resemblance to him, to allow the man to get past border controls and out of Argentina. Oliveira said she never asked the future pope exactly how he was getting people out of the country, understanding it was "too risky for him" to discuss the details, even with close friends. She said that Bergoglio did, however, confide in her about his fears for progressive Jesuits working in the *villas miserias* of Buenos Aires and taking part in anti-government activism, and his efforts to keep them as safe as possible. Oliveira joined farewell lunches Bergoglio organized for other Argentines he was helping to flee, usually at a Jesuit residence near the Plaza de Mayo (the same square in central Buenos Aires where the famed Mothers of the Plaza de Mayo later staged protests, demanding to know the fate of the *desaparecidos*, their disappeared children).

So when allegations about Bergoglio's role during the military years resurfaced, Oliveira was eager to set the record straight. "Mine is the opinion of a friend, and one has very few real friends," Oliveira told *La Nacion* two days after the pope's election. "Jorge is my friend, before he's a cardinal or a pope. He is a great man, someone who is always concerned about people who are suffering. He's also a man who helped many during the dictatorship . . . putting his own life at risk." Oliveira said Bergoglio's attitude toward the military regime was crystal clear: he often referred to them as "scoundrels."

Oliveira and Bergoglio remained friends after the transition to democracy in Argentina; Bergoglio celebrated Oliveira sister's wedding and is the godfather to Oliveira's son Alejandro. In February 2013, shortly before boarding the flight that would carry him to Rome for the conclave to elect a successor to Pope Benedict XVI, one of Bergoglio's last phone calls was to Oliveira. He vowed they would get together as soon as he was back in Buenos Aires. Weeks later, upon hearing the news of Bergoglio's election, Oliveira wept openly while standing in a coffee bar, partly out of joy and also out of sadness that her old friend was not coming home.

Oliveira died in November 2014 at the age of 71, following an operation to remove a brain tumor. Francis called members of her family that night to offer his consolation and to say he was praying for his friend's eternal rest.

POPE FRANCIS WAS BORN in 1936 and entered the Society of Jesus in 1958, meaning most of his formative experiences as a priest came before the reforming Second Vatican Council, held from 1962–65. The pre–Vatican II period was an era in which prospective clergymen typically entered the system young and lived in an environment in which interaction with the opposite sex was deliberately restricted, to the point that they were discouraged from looking too closely at women, a discipline known in the argot of the clerical world as "custody of the eyes."

As a result, when talk turns to women, clerics of the pope's generation often talk about their mothers or grandmothers, or perhaps a nun who taught them in grade school. They are keen to extol the domestic contributions of women—their importance in raising families, passing on the faith and imparting basic human virtues—which can make their rhetoric seem outdated and patronizing. Francis certainly feels such fondness for the women in his own family, especially, as we have seen, his paternal grandmother, Rosa.

On the other hand, Francis is atypical of many clergymen of his generation in that he did not enter a minor seminary as a teenager, where he would have been cut off from the outside world. Instead, he moved in the hurly-burly world of Argentina in the 1950s, a time when the Latin American nation was considered one of the most developed, cosmopolitan societies in the world. It was an environment in which women could serve in leadership capacities, inspired by Eva Perón's de facto role as spiritual leader of the nation.

After earning a degree from a technical school as a chemical assistant, Bergoglio worked in the foods section of the Hickethier-Bachmann laboratory, running chemical tests on nutrients. Bergoglio's supervisor at the lab was Esther Ballestrino de Careaga, a Paraguayan communist who had fled her country's military dictatorship in 1949 and settled in Buenos Aires with her daughters. Although Francis didn't realize it at the time, he would later become the first pope of the Catholic Church to have had a woman as a boss. He has often referred to Ballestrino as a major influence on his life. She was undoubtedly in his mind when he said in a 2013 interview that he wasn't offended by Rush Limbaugh calling him a Marxist because "I have met many Marxists in my life who are good people." Francis has said that Ballestrino drilled into him the importance of paying attention to details in his work, forcing him to repeat tests to confirm his results. "The work I did was one of the best things I've done in my life," Bergoglio later said in a 2010 interview with Argentine journalists Sergio Rubin and Francesca Ambrogetti. "[Esther Ballestrino de Careaga was] an extraordinary boss. When I handed her an analysis, she'd say, 'Wow, you did that so fast. . . . Did you do the test or not?' I would answer, 'What for?' If I'd done all the previous tests, it would surely be more or less the same. 'No, you have to do things properly,' she would chide me. In short, she taught me the seriousness of hard work. Truly, I owe a huge amount to that great woman." In another section of the interview, Bergoglio said that Ballestrino "taught me so much about politics."

Bergoglio reconnected with his former boss a decade later, when she and her family were under surveillance by the Argentine military regime. At one point, Ballestrino called to ask him to come to her house to give a relative last rites, which surprised Bergoglio because he knew the family wasn't religious. The truth was that Ballestrino needed someone to stash her extensive collection of Marxist literature; the young Jesuit provincial superior agreed to do so. Later, Bergoglio helped Ballestrino find one of her daughters who had been kidnapped by military forces. (She was detained and tortured for several months before being released.) Ballestrino became one of the founders of the Mothers of the Plaza de Mayo, often reaching out to Bergoglio for help.

Tragically, Ballestrino herself "disappeared" at the hands of security forces in 1977. Almost three decades later, when her remains were discovered and identified, Bergoglio gave permission for her to be buried in the garden of a Buenos Aires church called Santa Cruz, the spot where she had been abducted. Her daughter requested that her mother and several other women be buried there because "it was the last place they had been as free people." Despite knowing full well that Ballestrino was not a believing Catholic, the future pope readily consented.

There are other women who have been close to Bergoglio. Julia Torres, a leader of the Comunità di Gesù in Argentina, an offshoot of a charismatic movement founded in Italy, had frequent contact with Bergoglio while he was archbishop and became one of his closest advisers on a wide range of issues. María Lía Zerviño worked with Bergoglio in the archdiocese of Buenos Aires and also through the secretariat of the World Union of Catholic Women's Organisations. Bergoglio has good relations with several female journalists, including Francesca Ambrogetti, Elisabetta Piqué of *La Nacion* and Italian writer Stefania Falasca. Argentine journalist Alicia Barrios grew close enough to the pontiff to see him regularly and joke around with him. (For the record, there has never been any suggestion that his friendships with these women were anything other than platonic.) According to Barrios, Francis once asked her and the other women visiting him to stop wearing the black dresses that papal etiquette requires be worn by any woman other than a Catholic queen, who has the privilege of wearing white. He jokingly said that when he walks into a roomful of people wearing black, whether they're priests or visiting female friends, he has a flashback to his childhood fear of black cockroaches.

For an elderly Catholic clergyman, Francis is thus a rare commodity in his experience of women. He has come to know laywomen not only as family members but as professionally accomplished friends, bosses and equals. Francis clearly values the roles women play as wives and mothers, but it's not the only framework he has for understanding the contributions women make in both the Church and the wider world.

DESPITE HIS TALK OF EXPANDED roles for women in the Church, Francis is still firmly against ordaining women as priests or, for that matter, as clergy of any kind. He has even rejected the idea of reviving an older tradition of lay cardinals that would include women. (A lay cardinal is a nonclerical member of the College of Cardinals.) The proposal has drawn influential support from the likes of Lucetta Scaraffia, a historian and columnist for the Vatican newspaper *L'Osservatore Romano*, but Francis has unambiguously shot it down. Francis's clearest statement on the ordination issue came during an airborne press conference in July 2013, when he was returning from Rio de Janeiro. "The Church has spoken and says no. . . . That door is closed," he said.

The pontiff's rejection of female clergy is so unwavering that critics have accused him of having a blind spot on women's issues. Jon O'Brien of the liberal dissent group Catholics for Choice, an organization that defies orthodoxy by supporting abortion rights, said in 2013 that the pope's message seems to be "Women can wait while he takes care of more important issues." In October 2013 a progressive priests' group in Ireland leveled a similar charge when Francis signed off on the excommunication of Australian Fr. Greg Reynolds, in part for his advocacy of women's ordination.

In May 2014 an advocacy group called Women's Ordination Worldwide held a rally and press conference in Rome to complain that Francis's reforming stance on other matters isn't matched by his position on women's issues. "It's true that Pope Francis is portraying a new image of the Church being open to all and that he is trying to shake off the judgments and restrictions of the past," said activist Miriam Duignan in Rome. "But despite this openness . . . Francis holds fast to the old party line that says, 'Women in priesthood is not open to discussion. It is reserved for men alone. Women are not welcome.' How long do women have to wait to be considered equal and worthy of receiving the same welcome by the official Church as men?"

For many people, including rank-and-file Catholics who believe in gender equality, it is difficult to square Francis's overall reputation as a maverick and a progressive reformer—plus his specific pledges to enhance the role of women in Catholicism—with his steadfast defense of the status quo when it comes to female priests.

The fundamental reason for the Church's refusal to admit women to the priesthood is that it's bound by the example of Christ. Jesus did not include women among his original 12 apostles, so the argument runs, and the Church is compelled to follow that example, restricting the priesthood today to men. Although Francis presumably accepts that teaching, it's not the basis of his own stance on the issue. For him, the push for women priests is where two forces repellent to him intersect: machismo, which is an especially resonant concept for a Latin American, and clericalism, an exaggerated emphasis on the power and privilege of the clergy, which is virtually this pope's personal *bête noire*.

Clues to his feelings came via a September 2013 interview with Jesuit Fr. Antonio Spadaro of the influential journal *Civiltà Cattolica*. While calling for a "stronger presence" of women, Francis added a caution. "I am wary of a solution that can be reduced to a kind of 'female machismo,' because a woman has a different makeup than a man," Francis said. "But what I hear about the role of women is often inspired by an ideology of machismo."

Francis is not the first pope to suspect a latent machismo in certain models of female emancipation. The late Pope John Paul II frequently called for a new feminism to revitalize women's roles as wives and mothers, arguing that feminism is legitimate but needs to be scrubbed of "macho categories" that see the only path to empowerment through the imitation of male psychology and behavior. Prior to his election as pope, then-Cardinal Joseph Ratzinger likewise argued that some models of feminism were based on a utilitarian logic that understands human relationships in terms of a contest for power, saying that on the man's side of the ledger that sort of thinking "heads in the direction of machismo," and thus feminism becomes an equal and opposite "reaction against the exploitation of woman." In effect, the argument was that real feminism is not about an arms race with men, but rather about ending the arms race once and for all by rejecting power as the only way to evaluate one's worth or dignity. As applied to the priesthood, the conclusion is that it's a fallacy to believe that women will never be equal to men in the Church until they wield the same ecclesiastical power. Instead, the argument runs, real feminism means embracing "complementarity": the idea that men and women play different but complementary roles in the wider world and inside the Church.

Naturally, it's an argument that's met with an uneven reception, as many women have responded that it's rather disingenuous to play down the importance of power when you're the one wielding it. Moreover, many theologians in Catholicism, both men and women, point out that in all its official teaching on the subject, the Church describes the priesthood in terms of service rather than power. If that's true, they ask, couldn't the desire of women to become priests be understood in terms of a call to serve rather than a lust for power? In other words, they wonder, has official papal rhetoric set up a straw man?

Whatever the case, Francis appears to accept the diagnosis that the press for women in the priesthood often betrays a type of machismo in reverse. Given the prevalence of violence against women in Latin American culture (according to a 2012 report by the U.N. Economic Commission for Latin America and the Caribbean, 60 percent of females who die a violent death are under 13; seven out of 10 victims of child violence are girls; and in 14 Latin American nations, a man may legally rape his wife or fiancée), it's no surprise that Francis is sensitive to anything that in his mind tries to promote female empowerment by mimicking the worst aspects of male culture, which includes defining importance in terms of control.

If anything, Francis recoils from clericalism even more viscerally than machismo. As Francis has defined it, clericalism means two things: first, an over-emphasis on what he called "small-minded rules" at the expense of mercy and compassion; and second, an exalted notion of clerical power and privilege, as opposed to the spirit of service. Francis continually warns about the corrosive effects of clericalism in the life of the Church—it figures prominently in his interviews, his daily homilies delivered in the chapel of the Domus Santa Marta, and in his remarks to priests and bishops. Francis sees clericalism almost as the original sin of the Catholic priesthood. In informal remarks to leaders of religious orders in late 2013, he referred to the hypocrisy of clericalism as "one of the worst evils" in the Church and memorably said that unless future priests are inoculated against it when they're young, they risk turning out to be "little monsters."

Francis believes the demand for women's admission to the clerical ranks betrays an unconscious clericalism. In a December 2013 interview with the Italian newspaper *La Stampa*, he was asked about the notion that he might name female cardinals. "I don't know where this idea sprang from," Francis replied. "Women in the Church must be valued, not 'clericalized.' Whoever thinks of women as cardinals suffers a bit from clericalism." In his mind, conceding that the only way to elevate the role of women is to make them clergy feeds the mistaken notion that clerics are what's most important about Catholicism, when he sees his mission instead as exalting the role of the laity. When he talks about a "deeper theology" of women, this is likely part of what he has in mind—a sort of Copernican revolution in Catholic consciousness, with laity and women the real protagonists of the Church's mission in the world and the clergy a supporting cast. When he traveled to South Korea in August 2014, he repeatedly invoked the unique history of the Korean Church as one founded not by priests or foreign missionaries but by laypeople, and his delight in that fact was palpable.

To be sure, the argument is unlikely to satisfy many Catholics or women outside the Church, who will always see the ban on female priests as an anachronistic means of defending male privilege. But when Francis said, "That door is closed," he seemed to mean it.

SINCE THE IDEA OF INCLUDING WOMEN in the priesthood has been taken off the table, the question is: What is Francis doing to support enhancing the profile of women in the Catholic Church? Whenever the pontiff has addressed the issue, he has usually talked about "greater" and "expanded" leadership roles for women; assigning more value to the roles women already perform in Catholicism—recognizing, for instance, that the Virgin Mary was not a priest and yet surpassed the original apostles in her importance in salvation history; and fostering a "truly deep theology of women," involving a new understanding of the contribution of women to the life of faith and the feminine dimension of the Church itself.

During his first foreign trip as pope, to Brazil in July 2013, Francis told the country's bishops that he wanted them to "promote the active role of women in the ecclesial community," because "if the Church loses its women . . . it risks sterility." That prompted a reporter on the flight back to Rome to ask Francis to expand on what he sees as the role of women in Catholicism. "A Church without women is like the Apostolic College without Mary," the pope said, referring to the original band of 12 apostles who followed Jesus during his life and built up the Church after his death. He continued, "The role of the woman in the Church is not only maternity, mother of the family, but it is stronger. The role of the woman in the Church mustn't only end as mom, worker, limited. I think that we need to move further ahead in the development of this role and charism of the woman. The Church cannot be understood without women . . . active women in the Church."

Francis then cited the example of women in 19th-century Paraguay after a destructive war with the triple alliance of Argentina, Brazil and Uruguay left the country with a ratio of eight women for every man. Calling those Paraguayan women "the most glorious women of Latin

America," he said they made "a very difficult choice, the choice to have children to save the motherland, the culture, the faith and the language." He argued that their willingness to have children despite deep poverty and the fallout from war illustrates the way in which women often make risky choices that change history. "We haven't yet come up with a deep theology of the woman in the Church," Francis said. "[She] is more important than the bishops and priests," adding that Catholic theology needs to do a better job of explaining why that is the case.

In his most important publication to date, the November 2013 "Evangelii Gaudium" ("The Joy of the Gospel"), Francis included a section on women. In paragraph 103 he wrote, "The Church acknowledges the indispensable contribution women make to society through the sensitivity, intuition and other distinctive skill sets that they, more than men, tend to possess. I think, for example, of the special concern women show to others, which finds a particular, even if not exclusive, expression in motherhood. I readily acknowledge that many women share pastoral responsibilities with priests, helping to guide people, families and groups, and offering new contributions to theological reflection. But we need to create still broader opportunities for a more incisive female presence in the Church. . . . The presence of women must also be guaranteed in the workplace and in the various other settings where important decisions are made, both in the Church and in social structures."

Francis came back to the theme in a January 2014 session with the Italian women's group Centro Italiano Femminile, in which he said he hopes "the spaces for a more incisive and widespread feminine presence in the Church will be enlarged." In keeping with the Vatican's focus on traditional families, Francis emphasized that families benefit from women's "gifts of delicateness, special sensitivity and tenderness." He said, "The presence of women in a domestic setting turns out to be so necessary" for the "transmission to future generations of solid moral principles, and the very transmission of the faith."

Yet to date Francis hasn't done much to make his vision real. During the July 2013 news conference on the flight to Rome, he seemed to suggest that he wasn't talking about women holding formal offices or positions in the Church. "It is not enough to have altar girls, women readers or women as the president of Caritas," he said.

Asked in a March 2014 joint interview with *Corriere della Sera* in Italy and *La Nacion* in Argentina if he was considering naming a woman to head a powerful Vatican department, Francis implied that it wasn't what he had in mind. "Women must have a greater presence in the decision-making areas of the Church," the pope said. "But I would call this a 'functional' promotion,' " presumably meaning that it treats the importance of women in terms of the functions they perform rather than their inherent dignity and worth.

In June 2014 Francis sat down for his first extended interview as pope with a female journalist, veteran Vatican writer Franca Giansoldati of the daily *Il Messaggero*. His answers that day were fairly cryptic. When Giansoldati asked if there's misogyny in the Church, he replied, "The fact is that woman was taken from a rib." He added, laughing, "I'm joking. That was a joke." When Giansoldati pressed Francis on which new roles he had in mind for women, he laughed again and said, "Well, so many times priests end up under the authority of their housekeepers. . . ." The suggestion seemed to be that women don't necessarily need titles or offices to wield influence, but his old-school priestly rhetoric didn't do much to reassure women that a major breakthrough was around the corner.

Amid the general euphoria over the inclusive and compassionate new tone set by Pope Francis, some critics of the Catholic Church's track record on women's issues are inclined to give this reforming pontiff the benefit of the doubt. "People say, 'Well, he's not ordaining women, so therefore this is all irrelevant.' I don't think it is irrelevant," says Catholic feminist Lisa Cahill, a theology professor at Boston College and author of the book *Sex, Gender, and Christian Ethics*. Cahill argues that Francis is engineering a "holistic culture shift" in the Catholic Church, which among other things is about de-emphasizing the wars of culture over abortion and contraception that have long been a bone of contention between the Church and many women's groups. Alice Laffey, an associate professor at the College of the Holy Cross and a veteran Catholic feminist, says that although many Catholic women can't help but see the ban on female priests as discriminatory, Francis's broader anti-poverty agenda is arguably more critical for many women, especially in the developing world. "Throughout the world, women and their children make up the greatest percentage of human beings living in destitution," Laffey wrote in July 2013. "Their main concern is not women priests but food, health, education and physical safety. Francis's genuine concern for the real lives of the poor and suffering warmly embraces women."

When Francis talks about shining a light on the contributions women already make to Catholicism, it's an argument that anyone who knows how the Church actually works on a daily basis will understand. "If you walk into any parish office on a given day, if you were to snap your fingers and remove the female presence from there, nothing would [get done]," says Jesuit Fr. Timothy O'Brien, who edits the *Jesuit Post*. "Most of the places that I've worked as a Jesuit, that are ministries of the Church, are run by women." O'Brien argues that a priest shortage in many parts of the world is making the Church even more dependent on laywomen, meaning that the "greater roles" as described by Pope Francis are to some extent already accomplished.

In the U.S., women make up about 80 percent of ecclesial lay ministers. (The term refers to laypeople working for the Church in either a full-time or part-time capacity, performing roles previously held by priests and nuns, such as catechists, youth ministers, liturgical ministers, music ministers and parish associates.) About a quarter of the diocesan chancellors in America are now women, and women today serve as diocesan spokespeople, general council for dioceses, chief financial officers and in a wide variety of other capacities. Francis's rhetoric could be read to indicate that he supports this evolution toward women's leadership, although his skepticism about "functional" roles makes even that notion somewhat ambiguous.

When Francis talks about "more space" for women, it seems to be less about creating new roles and more about assigning greater value to the roles women already play. It's psychological, theological and moral space he appears to want to enhance, not so much corporate and institutional. As a veteran of the pastoral front lines, Francis knows it's women who raise children in the faith, women who make parishes run, women who keep alive popular devotions and practices, and women who mobilize the Church's human resources in Catholic charities and social service operations when people are in need. To the extent the pope succeeds in shining a spotlight on those contributions, many rank-and-file Catholics will no doubt see it as progress.

Francis's vow to enhance the profile of women in the Church, however, has not really been matched by policy and personnel choices. A year and a half into his reign, Francis had not elevated a single woman to the position of key confidante or aide. Although he retains friends from Buenos Aires and is pals with certain female journalists, there are few female decision-makers inside Francis's Vatican. Mary Ann Glendon, a Harvard law professor and former U.S. ambassador to the Holy See, served on a study commission created by Francis in the summer of 2013 to examine reform of the Vatican's financial structures and was later named a member of the supervisory council for the Vatican Bank. But Glendon is a longtime fixture on the Vatican scene and has acknowledged that she was chosen for these roles because of earlier relationships, rather than any direct personal connection with Pope Francis.

The pontiff has also been presented with several specific proposals for realizing the greater roles for women to which he has referred, and he hadn't acted on any of them as of late 2014. In December 2013 Maria Voce, an Italian lawyer who in 2008 took over leadership of the worldwide Focolare Movement—one of the largest and most influential lay organizations in Catholicism and whose president, by statute, must be female—floated the idea of creating a council of lay advisers for the pope. Her idea was that the council would serve as a companion to the G8 council of cardinal advisers Francis created in April 2013 to ensure that the voices of local churches are integrated more thoroughly into the decision-making process in Rome. As Voce conceived it, the council would be a mixed body of laywomen and -men from around the world, perhaps including at least one married couple, who could make sure the pope draws on the experiences and perspectives of laity in crafting his policy choices. The inclusion of women would send a powerful signal about the pope's determination to reach out to them, and Voce predicted that Francis is exactly the sort of pope who would be open to doing such a thing. Francis, for his part, obviously likes the *focolarini* (as members of the Focolare Movement are known), having received them in audience and praised their work. But Francis has not acted on the suggestion, and there is no indication of any momentum to do so.

In other ways, when Francis has had an opportunity to chip away at the glass ceiling for women in the Vatican, he hasn't done so. His Council for the Economy, for example—featuring a new configuration of eight cardinals and seven lay members—was a powerful step toward lay empowerment and was also groundbreaking in the pope's clear option for internationalization, with only two Italians among the 15 appointments. Among the laity chosen? Not a single woman.

Pressed to explain the lack of women in the group, the lay vice-coordinator of the new council, Maltese economist Joseph Zahra, told the *Boston Globe*, "The pope has spoken strongly about the role of women, and the absence of a woman on this one council in no way means they're being barred or shut out." He continued, "It's more about the fact that the pope wanted to move fast. Five of the seven lay members were members of the study commission, while another is an adviser to the Prefecture for [the] Economic Affairs, so they're all known quantities. As we get going, there's nothing to stop us from drawing on advisers and consultants, and some of those people will definitely be women."

On the plus side, when Francis unveiled the initial members for his new Pontifical Commission for the Protection of Minors in March 2014, the lineup was half men, half women. The women included Marie Collins, an Irish laywoman who was raped at the age of 13 by a priest and is now an activist; Hanna Suchocka, a former prime minister of Poland and the country's former ambassador to the Vatican; Catherine Bonnet, a French child psychologist who has written widely on the effects of sexual abuse and exploitation of children; and Baroness Sheila Hollins, the former president of the British Medical Association, who has frequently consulted on child development issues in the U.K. The primary responsibility for the choices of personnel fell to the man who had been the driving force in getting the commission going in the first place: Cardinal Sean P. O'Malley of Boston.

All that said, by December 2014 Francis had not named *any* layperson, much less a woman, to a senior Vatican position. Doing so might prove problematic, since the leadership offices in the Vatican generally exercise what's known as "vicarious authority" in the name of the pope, and many Church lawyers believe that to be able to do so one has to be a member of the clergy. That might explain why, after Pope John Paul II appointed Italian Salesian nun Sr. Enrica Rosanna as undersecretary of the department that oversees religious orders in 2004, any binding document on which her name appeared was always co-signed by a cleric, in order to short-circuit any ambiguity about the authority it carried. Francis is a pontiff who has shown himself to be unencumbered by legal fine points in other areas, and there are plenty of leadership roles to which women could be appointed that don't involve exercising this kind of authority: serving as the Vatican spokesperson, for instance, or running the Vatican's labor office. The fact is that so far Francis hasn't made any such move.

Despite the pope's repeated calls to develop a deeper theology regarding the role of women in the Church, there's been relatively little forward movement on that score either. Francis has not convened a high-level theological congress, nor has he commissioned a draft of a papal encyclical on the subject (as he has done on other issues that he has made a priority, such as the environment). Nor has he made any overt gestures of reconciliation toward feminist theologians in the same way he has moved to heal wounds with the theology of liberation, a progressive movement born in Latin America in the 1960s and 1970s that sought to place the Church on the side of the poor but was often seen in Rome as a form of Catholic Marxism. He has made no effort to wrap up the Vatican investigation of the Leadership Conference of Women Religious, the main umbrella group for American nuns, a controversial probe launched under Pope Benedict XVI. The charges include doctrinal aberrations and embrace of an almost New Age, post-Christian spirituality. Whatever one makes of the merits of the Vatican's case against the LCWR, the process is seen by many Catholic women as illustrative of the mistrust with which they're often seen in the corridors of power in Rome.

From a PR point of view, Pope Francis has a terrific narrative, and even some of the most acerbic critics of the Catholic Church seem inclined to give him the benefit of the doubt. But if the gap between the pope's rhetoric on women and his track record persists, the public love affair could turn sour. Francis would have no one but himself to blame, because this is one arena in which he has created expectations all by himself.

6

The Social
Gospel

WHILE THE GEOGRAPHICAL CENTER of Francis's papacy is the Vatican, one can catch a better glimpse of its spiritual heart by traveling six miles across town to the northeastern edge of Rome. Just off the Via Giuseppe Barellai, in a place deliberately situated as far away as possible from the city's traditional centers of culture, commerce and tourism, stands a drab cluster of reddish-tan brick buildings, surrounded by a thick wall discreetly manned by a constant police presence. The place's formal name is the Casal del Marmo penal institute for minors, and it's the largest youth prison in Italy's capital. The structure includes three multistory buildings, two for males ages 14 to 21 and another for females.

Francis chose to go to the Casal del Marmo for his first Holy Thursday mass as pope, a decision that brought into focus his concern for the poor, the marginalized, immigrants and other disadvantaged groups.

Going to the prison that night was an unconventional decision, one of many from this pope, but it offered an ideal metaphor for the kind of papacy he wants to lead.

Although it's an Italian facility, the prison population is largely non-Italian, composed mostly of young migrants who have either lost their families or been abandoned. In early 2013 there were 49 inmates—11 Italians and the rest North Africans and Slavs. While the majority had committed such relatively minor offenses as petty theft to support a drug habit, a couple of inmates had been convicted for manslaughter and murder. Authorities try to give the young offenders a chance, offering basic literacy classes, sports programs and vocational training: for example, carpentry and upholstery skills for boys; sewing and cooking courses for girls. Still, when walking the halls at Casal del Marmo, it's impossible to miss the atmosphere of fear and barely suppressed rage.

"The kids here basically have been forgotten by everyone," says Fr. Gaetano Greco, the Italian chaplain at Casal del Marmo. "I'm not sure how you rank levels of abandonment, but if we had an index for it they would be right at the top."

Greco is a balding, bearded 50-something Italian who has thoroughly embraced his flock of young castoffs. Inside the prison, he's known as the "barber-priest," because he volunteers to give haircuts to the young inmates, seeing it as an opportunity to develop a deeper bond with them. Outside the prison walls, Greco is a father to the young offenders in another sense: he has opened the doors of his own residence to former inmates and developed it into a center known as Borgo Amigò, a sort of halfway house intended to help them make the transition to a normal life.

Popes generally celebrate Holy Thursday mass inside St. Peter's Basilica, under Michelangelo's great dome containing the words from Matthew's gospel regarded as laying the foundations of papal power: *Tu es Petrus et super hanc petram aedificabo ecclesiam meam et tibi dabo claves regni caelorum,* meaning "You are Peter, and upon this rock I will build my church, and I give you the keys to heaven and earth." Francis's choice of Casal del Marmo for his first Holy Thursday service was an early hint of what's now known as one of his aims: to refine authority in Catholicism in terms of service rather than institutional power.

Two weeks earlier, in the homily delivered during his inaugural mass, Francis had voiced his dream of a "poor Church for the poor," saying that "authentic power is service" and adding that the test of authenticity is acting on behalf of "the hungry, the thirsty, the stranger, the naked, the sick and those in prison." What happened at Casal del Marmo suggested that those words would become the core of a papacy devoted to the "social gospel," meaning Christianity's concern for the poor and the marginalized.

The papal visit to Casal del Marmo wasn't novel in itself. Both previous popes had visited, but neither had attended a Holy Thursday service and neither showed up in quite the manner Francis did. When Benedict XVI arrived in 2007, he was accompanied by an entourage of Vatican aides as well as the Italian minister of justice, creating a crush of VIPs that crowded half the inmates out of the prison's tiny chapel and forced them to follow along on a small TV monitor in a nearby corridor. When Francis turned up for mass at 5:30 p.m., he walked into the chapel virtually alone, instructing most of his aides and security team to wait outside.

Holy Thursday is part of the week that leads up to Easter Sunday. In Catholic tradition, it commemorates both the institution of the Eucharist by Christ at the Last Supper as well as the foundation of the priesthood, on the eve of Jesus' death on the cross. All around the world, priests perform a foot-washing ritual in commemoration of Christ washing the feet of his disciples before the Last Supper. Because of the association with the priesthood, Church rules specify that the rite must be restricted to men.

In a groundbreaking gesture, during Francis's mass that evening, he washed the feet of 12 young inmates, including a male Muslim and two women—a young Italian Catholic and a Serbian Muslim. It marked the first time any pontiff had washed the feet of women and the first time a pope had included non-Christians in the rite.

"This is a symbol, it is a sign," Francis told the group. "Washing your feet means I am at your service. Help one another. This is what Jesus teaches us. This is what I do."

Jesuit Fr. Federico Lombardi, a Vatican spokesman, said that because the facility houses young men and women, "it would have been strange if girls had been excluded. . . . This community understands simple and essential things; they [are] not liturgy scholars. Washing feet was important to present the Lord's spirit of service and love."

The atmosphere in the chapel was electric. One of the 12 young inmates who was supposed to have his feet washed by the pope was so emotional that he had to be led away, and others wept as the pope performed the rite. When Francis offered a brief farewell and turned to exit the chapel, one of the inmates suddenly cried out, "I just want to know why you came."

Francis stopped and surveyed the scene. "It was a feeling that came from my heart," Francis replied. "I felt it. [I wanted to be] where there are people who maybe can help me to be more humble, to be a servant like a bishop ought to be. I thought about it and I asked, 'Where are people who would like a visit?' They told me, 'Maybe Casal del Marmo.' It came only from the heart. Things of the heart don't have an explanation, they just come." More tears were shed as inmates listened to the pope.

Many longtime Roman observers said they hadn't seen a pope do something quite so moving since Pope John XXIII, known as "Good Pope John," visited Rome's Regina Coeli prison the day after Christmas in 1958. On that occasion, Pope John had asked the warden to let the prisoners out of their cells so he could speak to them in the prison's courtyard. The rotund pontiff—a son of peasant farmers—told the prisoners that one of his own relatives had once served a term in jail for poaching, and said, "I have placed my heart alongside your hearts." One of the inmates, a convicted murderer, wept as he kissed the pope's ring and asked, "Are your words of hope meant for such a great sinner as me?" Pope John lifted him up, embraced him and said, "My son, they're especially for you." The reaction was that a pope had just delivered a gesture truly in the spirit of the gospel, and that was the feeling at the Casal del Marmo in the wake of Francis's visit.

BECAUSE FRANCIS HAS EARNED a reputation as a maverick, there's a tendency to style absolutely everything he does as trailblazing. In truth, he's hardly the first pope to whom the social gospel has been important, a point often lost on conservative critics of Francis's papacy.

Take the reaction of Rush Limbaugh, for example. In November 2013 the American pundit derided the economic analysis provided by Pope Francis in the document "Evangelii Gaudium" as "pure Marxism," contrasting it negatively with the fierce anti-communism of the late Pope John Paul II. Yet the reality is that while John Paul II certainly opposed the suppression of human rights and political freedom under communism, he was hardly an apologist for free-market capitalism. In 1993 John Paul II famously said that "Catholic social teaching is not a surrogate for capitalist ideology . . . [which is] responsible for grave social injustices." In 2007 Pope Benedict XVI condemned both Marxism and capitalism as "failed ideologies."

Despite Francis's dream of a "poor Church for the poor," much of his language about economic systems, his laments about "unfettered capitalism" and his call for the "globalization of solidarity" are actually among the least innovative features of his papacy. In fact, such statements are standard papal rhetorical tropes. Francis is not building from scratch or operating in a vacuum. Only by locating his activity within the broader Catholic tradition and the recent history of papal social activism will the truly distinctive features of the "Francis effect" come into focus. It's not the content of the social gospel but his verve in applying it that defines the Francis era.

It's also important to acknowledge that taking positions, however courageous or forceful, and producing concrete political results are two different things. When Pope John Paul II stood in Warsaw's Victory Square in 1979 and inspired a crowd of millions to chant, "We want God!" thereby openly defying the atheistic orthodoxy of the communist state, he helped set the dominoes in motion that led to the collapse of the Soviet system. It remains to be seen if Francis will have anything like that kind of impact in bringing down unjust economic structures, defending immigrant rights across the globe or fostering stronger ecological protections.

ANOTHER ROMAN LOCALE that helps capture what Francis is about is the rough-and-tumble neighborhood of Magliana. It's iconic for Italians because of its association with the mafia, and it's where Francis made a parish visit and smiled broadly at a handwritten sign that read, "*Come butta France?*" which roughly translates to "How's it hanging, Frankie?" Or one might also bring into view the Roman hospital Bambino Gesù, where Francis spent three hours over Christmas 2013 visiting sick children and their families; and the Don Gnocchi center for the elderly and disabled, where the pontiff went on Holy Thursday 2014 to wash and kiss the feet of 12 patients. The patients ranged in age from 16 to 86, and several of them were in wheelchairs with their feet extremely swollen or disfigured. On all these visits, Francis arrived in a blue Ford Focus that has become his trademark means of transportation around town, as opposed to the black Mercedes sedan that used to be the official papal vehicle.

Another Roman destination where the Francis effect plays out is

Termini, the city's main bus and train station, which acts as a magnet for poor migrants as well as troubled locals. There is some protection from the elements along the tracks, and charitable groups make regular visits to hand out sandwiches and provide rudimentary medical care. Termini is a good place to see Francis's concern for marginalized people at any time, but it's the story of Andrea Quintero that drives the point home. It's a story less about Francis himself and more about the new winds in Catholicism unleashed by his passion for the social gospel.

Quintero was a Colombian who left her family in her mid-20s after they shunned her because she was transgender. She bounced around various ports of call before ending up in Rome, living on the streets around the train station, where she became known as "the trans of Termini." Quintero was well known to aid workers in the area, not only for her homelessness but also her repeated struggles with drug addiction. She scraped together a living by panhandling and was often harassed and physically abused. On the evening of July 29, 2013, Quintero was beaten to death by unknown assailants—her body was later discovered alongside the tracks at the station. Her remains were kept at the Roman morgue for four months in case any family members came forward to claim her for burial. No one did.

Eventually, a city official reached out to the Centro Astalli, a Jesuit-run center for migrants and refugees, to organize a respectful funeral for Quintero. Astalli's director, Fr. Giovanni La Manna, initially planned to put together a small service in the center's chapel, but it also occurred to him that the funeral could be a teaching moment. His idea was daring: Why don't we celebrate it at the Church of the Gesù, the mother ship of the entire Jesuit order?

La Manna knew he would need an informal blessing from the Vatican, in part because with Francis the first Jesuit pope in history, the leadership of the order wouldn't want to do anything to embarrass the pontiff. La Manna confessed that had the pope been anyone other

than Francis, he never would have asked, as he could have imag-
ined the reaction of the Vatican and Italian bishops: making a public
spectacle out of the funeral would risk confusion about the Church's
teaching on sexual morality, so better to do it in quiet. With Francis,
however, La Manna said he felt the pope would "get it."

Quintero's funeral took place in the Church of the Gesù on Dec.
27, 2013, attracting a cross-section of street people as well as Rome's
ecclesiastical and political elite. La Manna described it as "a signal for
the entire Roman community that's distracted in the face of so many
people who face discrimination and who live their difficulties to the
indifference of our city." At one level, it may seem that because Francis
didn't attend or ever publicly extend his blessing to the event, his
connection to the story is marginal. One has to know Roman politics
to appreciate that something this unusual would never have happened
in a major Roman church before Francis, especially a church with a
direct connection to the pope through his religious order, and thus
how meaningful a symbol it is for the change he's inspiring.

CHRISTIANITY'S SOCIAL AGENDA in recent years,
especially in the U.S., has focused on struggles over abortion, gay
marriage, contraception and other contentious matters of sexual morality. The Catholic Church has held a strongly pro-life position, with
America's bishops seen by some as the new voice of the religious right.
In the early days of Francis's papacy, there was ferment—expressed
either in delight or alarm, depending on one's point of view—that
Francis might pull Catholicism back from those commitments, especially after he made comments to the effect that he didn't believe it
was necessary for him to preach about abortion and homosexuality,
because "the positions of the Church are already well known."

Noted pro-life leaders such as Archbishop Charles Chaput of

Philadelphia were pressed to explain what was going on. "I can't imagine that [Francis] won't be as pro-life and pro-traditional-marriage as any of the other popes have been in the past," he said in a July 2013 interview with the *National Catholic Reporter*. "He hasn't expressed those things in a combative way, and perhaps that's what some are concerned about." Chaput reassured pro-lifers that Francis would not fall silent. "We all as bishops, including the bishop of Rome, have to talk about those things."

In truth, there never was any serious reason to believe that Francis would water down the Church's commitment to the defense of human life. In an audience Francis held with an association of Italian gynecologists around the time that his *Civiltà Cattolica* interview appeared, he quoted from a 1974 document from the Congregation for the Doctrine of the Faith: "The first right of a human being is life. There are other goods, some of which are more precious, but this is the fundamental good and the basis for all the others." Francis argued that in recent years the Church has become engaged in the defense of the right to life precisely because human life has become cheap in the contemporary world, citing the "unborn" among the most vulnerable categories of people. He urged the gynecologists never to stop reminding the world that human life in its initial phase is "sacred."

Francis almost invariably includes the unborn in his standard list of the victims of a "throwaway culture." In "Evangelii Gaudium," Francis wrote that the Church's defense of unborn life "cannot be expected to change" because it's "closely linked to the defense of each and every other human right." In a January 2014 speech to diplomats accredited to the Vatican, Francis returned to the theme. "It is horrific even to think that there are children, victims of abortion, who will never see the light of day," he said.

In April 2014, during an audience with members of an Italian pro-life movement, the pontiff used even stronger rhetoric. "It is necessary to reiterate the strongest opposition to any direct attack on life, especially [the] innocent and defenseless, and [the mother's] unborn child in the womb is the innocent par excellence," the pope told the gathering. "Life, once conceived, must be protected with the utmost care; abortion and infanticide are abominable crimes."

Francis used his August 2014 trip to South Korea to express his support for the pro-life cause by visiting a symbolic "cemetery for abortion victims," located behind a Church-run charitable center about 120 miles outside Seoul. The memorial is composed of a grassy field dotted with white crosses as well as a statue of what Catholics refer to as the Holy Family: Joseph, Mary and Jesus as a child. Francis paused briefly at the site, bowing his head and folding his hands in a moment of silent prayer.

Francis is a robustly pro-life pope. His calls for less constant references to matters such as abortion, contraception and gay marriage are therefore not about revising the substance of the Church's positions but an acknowledgment that sometimes shrillness and finger-waving rhetoric backfires. Australian prelate Anthony Fisher, a member of the Vatican's Academy for Life and someone seen as an intellectual leader in the pro-life movement, made that point in a February 2014 interview with the *Boston Globe.* In the eyes of many, Fisher said, the hard-line approach to the wars of culture "has not worked. It has hardened hearts, made people closed to the Gospel of Life, made them write off Christians as fanatics or single-issue people. The Church is the loudest, clearest voice for life, there's been no change in that situation under this pope. However, we have to take seriously the idea that maybe we need a different rhetorical register and a different strategy."

At the same time that Francis re-crafts Catholic strategy on pro-life issues, he is also self-consciously lifting up other elements of its social teaching that he believes have not always received the proper attention amid the strong concentration on the pro-life agenda. His aim seems to be to make concern for the poor, immigrants, the environment and peace as much defining elements of what it means to be pro-life as opposition to abortion and gay marriage.

FRANCIS'S COMMITMENT TO ALL FORMS of the social gospel reflects his roots. In Argentina, they say that if you want to understand the priestly soul of Jorge Mario Bergoglio, then you have to know the *villas miserias*, where the poorest of the poor in Buenos Aires are found. Villa 21, the largest of the approximately 20 slums in the city, has a population of almost 50,000. It's a difficult place to work. The slum's former pastor, a popular priest named Fr. José "Pepe" di Paola, had to be transferred out because of persistent death threats related to his efforts to break the grip of the drug gangs. But despite its manifold dangers, virtually everyone in the neighborhood knows Bergoglio, and many adorn the walls of their tin-and-wood shacks with prized photos showing him baptizing their children, confirming their nephews, or sitting in their living rooms to offer consolation when a family member died.

"I'd say that over the 15 years he has been walking down the streets here, at least half of the people have met him at some time and have a picture with him, meaning at least 25,000 people in this *villa* alone," said Fr. Juan Isasmendi, one of the priests who lives and works in Villa 21. Members of the parish celebrated a mass of thanksgiving when Francis was elected; thousands turned up, holding their pictures aloft like a living photo album.

Melchora Lescano, a mother and grandmother who lives in the *villas*, said that Bergoglio "walked the streets here, he drank *mate* with us," referring to the strong tea that's defined by law in Argentina as the national infusion.

It was that history that drove Bergoglio to deliver a hard-hitting speech on poverty during a 2007 assembly of the Latin American bishops in Aparecida, Brazil, attended by Pope Benedict XVI. Bergoglio denounced the region's "scandalous inequality, which damages both personal dignity and social justice." He declared, "We live, apparently, in the most unequal part of the world, which has grown the most yet reduced misery the least. The unjust distribution of goods persists, creating a situation of social sin that cries out to heaven and limits the possibilities of a fuller life for so many of our brothers."

Cardinal Sean O'Malley of Boston, one of the cardinals who took part in the conclave that elected Bergoglio, says the pope's background is essential to grasping his sense of priorities. "I knew that the Church's social gospel would be front and center with this man, realizing the experience of the Church in Latin America," O'Malley said in a July 2013 interview with the *National Catholic Reporter*. "It's a Church that's dealt with life and death issues for so long. In other parts of the world, we sometimes get caught up in some very superficial things, but in Latin America it's awfully basic. When you've seen dictatorships imprisoning people and killing them, when you've seen people starving to death, it focuses you on the essentials."

ONE MEASURE OF POPE FRANCIS'S impact on the popular imagination is the responses that have come from well beyond the usual circles of Vatican-watchers and Catholic insiders.

When the Italian edition of *Vanity Fair* named Francis its person of the year in 2013, the write-up included a tribute from Elton John, who described the pontiff as a "miracle of humility in an era of vanity." Likewise, when *Esquire* dubbed Francis its Best Dressed Man of 2013, it included opinions on the pope's sartorial choices from the author of *The Fairchild Encyclopedia of Menswear* and from an expert at New York's Fashion Institute of Technology, who lauded Francis for spurning the crimson-and-lace fluff of Vatican tradition in favor of a simple, less-is-more look.

But not all opinions of Francis have been positive, which brings us back to Rush Limbaugh and his swipe at Francis for promoting "pure Marxism." Limbaugh said, "Wherever socialists have gained power, they have done nothing but spread poverty. . . . And to hear the pope regurgitating this stuff, I was profoundly disappointed."

The text that had Limbaugh so worked up, the pope's "Evangelii Gaudium," was not the first major teaching document issued by Francis—that had come five months earlier in an encyclical, "Lumen Fidei," which was largely written by Pope Benedict XVI. The 224-page "Evangelii Gaudium" was the first substantial bit of writing that was all Francis. In it, he delivered some blistering rhetoric on the inequities of free-market capitalism, including the way in which prosperity deadens us to the suffering of others. "We have to say 'thou shalt not' to an economy of exclusion and inequality. Such an economy kills," Francis wrote. "Some people continue to defend trickle-down theories which assume that economic growth, encouraged by a free market, will inevitably succeed in bringing about greater justice and inclusiveness in the world. This opinion, which has never been confirmed by the facts, expresses a crude and naive trust in the goodness of those wielding economic power and in the sacralized workings of the prevailing economic system. Meanwhile, the excluded are still waiting."

Francis went on to defend public intervention in the economy. "While the earnings of a minority are growing exponentially, so too is the gap separating the majority from the prosperity enjoyed by those happy few," Francis wrote. "This imbalance is the result of ideologies which defend the absolute autonomy of the marketplace and financial speculation. Consequently, they reject the right of states, charged with vigilance for the common good, to exercise any form of control. A new tyranny is thus born, invisible and often virtual, which unilaterally and relentlessly imposes its own laws and rules. . . . We can no longer trust in the unseen forces and the invisible hand of the market. Growth in justice requires more than economic growth, while presupposing such growth: it requires decisions, programs, mechanisms and processes specifically geared to a better distribution of income, the creation of sources of employment and an integral promotion of the poor which goes beyond a simple welfare mentality."

Since the dawn of modern Catholic social teaching in Pope Leo XIII's 1891 encyclical "Rerum Novarum," every pontiff of the 20th and 21st centuries has voiced skepticism about the ability of a free market to deliver just outcomes when left to its own devices. And Francis hasn't even been as tough on global capitalism as his immediate predecessors. John Paul II once asserted that "the bourgeois mentality and capitalism as a whole, with its materialist spirit, acutely contradict the gospel" and warned that "the rich north will be judged by the poor south." Benedict XVI, whose great-uncle founded a farmer-laborer party in 19th-century Bavaria to fight the excesses of robber-baron capitalism, sometimes used language about the failures of the capitalist system that would drive the likes of Limbaugh to utter distraction.

Focusing on Francis's treatment of capitalism misses what was truly innovative about "Evangelii Gaudium," which wasn't the pope's approach to economics but rather to Catholicism itself. The key line was one in which Francis asserted that solidarity with the poor, as well as the promotion of peace, are constituent elements of what it means to be a missionary Church. This was a direct challenge to contemporary Catholic sociology. Evangelization and the social gospel have generally been regarded as distinct concerns. The former is concerned with bringing people to faith in Jesus Christ and membership in the Church, while the latter addresses their material needs. Pope Francis aspires to break down those barriers between people who evangelize and people who serve the poor, because in his mind they should be one and the same. Serving the poor, in other words, is part and parcel of what it means to "do mission."

"The new evangelization is an invitation to acknowledge the saving power at work in the lives [of the poor] and to put them at the center of the Church's pilgrim way," Francis wrote. "We are called to find Christ in them, to lend our voice to their causes, but also to be their friends, to listen to them, to speak for them and to embrace the mysterious wisdom which God wishes to share with us through them." This core

CALLED TO SERVE *Jorge Mario Bergoglio was raised in Flores, a predominantly Italian, Catholic, middle-class neighborhood in Buenos Aires, Argentina. Strongly influenced by his grandmother's approach to faith, Bergoglio felt a calling to the priesthood when he was just 12 or 13 years old, but it didn't stick at the time.*

FAMILY TIES *Maria Elena Bergoglio (above), the pontiff's only surviving sibling, still resides near the old family home in a Buenos Aires suburb. The Bergoglio children (right) pose with parents Regina Maria Sivori (seated) and Mario Jose Francisco in an undated photo: (from left) Alberto Horacio, Maria Elena, Jorge Mario, Oscar Adrian and Marta Regina.*

CHAMPION OF THE POOR *In 1998 then-Bishop Bergoglio visits the Villa 21-24 slum in Buenos Aires with Fr. Jose Maria de Paola, nicknamed "Father Pepe." Bergoglio was known for encouraging dynamic young priests to work among the city's impoverished.*

ON THE MOVE
Bergoglio takes the Buenos Aires underground before celebrating mass at the city's Metropolitan Cathedral in 2008. As a cardinal, Jesuit Bergoglio often used public transportation. Upon assuming the papacy, he made global headlines for riding in a modest Ford Focus.

HABEMUS PAPAM! *Francis exits the Sistine Chapel after his election as pope on March 13, 2013. The new leader, who was also a top candidate for the job in 2005, was chosen by cardinals in the fifth ballot conducted over a period of just two days.*

SETTING AN EXAMPLE *The newly elected pope pays his tab at the Domus Internationalis Paulus VI, where he had stayed during the 2013 conclave that elected him. The move was seen as an early act of humility, establishing the tone for a new papal style.*

THE PEOPLE'S POPE
Author John L. Allen, Jr., speaks with Francis on a plane during a July 2013 papal visit to Brazil, where the pontiff celebrated World Youth Day in Rio de Janeiro. The trip to Francis's home continent was his first overseas excursion as pope.

ROCK-STAR STATUS

Francis waves to the crowd of faithful Catholics as he arrives in St. Peter's Square for his weekly audience on April 10, 2013. He has used his regular public appearances to make personal connections, often embracing sick or disabled visitors.

PRAYER FOR PEACE *On his way to celebrate mass in Bethlehem on May 25, 2014, Francis makes an impromptu stop at the West Bank separation wall, seen as both a physical and symbolic barrier to peace between Israel and Palestine.*

SELFIE *In St. Peter's Basilica, Francis poses for a photograph with young people on a pilgrimage from the Piacenza-Bobbio diocese in Italy in August 2013. The pontiff has since appeared in a number of spontaneous photo ops with fans.*

SPIRITUAL SUPERHERO

A nun snaps a photo of street art depicting a powerful, flying, caped Francis near the Vatican in January 2014. The Vatican communication office also tweeted a photo of the playful image, created by local artist Mauro Pallotta.

THE REFORMERS *Francis named Irish clerical abuse survivor Marie Collins (top left) and U.S. cardinal Sean O'Malley (top middle) to an anti-child-abuse panel in March 2014. Swiss lawyer Rene Bruelhart (top right) heads the AIF, the Vatican's financial watchdog charged with investigating money laundering. Honduran cardinal Óscar Andrés Rodríguez Maradiaga (above) leads the Council of Cardinal Advisers, a group responsible for overhauling the Vatican bureaucracy.*

HIGH HOPES *On May 15, 2013, Francis releases a white dove over St. Peter's Square. Members of the crowd in the square had unexpectedly offered the popular pontiff a cage containing the birds, which are symbols of the Holy Spirit and peace.*

conviction that serving the poor and preaching the faith amount to the same thing shoots through Francis's papacy in terms of his theological outlook, political advocacy and pastoral priorities.

At the theological level, Francis has encouraged détente with the liberation theology movement, which pioneered the idea of an "option for the poor" at the heart of both Catholic theology and the Church's social activism. But the movement ran afoul of many Latin American churchmen, not to mention the Vatican, for its use of Marxist social analysis and its sometimes rebellious stance vis-à-vis authority in the Church. The leading symbols of the two sides were a mild-mannered Peruvian theologian named Gustavo Gutiérrez, whose seminal 1971 book *Teología de la Liberación* gave the liberation theology movement its name, and a German prefect of the Vatican's Congregation for the Doctrine of the Faith, Joseph Ratzinger—who later became Pope Benedict XVI. Over the years, Gutiérrez fought off doctrinal investigations both by his own bishops in Peru and by Ratzinger's department in the Vatican.

Given that history, the image of Gutiérrez standing on a Vatican stage for a public discussion in February 2014, linked arm-in-arm with another German doctrinal czar, Cardinal Gerhard Müller (who sported a Peruvian poncho for the occasion), was startling. (That said, the two men are close friends. Every year since 1998, Müller has traveled to Peru to take a course from Gutiérrez and spend time living with farmers in a rural parish near the border with Bolivia.) Anyone aware of the troubled past between Gutiérrez and the doctrinal office couldn't help but be dazzled. As one veteran Vatican writer put it privately, the event felt almost like "the end of history."

Gutiérrez argued that Pope Francis is realizing the movement's promise to place the poor at the center of the Church's theological reflection. "There's a big temptation to remain in one place, but this is not the need, [not] what the gospel expects from us," Gutiérrez said. Referring to the New Testament story of the Good Samaritan who stops to help a suffering person after others pass him by, he said that "a Samaritan Church is an open Church, a Church attentive to human needs."

In terms of political advocacy, defense of the dignity of the poor is a constant theme for Francis. In July 2013, during a trip to Brazil, Francis visited Varginha, a notorious slum in Rio de Janeiro. Varginha is known as Rio's "Gaza Strip," due to bloody clashes between gangs and the police. While there, Francis told the poorest of the poor that "the Church is with you," but then he went much further than a pontiff usually does. Popes are generally reluctant to do or say anything that might be perceived as critical of their hosts when they travel, and that was an especially timely concern in Brazil, because Francis arrived just a month after the country's streets had erupted in violent anti-government protests. Yet he felt there was a principle sufficiently worth articulating during his stop at Varginha that he was willing to rupture that protocol. Delivering an unusually pointed rebuke, he denounced the government's brutal strategy of "pacifying" the favelas in an attempt to uproot organized crime and narco-traffickers. In 2012, before Francis's visit, security services had unleashed a massive offensive and then boasted that peace had returned. Francis rejected that claim. "No amount of 'peace-building' will be able to last, nor will harmony and happiness be attained in a society that ignores, pushes to the margins or excludes a part of itself," he said. "A society of that kind simply impoverishes itself, it loses something essential."

The pontiff's concern for the poor isn't evident only on his foreign travels. In Rome, nothing expresses the point more than the improbable rise of the Polish archbishop Konrad Krajewski. Krajewski holds the previously undistinguished office of papal almoner, in charge of coordinating the pope's personal charitable activity. Under Francis's papacy, it has gone from being an afterthought to a defining priority. The 50-year-old Krajewski has emerged as a force to be reckoned with, largely because he has regular and unfiltered face time with the boss. Francis meets with him at least once a week, taking a strong personal interest in his efforts to serve the poor of Rome, which gives the affable Polish prelate an opportunity to chat with Francis on a wide range of issues.

Known around Rome as "Don Corrado" (the Italian version of his first name), Krajewski was inadvertently responsible for launching one of the most persistent urban myths about Francis. Meeting for a chat with Italian journalists in December 2013, someone asked if Francis ever accompanies Krajewski when he goes out at night to deliver sandwiches and spiritual comfort to the homeless who congregate around St. Peter's Square. His reply was more or less "next question," delivered with a smile, which some read as an indirect confirmation that Francis moves around at night incognito. A flustered Krajewski called up *Corriere della Sera*, Italy's newspaper of record, to set the story straight. "It's not true at all, good grief," Krajewski told a reporter. "For sure, the Holy Father would like to [go out], just as he'd like to go out to hear confessions from the faithful, but it's not possible and it has never happened." But one thing Krajewski did do at the pope's request was invite three homeless men and their dog to join his household staff for a breakfast celebrating his 77th birthday on Dec. 17, 2013.

In the Vatican, as with many institutions, access is power. Thus the sight of Krajewski perpetually at the pope's side has driven home to Church leaders that direct care for the poor is a front-burner concern. In the past, it never would have occurred to anyone seeking a favor from the pope to try to use the almoner as an intermediary; today, Krajewski says he is inundated with such requests. His proximity and access to the pontiff signals to others that if they want to catch the eye of this pope, then doing something creative and hands-on for the poor is almost certainly the right way to go about it.

IMMIGRATION IS AN ISSUE on which Francis's commitment to the social gospel is especially keen. In July 2013, when the new pope made his first Italian trip outside Rome, he went to the southern Mediterranean island of Lampedusa, a major point of arrival for impoverished migrants and refugees from Africa and the Middle East. Often subjected to appalling exploitation and abuse on their overland journeys, migrants then attempt to cross the Mediterranean in rickety and overcrowded boats. The trip is an extremely hazardous one: some 20,000 people have died that way over the past two decades. Francis laid a wreath in the sea to commemorate them and blasted what he called the "globalization of indifference" to migrants, characterizing them as primary victims of a "throwaway culture." The visit proved prophetic, as just two weeks later a boatload of migrants from Eritrea, Somalia and Ghana capsized and caught fire, leaving more than 360 dead.

"Let us ask the Lord to remove the part of Herod that lurks in our hearts," Francis said on his visit, referring to the New Testament story about the king who ordered infants slaughtered in an effort to strike out the Christ child. "Let us ask the Lord for the grace to weep over our indifference, to weep over the cruelty of our world, of our own hearts and of all those who in anonymity make social and economic decisions which open the door to tragic situations like this."

One concrete result of Francis's visit came on Christmas Day 2013, when a group of Muslim immigrants from Morocco and Tunisia held in a Rome detention center agreed to suspend their hunger strike in exchange for a local priest carrying a letter from them to the pope. The immigrants had sewn their lips shut in protest over the inhumane conditions in which they were kept, and medical personnel worried that their lives would soon be at risk. The priest, Fr. Emanuele Giannone, said the migrants accepted the deal because "they saw the images of Francis at Lampedusa, they heard his words that day and they knew that they came from the heart."

The pope's leadership on the issue has encouraged Church personnel at other levels to ramp up their own efforts. In April 2014 a delegation of U.S. bishops staged a dramatic pro-immigrant statement on the border between the U.S. and Mexico in order to press the case for immigration reform. Led by Cardinal Sean O'Malley of Boston, the bishops celebrated mass at the security barrier separating the two countries, offering communion to people on the Mexican side through slats in the fence. The bishops cited Francis as their inspiration, saying that Nogales, Arizona, where the mass took place, is "our Lampedusa."

The pope has sometimes waded into American debates in his defense of immigrant rights. In the summer of 2014 the U.S. Customs and Border Protection service was struggling to cope with a spike in unaccompanied minors trying to cross into the U.S. from Central America, driven by a wave of violence across the region that frequently targeted children. More than 52,000 such minors had been processed between October 2013 and July 2014, and that's just those who were caught, with the real number presumably much greater. At the time, Congress was considering weakening provisions in the Trafficking Victims Protection Reauthorization Act of 2008 to allow individual border-patrol agents the ability to render a decision and quickly deport a child. Francis dispatched a message urging lawmakers to move in the opposite direction, toward safeguarding the right of due process. "Such a humanitarian emergency demands as a first urgent measure that these minors be protected and duly taken in," he said, adding that youth "cross the border under extreme conditions, in pursuit of a hope that in most cases turns out to be vain."

Once again, Francis seemed to have an impact in cajoling others to follow his lead. The Jesuit Conference, an organization representing the approximately 2,500 Jesuit priests and brothers in the U.S., issued a plea to the 43 members of Congress who are alumni of Jesuit schools, both Republicans and Democrats, not to water down the 2008 act. Fr. Thomas Smolich, the president of the conference, called the attempted changes to the law "inhumane and an insult to American values."

One of the Jesuit alums is House Speaker John Boehner, a graduate of Xavier University in Cincinnati. Smolich addressed Boehner directly, insisting that short-circuiting due-process rights won't make the causes of the situation go away. "This is not a new crisis, nor is it primarily at our border," Smolich wrote. "It has been escalating over the last decade . . . 90 children are murdered or disappeared in Honduras every month." He pointedly reminded Boehner that "this is the equivalent of eight children being executed in your Congressional district every 30 days." It's telling that the Jesuit conference had never before directly appealed to their alumni in Congress on any other issue. Under the first Jesuit pope, and one who has obviously made immigration a priority, they broke the mold.

It's unclear whether the Jesuit Conference's plea had an effect on the corridors of power, but in November 2014 President Obama announced that he would act unilaterally on the issue of illegal immigration, relaxing policy and removing the threat of deportation for as many as 5 million people.

FRANCIS'S REGULAR REFERENCES to the throwaway culture refer most tragically, perhaps, to human trafficking, a 21st-century version of slavery involving an estimated 2.4 million people and $32 billion in illegal profits. Since many of the victims of the trade come from the developing world, it's an abiding concern for Francis. As archbishop of Buenos Aires, Bergoglio sponsored an activist group called La Alameda that fed him information about slave labor in Argentina's clandestine sewing shops and human trafficking for prostitution; the future pope eventually found work and asylum for the survivors. During a mass held in a Buenos Aires train station in 2012, Bergoglio compared the city to a "butcher shop" that takes away the human dignity of people trapped by these networks. He also denounced the local police department and the legal system for accepting bribes from traffickers, saying that "without them, these mafias wouldn't exist."

As pope, Francis has used virtually every platform he can to talk about trafficking. It featured prominently in a December 2013 speech he gave to 17 new ambassadors to the Vatican, who were presenting their credentials to the pope. Francis said it's a "disgrace" that people are treated "as objects, deceived, raped, often sold many times for different purposes and, in the end, killed, or in any case, physically and mentally damaged, ending up thrown away and abandoned. Human trafficking is a crime against humanity. We must unite our efforts to free victims and stop this crime that's become ever more aggressive, that threatens not just individuals, but the foundational values of society. . . . This cannot go on."

In early 2014 Francis helped launch a new anti-trafficking foundation and advocacy center called the Global Freedom Network, funded by Australian philanthropist and mining magnate Andrew Forrest. Francis was joined in the effort by Archbishop Justin Welby of Canterbury, leader of the worldwide Anglican Communion, and Ahmed Muhammad Ahmed el-Tayeb, the Grand Imam of Al Azhar Mosque and University in Cairo, Egypt, known as the Vatican of the Sunni Muslim world. Later that year, Francis welcomed a conference to combat human trafficking, held in the Vatican. Organized by the Catholic bishops of England and Wales, the gathering brought together police chiefs from 20 nations, trafficking victims, and religious and secular humanitarian groups involved in anti-trafficking campaigns.

Bishop Marcelo Sánchez Sorondo, a fellow Argentine who heads a pontifical academy and is the pope's representative to the anti-trafficking network, said Francis is aware that many people consider human trafficking to be "an enormous, energy-consuming problem that simply cannot be resolved," but he said the pope has issued clear marching orders.

According to Sánchez, the pope expects Catholic leaders around the world to follow his lead. Too many bishops "either believe their country doesn't have human trafficking, or they consider it a problem to be resolved by politicians and the police" and thus not part of their job description. Pointedly, Sánchez added that he had run into that attitude from "an American cardinal," although he didn't supply a name. The not-so-subtle message from one of the pope's closest aides was that the boss doesn't want to hear this sort of denial.

IT WAS PROBABLY INEVITABLE that the first pope named Francis—inspired by a saint who preached to birds and gave pet names to the sun and the moon—has turned out to be a strong environmentalist. In fact, Francis has said that concern for the environment is a defining Christian virtue. (It's also worth remembering that the young Bergoglio trained as a chemist, so he has a foundation to appreciate the scientific issues involved.) This element of the social gospel bubbled to the surface as early as his inaugural mass, when Francis issued a plea to "let us be 'protectors' of creation, protectors of God's plan inscribed in nature, protectors of one another and of the environment."

St. Francis's imprint on this pope is clearly strong. In unscripted comments during a meeting with the president of Ecuador in April 2013, he said, "Take good care of creation. St. Francis wanted that. People occasionally forgive, but nature never does. If we don't take care of the environment, there's no way of getting around it."

The two previous popes were also environmentalists. The mountain-climbing, kayaking John Paul II was a strong apostle for ecology, once issuing an almost apocalyptic warning that humans "must finally stop before the abyss" and take better care of nature. Benedict XVI's ecological streak was so strong that he earned a reputation as "the Green Pope" because of his repeated calls for stronger environmental protection, as well as gestures such as installing solar panels atop a Vatican audience hall and signing an agreement to make the Vatican Europe's first carbon-neutral state.

Francis is carrying that tradition forward. Among other things, he told French president François Hollande during a January 2014 meeting that he is working on an encyclical on the environment. (An encyclical is

considered the most developed and authoritative form of papal teaching.) The Vatican has since confirmed that Francis indeed intends to
deliver the first encyclical ever devoted entirely to environmental issues.

In a July 2014 talk at the Italian university of Molise, Francis described
harm to the environment as "one of the greatest challenges of our
times." It's a challenge, he said, that's theological as well as political in
nature. "I look at . . . so many forests, all cut, that have become land . . .
that can [no] longer give life," the pope continued, citing South American woodlands in particular. "This is our sin, exploiting the Earth. . . .
This is one of the greatest challenges of our time: to convert ourselves
to a type of development that knows how to respect creation."

Not so long ago, the idea of Catholic environmentalism would have
struck some as a contradiction in terms. In the 1960s and 1970s, it was
fashionable among pioneers of the environmental movement to fault
the entire Judeo-Christian tradition for humanity's savage indifference
to the earth. Lynn White, Jr., of the University of California published an
influential article in the journal *Science* in 1967 in which he blamed the
Bible for making Westerners feel "superior to nature, contemptuous of it,
willing to use it for our slightest whim." While acknowledging contrary
currents in Christian history such as St. Francis, White nonetheless ended
with a sweeping indictment: "We shall continue to have a worsening
ecological crisis until we reject the Christian axiom that nature has no
reason for existence save to serve man."

Today things are virtually upside down, with Pope Francis seen as
an important environmental advocate. Writing in *The Atlantic Monthly*,
Tara Isabella Burton praised Francis for "publicly—with the dizzying
reach granted to a man in his position—emphasizing an understanding of nature that, in contrast to the combative dichotomy so prevalent in mainstream politico-religious discourse, is intrinsically positive
in its treatment of the physical world." Burton called the pope's
vision one "that is, radically and profoundly, pro-life." Burton's reference to "pro-life" connotes that Francis is leading Catholics to view

environmental concern as part and parcel of what it means to foster a "culture of life," and therefore of equivalent importance as resisting abortion and gay marriage.

In the argot of contemporary environmental thinkers, if Benedict XVI was the Green Pope, then Francis may be remembered as the "Dark Green Pope"—a figure who intensifies the Church's commitment to the environment by linking it to the corrosive effects of consumerism and runaway global capitalism. Before Francis arrived on the scene, the American political theorist Jeremy Rifkin forecast that issues such as GMOs and climate change would dissolve the old left-right divisions, creating a new "biopolitics" in which defenders of nature on the left and defenders of human life on the right would find themselves allies, standing against a 21st-century hyper-industrialism that sees everything, including nature and organic life, as a commodity. Francis, the pope of the social gospel, could develop into the leader who makes Rifkin's prediction come true.

7

The Abuse
Scandals

IN 1960, WHEN A 13-YEAR-OLD IRISH GIRL named Marie Collins developed a bone infection in her arm, she was admitted to Our Lady's Hospital for Sick Children in the Crumlin neighborhood of Dublin. Although children generally stayed in large common rooms then, Collins was assigned to a private cubicle. In that era in Ireland, parents were not allowed to accompany their children into the sick wards out of concern for infection, but Collins's mother and father weren't worried about leaving her alone. The devout Catholic couple had been charmed by the hospital's chaplain, a young and dynamic priest named Fr. Paul McGennis, who was just one year out of the seminary. Collins's mother told her how lucky she was to have such a good priest at her side. "[My mother] had been so glad that this young chap was caring for me and looking after me and reading me stories," Collins later recalled. "She had felt that I wasn't alone."

As Marie Collins lay in bed one night, McGennis stepped into her cubicle and pulled the curtains behind him. Collins said she thought he had stopped by to check on her, perhaps to read her a story or to offer her some spiritual consolation. It soon became clear, however, that the cleric had something else in mind. McGennis proceeded to rape Collins, assuring her, as Collins testified in a 1997 sexual assault trial against McGennis, that because he was a priest there was no sin involved, since as a man of God he "could do no wrong." Adding to the horror, McGennis also took explicit photographs of Collins.

At the time, Ireland was still essentially a clerical state, with virtually every social institution in the country run by the Catholic Church. The modernizing reforms of the Second Vatican Council were years away, and priests remained almost unquestioned, and unquestionable, moral authorities. As a result, Collins said, she told no one about what had happened. She struggled to make sense of it, wondering if McGennis was right that in the eyes of God, a priest is allowed to take anything he wants or needs.

"The fact that the man abusing me was a priest added to the great confusion," Marie Collins said at a 2012 symposium in Rome on child sexual abuse in the Church. "Those fingers that would abuse my body the night before were the next morning holding and offering me the sacred host.... This added weight to my feelings of guilt and the conviction that what had happened was my fault, not his. When I left the hospital I was ... no longer a confident, carefree and happy child. Now I was convinced I was a bad person and I needed to hide that from everyone."

Although as an adult Marie Collins went on to marry and have a son, she struggled with depression. "I was just surviving from day to day, not feeling very good about myself," she said. "I never connected it to what happened in my childhood. I felt I was letting down my husband, my son. There were periods when I thought they'd be better off without me."

The difficulties of coping with long-suppressed trauma led Collins in 1985 to help launch an Irish support group for depression sufferers called Aware. She still wasn't ready to reveal the source of her depression to anyone, however, and it took another decade for her to come forward. Looking back, Collins said, she doesn't know exactly what she was expecting when she finally worked up the courage to make an appointment with the archbishop of Dublin to tell him the story, but she certainly didn't imagine he'd react the way he did.

Cardinal Desmond Connell, who served as archbishop of Dublin from 1988 to 2004, essentially told her to shrug it off. The Church's top priority, Connell said, had to be to protect the "good name" of the priest, and because the abuse Collins suffered at his hands was, in his words, "historical," there was no point in dredging up the past. Archbishop Connell also refused to cooperate with an Irish police investigation, despite the fact that the bishops of Ireland by that stage had adopted strict guidelines about reporting abuse complaints to civil authorities. Collins persisted in trying to get Church officials to take action against the priest who had raped her and to launch broader reforms to prevent such abuse in the future. She dispatched plaintive letters to the Vatican pleading for an intervention by Pope John Paul II. It was all to no avail.

Collins and other activists didn't get the response they wanted from Church officials, but they eventually succeeded in persuading civil prosecutors to act. Fr. Paul McGennis—the priest whose "good name" Archbishop Connell was determined to preserve—eventually pleaded guilty in 1997 to two counts of sexual assault and received an 18-month sentence. McGennis was convicted again in 2011 of eight separate counts of indecent assault against another female parishioner between 1980 and 1984; the victim had been 11 years old at the time of the assault and had twice tried to commit suicide in the years that followed.

Under Irish law, judges are allowed to use age and ill health to mitigate prison terms. Despite the fact that McGennis was 79 and ill, he was sentenced to two years in prison. Judge Desmond Hogan said he couldn't ignore the "aggravating circumstance" of abuse of power. "[McGennis] must have known he was taking advantage of the fact his word would never be questioned, and that placed additional trauma on the injured party," Hogan said. "[The victim] felt she wasn't going to be believed because of the position that the defendant held within society."

For his part, Archbishop Connell finally apologized in 2002 for not taking Marie Collins seriously, seven years after she first approached him. Connell's troubles weren't over, as a government inquiry later that year criticized him for being "economical with the truth" in answering questions about the Church's past. Nonetheless, Pope John Paul II allowed Connell to stay on. He retired in 2004 at the age of 78.

A series of Irish governmental panels and judicial inquiries beginning in the 1990s established that the abuse perpetrated by McGennis, as well as the response from officials such as Connell, was part of a much wider pattern. A 2009 report from a government panel detailed the emotional, physical and sexual abuse of thousands of Irish children by Catholic priests and nuns between 1930 and 1990. The report also highlighted the clear and long-standing Church policy of keeping allegations quiet and shuffling abusers from assignment to assignment, rather than expelling them from the priesthood and turning them over to police and civil prosecutors.

Although such behavior was hardly restricted to Ireland, the crisis there was uniquely intense because of the vast social influence of the Catholic Church. In March 2010 Pope Benedict XVI devoted a pastoral letter to the sexual abuse scandals in Ireland, saying he was "truly sorry" for the harm caused by "sinful and criminal" abuse at the hands of priests, brothers and nuns, although he stopped short of demanding the resignations of Church officials who turned a blind eye to these horrors.

As public outrage over the revelations began to build, Marie Collins emerged as a spokesperson for the victims and a frequent antagonist to Church officials. She became a fixture in the Irish media, blending feistiness and obvious personal credibility with a deep command of the issues involved, both in terms of the Church and civil law. Collins is tough, smart and articulate, and few know the agony of abuse victims better than she. The fact that she's still a deeply faithful Catholic—and one who often talks with pain about how younger members of her own family have drifted away from the faith—only adds to her credibility.

As the abuse crisis played out in Ireland, Collins insisted that both Archbishop Connell and Cardinal Seán Brady of Armagh in Northern Ireland should be dismissed from their positions. Cardinal Brady has come under fire in recent years for his part in covering up a sexual abuse scandal when he was a young priest. In 1975 he and other Church officials learned of abuse perpetrated by a priest named Brendan Smyth but didn't report it to the police. Smyth was arrested in 1994 after abusing four siblings in Belfast, and he eventually pleaded guilty to 141 counts of child molestation in Ireland and Northern Ireland between 1945 and 1989. He died of a heart attack in prison in 1997, one month into his 12-year sentence. Cardinal Brady resigned in September 2014, at the official bishops' retirement age of 75.

As time went on, Collins received an increasingly better reception within Catholic circles. When the reform-minded Diarmuid Martin was named the new archbishop of Dublin in 2004, he made Collins one of his key advisers. For several years Collins worked with Martin on designing new anti-abuse protocols, which became a model for Catholic organizations around the world. In 2012 when Rome's Jesuit-run Gregorian University organized a major symposium on the abuse scandals, Collins was invited to tell her story at a penance service in which a senior Vatican official apologized to her and abuse victims everywhere for the Church's legacy of inaction.

By 2014 Collins had the ear of Pope Francis, serving as a member of the Pontifical Commission for the Protection of Minors, placing her among the key architects of his strategy to make child protection the center of the Church's concerns. Nothing says more about how the wheels are turning under this reforming pontiff than Collins's metamorphosis from a perceived enemy—a woman who wouldn't have been allowed past the Vatican's front door not so long ago—to a valued member of the pope's inner circle. And nothing says more about the metamorphosis of Francis on this subject than having Collins by his side.

ANYONE WHO HAS EVER heard an abuse victim tell his or her story knows that listening to it is a transformative experience. One can usually detect the real reformers in the Catholic system, those truly committed to never allowing this to happen again, not so much by their stand on specific policy issues but by whether they've spent time in living rooms with victims.

When Jorge Mario Bergoglio was elected to the papacy, the initial reaction among those striving to redress sexual abuse in the Church was alarm, because Bergoglio seemed to lack the experience of proximity to victims to help shape his approach. Some feared the recovery effort might go back to where they had been before the reforms of his predecessor. Pope Benedict XVI had signed off on the zero-tolerance approach worked out by the U.S. bishops and had made it global policy, expelling hundreds of abusers from the priesthood using his papal authority. Some bishops and Church lawyers from other parts of the world saw the expediting procedures for removing accused priests as a violation of their due-process rights, and people in the reform camp worried that the first pope from the developing world, from a region where the abuse scandals had not been as intense, might share those perceptions.

One expert on child protection in the Catholic Church, speaking on condition of anonymity in the summer of 2014 just ahead of the pope's first meeting with sexual abuse victims, described the mood among reformers after Bergoglio emerged as the new pontiff. "I'll be honest with you," the expert said. "We were all scared."

The reformers include such bishops as Diarmuid Martin in Ireland and Cardinal Sean O'Malley in the U.S., who have fought internal battles to get both the Vatican and their brother bishops to accept the

need for strong new policies on matters such as reporting abuse allegations to the police and taking stern measures to ensure that an abuser
can never again function as a priest. They also include Catholic personnel in the U.S. who helped develop VIRTUS ("virtue" in Latin), a set
of best practices for training Catholics to identify the warning signs of
abuse and to respond when abuse occurs. The program has become
widely adopted in the U.S. and in other parts of the Catholic world.

Most important, the reformers include victims themselves, such
as Marie Collins and Peter Saunders of the U.K., who grew up in a
devout Catholic home and who from the age of 8 until 13 was sexually abused by a member of his family, as well as a lay teacher and two
priests at the Catholic school he attended. While many abuse victims
have understandably walked away from the Catholic Church, some,
such as Collins and Saunders, are determined to remain on the inside
and press the Church to turn over a new leaf. It's often a lonely position, as deniers in the Catholic fold sometimes see them as giving aid to
enemies of the Church, while some of their fellow victims think they're
giving PR cover to an institution that has still not acknowledged the
depth of its failures.

Improbably enough, the reformers—many of whom had issues with
Pope Benedict XVI on other matters of doctrine or politics—nevertheless saw Benedict as a hero on sexual abuse issues. As head of the Vatican's
doctrinal department in the late John Paul II years, then-Cardinal Joseph
Ratzinger, despite significant internal Vatican opposition, played a decisive role in upholding the American bishops' new zero-tolerance policy
and also pressed John Paul II to approve new expedited procedures for
weeding abusers out of the priesthood. Later, as pope, Benedict met with
victims six times and became the first pontiff to apologize in his own
name for the scandals. During his eight years in the papacy, almost 1,000
priests were defrocked over abuse charges.

In 2001, when Cardinal Ratzinger led the Congregation for the
Doctrine of the Faith, his top prosecutor on abuse cases was a diminutive

but determined Maltese monsignor named Charles Scicluna, who later returned to his country as an auxiliary bishop. It was Scicluna who went after the powerful Mexican priest Fr. Marcial Maciel Degollado, founder of the Legionaries of Christ, who in the late 1990s had been accused of abusing seminarians in his own order but was seen as invulnerable because of his strong ties to senior figures in the papacy of John Paul II. Maciel denied the accusations, but as a result of Scicluna's investigation, the Vatican concluded that he was guilty, and Benedict XVI sentenced him to a life of prayer and penance in 2006. He died less than two years later in 2008. It was also Scicluna who publicly accused the Italian Church of fostering a culture of *omertà*, a code of silence resulting from a misguided sense of loyalty, in relation to abuse cases. Scicluna subsequently developed a reputation as the Eliot Ness of the Catholic Church, a prosecutor who is basically incorruptible.

Scicluna said that Ratzinger had a "conversion experience" in 2001 and 2002 as a result of sitting at his desk and reading the case files of every priest accused of abuse anywhere in the world. Ratzinger had persuaded John Paul II to issue an edict requiring bishops to forward those files to his office. Scicluna remembers sitting with Ratzinger and watching him pore over victim testimony. The experience was clearly devastating, with Ratzinger's eyes filling with tears as he read, over and over again, how emotionally devastating the abuses had been. According to Scicluna, Ratzinger developed a sense of urgency after that conversion, becoming the first pope to meet with victims, on his visit to the U.S. in 2008, and giving his support to reformers around the world. Although critics insist Benedict left behind plenty of unfinished business—including the vexed question of accountability, not just for priests who abuse but for bishops who cover it up—virtually everyone concedes that Catholicism moved further down the path of reform because of his influence.

In Argentina, however, Bergoglio had not walked anything like the same path. For one thing, the Catholic Church's "sexual abuse crisis," as Europeans and North Americans knew it, engendered highly critical media coverage; multimillion-dollar lawsuits that triggered even more damaging revelations; public protests; and disastrous hits to both the Church's public image and internal morale, as the reality of what had happened to victims at the hands of predatory Catholic clergy became widely known. Such a maelstrom has not yet reached most parts of the developing world. As a result, prelates from those regions can sometimes seem clueless on the issue. Today, more than a decade into the arc of the scandals, it's not hard to find Latin American prelates who suggest that the phenomenon of clerical sexual abuse has been inflated by media outlets hostile to Catholic teaching and by lawyers looking to line their own pockets, or that it is a product of a sexually libertine culture in the West, especially with regard to homosexuality.

There were concerns that Bergoglio breathed the same air, in part because of a comment he made in 2010. In the now-infamous interview, Bergoglio said, "In my diocese, it never happened to me," by which he meant that he never had cases of accused clergy. It was an improbable claim given that Buenos Aires is among the world's largest Catholic jurisdictions and Bergoglio was in charge during a period in which tens of thousands of victims worldwide came forward to report abuse at the hands of Church personnel. It's also inconsistent with the public record, since several cases did in fact arise during Bergoglio's time as archbishop; advocates for abuse victims say the future pope's response was deeply flawed. They complain that he turned a deaf ear to victims and appeared, at least in public, to side with the accused, leading victims to conclude that he was another Catholic prelate in denial.

The most notorious such case centered on Argentine cleric Julio César Grassi, the founder of national charity Happy Children, which provides shelter to youth living on the streets. The handsome, entrepreneurial priest became a sort of rock star in the Argentine media and developed close ties to the country's political and economic elite, often appearing in celebrity columns for his charity work and attendance at gala events. Catholic insiders in Argentina say there had been rumors about Grassi's private life for some time, when an Argentine television network raised charges of molestation against him in 2002. Years of careful investigation followed, and by the time a nine-month trial wrapped up in 2009 Grassi had been convicted of abusing five teenage boys and sentenced to 15 years in prison (he was acquitted of several charges raised by two other accusers).

Grassi, now 58, was a priest of the Morón diocese in Argentina, where he relocated after leaving the Salesian religious order in 1991, so he technically didn't fall under Bergoglio's direct responsibility in Buenos Aires. Yet Bergoglio was president of Argentina's bishops' conference when the charges arose, and he approved hiring a well-known legal scholar named Marcelo A. Sancinetti to study the case. Sancinetti produced four volumes, totaling in excess of 1,000 pages, and concluded that Grassi was innocent on all counts, claiming that the accusations were inconsistent with the evidence and marred by internal contradictions. Throughout the process, Bergoglio extended his support to Grassi, asserting in 2006 that the priest had fallen victim to a "media campaign." During his criminal trial, Grassi said the archbishop "never let go of my hand." (Claims that Bergoglio was paying Grassi's legal bills turned out to be unfounded.) In 2003 one of Grassi's alleged victims, who was 13 when he said the assault occurred, begged Bergoglio for a meeting but was rebuffed.

Though Grassi remains the most damaging blemish on Bergoglio's record, he's not the only one. Fr. Mario Napoleón Sasso was identified as a pedophile in the early 1990s and sent for treatment to a Buenos Aires center called Domus Mariae in 1997. Sasso later went on to commit at least five acts of abuse against girls between the ages of 11 and 14, offenses for which he was criminally convicted in November 2007 and sentenced to 17 years in prison. There's also Fr. Rubén Pardo, who admitted to his bishop that he had sexually assaulted a teenage boy and who was discovered hiding from law enforcement in a residence in the archdiocese of Buenos Aires where one of Bergoglio's assistant bishops also lived. Pardo was under criminal investigation when he died of AIDS in 2005, ending the case against him.

Sadly, there are more. Brother Fernando Enrique Picciochi, a member of the Marist religious order, fled to the U.S. when faced with the prospect of prosecution for abuse. The alleged victim sought the help of a Bergoglio aide to get out of a confidentiality agreement imposed by the Marists in order to file an extradition request, but the aide declined to get involved. (That aide, by the way, was a cleric named Mario Poli, later appointed by Pope Francis as his successor in Buenos Aires.) In 2001 Fr. Carlos Maria Gauna, a Buenos Aires priest, was accused of inappropriately touching two girls at a school where he served. Bergoglio promised to look into it, yet today Gauna is still a priest in Buenos Aires, serving as a hospital chaplain—a sign, some believe, that Bergoglio took the allegations seriously enough to move him out of direct contact with children but not seriously enough to remove him from the priesthood. In 2001 a criminal case was opened under the supervision of a juvenile court, but charges were not filed. Gauna has not commented on the allegations.

In each of these cases, the victims requested meetings with the future pope to tell their stories, and all were turned down. As those reports began to surface, child-protection experts in the Church who want to see Catholicism become a model of best practices in abuse prevention and detection were alarmed by the pontiff's seeming indifference.

The early months of Francis's papacy did little to allay the concerns of those who felt Bergoglio had failed abuse victims in his native country. He made a point of reaching out to virtually every constituency traditionally alienated from the Church—from atheists and secularists to followers of other religions and the poor. Yet despite repeated suggestions and requests, Francis did not sit down with victims of clerical sexual abuse for 16 months. Although Francis said the right things about zero tolerance—and signed off on revisions to the laws of the Vatican City State that strengthened its provisions for the crime of child sexual abuse—in an interview with the Italian newspaper *Corriere della Sera*, he appeared to relapse into the sort of defensive rhetoric common among senior churchmen before the reforms of Benedict XVI. "The Catholic Church is perhaps the only public institution that has moved with transparency and responsibility," Francis told the newspaper. "No one has done more, and yet the Church is the only one that has been attacked."

In that context, the reform path Francis embarked upon in late 2013 was not only significant in itself but may mark the most dramatic, if as yet unfinished, chapter in the evolution of Jorge Mario Bergoglio since taking over the Church's top job.

A KEY FIGURE IN STEERING FRANCIS toward more compassion for victims of sexual abuse is Cardinal Sean O'Malley of Boston. In the run-up to the 2013 papal election, O'Malley—a member of the Capuchin religious order, an offshoot of the Franciscans—was the crowd favorite in Rome. The buzz around him was overwhelming, in part because of the famed Capuchin stigmatic and healer Padre Pio, who became a saint in 2002. On March 9, 2013, five days before the cardinals filed into the Sistine Chapel to begin the process to elect the new pontiff, *Corriere della Sera* staged an online poll inviting readers to pick their favorite candidate. O'Malley topped the charts with 37 percent, easily outpacing the next closest finishers, Angelo Scola of Milan, who drew 18 percent, and Luis Antonio Tagle of the Philippines, with 14 percent. (Bergoglio wasn't even on the list.) Everywhere O'Malley went during that period, vast crowds turned out to catch a glimpse of the man many Romans ardently hoped would become the next pope.

His popularity was noted by his peers. The current superior of the Capuchin order, Swiss-born Fr. Mauro Jöhri, claimed that if popes were still chosen by Roman mobs storming the castle, there's no doubt O'Malley would be sitting on the throne of Peter. O'Malley's appeal forced the other cardinals to take a closer look at the Boston prelate, and what they saw was the Catholic Church's preeminent fix-it figure for sexual abuse scandals.

Born in 1944 in Lakewood, Ohio, the young O'Malley signed up for the Capuchins for the same reasons that other gung-ho young men join the Marines: to see the world and do the toughest job. From the beginning, he was passionate about social justice. While studying in Washington, D.C., O'Malley took part in the Poor People's Campaign organized by Protestant minister Ralph Abernathy, sleeping in one of the tent cities and watching as off-duty police lobbed tear gas at protesters. During the 1970s and 1980s, O'Malley served in Washington's Centro Católico Hispano, ministering to immigrants and refugees and sharpening his fluency in Spanish and Portuguese. He developed a keen sensitivity for victims of uncaring elites who regard themselves as above the law. O'Malley recalls once talking to a foreign ambassador in Washington who had badly abused a Latin American immigrant who was his maid and had come to O'Malley for help. Listening to the arrogant diplomat insist he had treated the maid "as a member of my own family," O'Malley fired back, "If that's true, then thank God I'm not in your family!"

Although Capuchins aren't usually supposed to become bishops (on the grounds that they might be tempted by pride), historically an exception has been carved out for priests serving in mission territories. That's where O'Malley thought he would spend the rest of his life when, in 1985, Pope John Paul II named him the bishop of St. Thomas in the American Virgin Islands, one of the smallest Catholic jurisdictions in the world. The American Virgin Islands boast just 30,000 faithful—about the same as a large parish in the U.S.

As it turns out, however, O'Malley was destined for mission territory of a different sort. In 1992 he was appointed the new bishop of Fall River in Massachusetts, taking over amid a scandal centering on the Rev. James Porter, who was convicted of molesting 28 children and confessed to abusing as many as 100 others over a 30-year period. Then in 2002 O'Malley was moved to Palm Beach, Florida, replacing two successive bishops who had resigned after admitting they had sexually abused minors. Neither bishop was prosecuted, in part because the incidents had occurred long enough ago that the statute of limitations in civil law had passed, but the damage to diocesan morale and the Church's image was enormous.

As bad as those situations were, they paled in comparison with the challenges awaiting O'Malley in Boston, where he was dispatched by John Paul II in 2003 at the peak of arguably the most intense sexual abuse scandal anywhere in the world. It began with ugly revelations about a serial predator and former priest named John Geoghan, who was accused of abusing more than 130 children over a 30-year career. (In 2002 Geoghan was sentenced to nine to 10 years in a Massachusetts prison, where he was killed by another inmate in 2003.) It wasn't simply the abuse that made the case so shocking; a pattern also emerged in which Church officials shuffled Geoghan from assignment to assignment, thereby putting additional children at risk. Other bombshells followed, including the case of a former priest named Paul Shanley convicted of raping a young boy. Shockingly, it turned out that in the late 1970s Shanley had links to the North American Man/Boy Love Association, an organization that promotes the decriminalization of sexual relationships between men and underage boys. Despite those red flags, officials had allowed Shanley to continue as a priest for years, both in Boston and in San Bernardino, California.

Within a year of these disclosures, Boston's once-mighty Cardinal Bernard Law resigned in disgrace. For many Bostonians, the fact that Law was assigned a comfortable post in Rome by Pope John Paul II following Law's resignation (he was named the archpriest of the Basilica of St. Mary Major) and that he remained a voting member of the Congregation for Bishops, with a voice in the selection of new prelates around the world until he reached the age of 80 in 2011, remains a source of deep hurt.

O'Malley was sent in to pick up the pieces. He eventually settled more than 100 abuse claims against the archdiocese and imposed a zero-tolerance policy. In the beginning, O'Malley seemed staggered by the ferocity of the anger in Boston and the almost impossible obstacles he had inherited, including a serious financial shortfall in the archdiocese. In 2004 he wrote a letter to parishioners in which he said, "At times I ask God to call me home and let someone else finish this job, but I keep waking up in the morning to face another day." Some of O'Malley's closest Capuchin friends suspected he was clinically depressed, and a few considered an intervention to suggest that he seek psychological help. O'Malley denied that he was depressed, saying he simply wanted to acknowledge the depths of the challenges he faced. As time went on, however, O'Malley found his legs and became steadily more willing to lead. He presided over penitential liturgies apologizing to abuse victims, both in Boston and around the world, and has become the Vatican's designated troubleshooter whenever an abuse scandal breaks out.

Despite O'Malley's commitment, his record on abuse scandals has nevertheless drawn fire. The Survivors Network of Those Abused by Priests (SNAP)—the largest advocacy and support group for victims of clerical abuse in the U.S. and a driving force in many sexual abuse lawsuits against the Church—blasted his appointment to the Vatican's anti-abuse panel in 2014. The organization claimed that on O'Malley's watch, the Boston archdiocese had omitted at least 161 names from its official list of accused priests; that it has a "disturbingly high" rate of clearing priests from accusations; and that it violated the U.S. bishops' standards for providing training to adults to detect the warning signs of abuse in children. SNAP called O'Malley's record "deeply flawed" and highlighted what it saw as his "carefully crafted image and extraordinarily savvy public relations." O'Malley has defended the integrity of his review board in clearing priests and says the omitted names are mostly religious-order priests and thus the orders must disclose the names of accused priests, not the archdiocese. Despite the criticism, O'Malley remains among the most outspoken senior voices in the Church on the urgency of reform.

Because O'Malley is the lone American cardinal whose Spanish is fluent enough to converse comfortably with native speakers, he was the designated bridge between North American and Latin American cardinals in the informal conversations leading up to the papal election. During the exchanges, Bergoglio and O'Malley rekindled a friendship originally born when O'Malley stayed at the Jesuit cardinal's residence in Buenos Aires in 2010. He and Bergoglio found that they saw eye to eye on many things: their passion for the poor; their strong attachment to the popular faith and piety of ordinary people, as opposed to flights of theological fancy; their impatience with ecclesiastical pomp; and the sense that the Vatican was long overdue for major reform. Despite O'Malley's vintage Irish name—how much more Emerald Isle can you get than Sean Patrick O'Malley?—he isn't the ward-heeler politician that many Irish-American prelates turn out to be and doesn't really possess the gift of gab. Italian Vatican journalists say the 70-year-old O'Malley is the "least American of the Americans," because of his humility, his cosmopolitan outlook, his command of languages and his membership of a religious order that transcends nationality.

Although cardinals are not supposed to reveal their voting preferences in a papal election, O'Malley's enthusiasm for the new pontiff immediately after his election seemed to suggest that he had been a Bergoglio supporter. As a result, Bergoglio not only likes what he sees in the Boston prelate but knows that he owes O'Malley a political debt. He also knows that if things had gone just slightly differently, O'Malley might have been pope. As O'Malley himself joked in a July 2013 interview, "If the conclave had lasted another day or so, I would have been in great danger."

When the new pontiff decided in April 2013 to create a council of eight cardinals from around the world to act as his "kitchen" cabinet, it was natural that he tapped O'Malley as the lone American member. In turn, O'Malley said he prayed deeply over why God had placed him in this position, wondering what advice he could supply to Francis that other cardinals couldn't or wouldn't give, and came to the conclusion that providence was asking one thing from him above all: to help the new pope hear the voices of victims of sexual abuse and to make sure Catholicism's commitment to reform becomes irreversible.

WHEN THE POPE'S brand-new Council of Cardinals met for the first time in October 2013 to begin talking about Vatican reform, the abuse scandals were nowhere on the agenda. The omission wasn't terribly surprising, given the composition of the group. The pope's chosen coordinator for the council, Cardinal Óscar Andrés Rodríguez Maradiaga, had never fully recovered from his 2003 suggestion that a Jewish-controlled American media establishment was using reports of abuse to lash out at the Vatican for its support of Palestinian state-hood. Cardinal Giuseppe Bertello, the lone Italian, sympathized with the Vatican old guard and certain clerics in places like Latin America that resented American bishops for adopting anti-abuse rules regarded by many as a violation of Church law. For instance, the Code of Canon Law, the official body of internal law for the Church, traditionally assigns tremendous discretion to superiors to make punishments fit crimes, making rigid zero-tolerance policies on such issues as sexual abuse an aberration. The only other prelate on the body who had much experience coping with the fallout from a major scandal was George Pell of Australia, who at the time was facing a Royal Commission into Institutional Responses to Child Sexual Abuse and battling what he described as a "smear campaign."

Aware that the unpromising makeup of the panel might not lead to the reforms so desperately needed, O'Malley was adamant during the meeting and in private exchanges with Francis that something else had to be done. (O'Malley revealed during a public event in Boston in September 2014 that his primary instrument of communication with Francis is via a fax machine in the pope's residence at the Domus Santa Marta and that the pontiff always responds personally and quickly.) Although O'Malley's notes to the pontiff dealt with the full range of issues the cardinals face in designing a leaner and more accountable bureaucracy in the Vatican, O'Malley never let up on the argument that overcoming the abuse scandals has to be part of the mix.

The next time the cardinals met, in December 2013, Francis pulled O'Malley aside and asked, "What do we need to do?" It was the question for which O'Malley had been waiting. He told the pontiff the most important first step was to establish a papal commission to act as the vanguard for reform, made up of world-class experts who could promote best practices and, just as important, would have the gumption to force bishops and other officials to adopt the same commitment to change. Knowing the way Roman politics works, O'Malley advised Francis not to wait to fill out all the details for the new commission before announcing it, fearing the idea might die the death of a thousand cuts as officials jockeyed over who would control it, what its precise powers would be and which Vatican department would house it. In response, Francis simply said, "Let's do it."

Less than 24 hours later, O'Malley sat on the dais in the Vatican press office to inform the media that Pope Francis had decided to establish a Pontifical Commission for the Protection of Minors, saying the specifics had not yet been worked out but that the new body would include "all those who are experts in the work of safeguarding children, and all those who have been taking care of children."

In light of the spontaneous fashion in which the announcement was rolled out, it's not surprising that it took an additional three and a half months to announce a lineup of initial members. When it came, however, it was like a thunderclap. Beyond O'Malley, the eight members included Marie Collins, representing the first time that a sexual abuse victim had been appointed as a papal adviser; a German Jesuit priest named Fr. Hans Zollner, who had organized the Gregorian University's 2012 summit and founded its Center for Child Protection; and Baroness Sheila Hollins, chair of the board of science of the British Medical Association, a woman who had been a driving force in pushing Catholic bishops in the U.K. to adopt a zero-tolerance policy. In a sign that Francis was taking a strong personal interest in the new group, he tapped one of his closest friends in Rome, fellow Argentine Jesuit Fr. Humberto Miguel Yáñez, who Bergoglio inducted into the order in 1975.

What was notable was that virtually everyone appointed had at some point run into blowback from officialdom for their advocacy of aggressive reform. Most had felt the sting of being described as disloyal players in the media- and lawyer-induced plot to kick the Church when it was down. Thanks to Francis and O'Malley's influence, the once avant-garde Catholic reformers became mainstream and the deniers in the fold began to wonder if they had a future.

The eight members of the new commission met for the first time in Rome in May 2014, with the official agenda being to develop a set of statutes for themselves. Because of the push to get the group started quickly, Francis had set aside the normal protocol of having a team of Church lawyers develop statutes before a new outfit is announced or members are named. In this case, Francis told the members of the commission to work out the legal fine points themselves. As one of them put it in May 2014, "the pope basically handed us a blank check."

The conversation during that first get-together was broad, focusing on what Francis needed to do right away to make it clear that the issue mattered. An agreement was reached that Francis should hold a meeting with abuse victims, on the premise that there's no substitute for hearing stories firsthand. O'Malley said he would take the lead role in putting the encounter together.

During Benedict XVI's meetings with abuse victims, the Vatican developed a protocol for these sessions, a key element of which was that they were never announced until after they happened in order to preserve the victims' privacy. In this case, however, Francis let the cat out of the bag. During the return flight from his May 2014 trip to the Middle East, the pontiff took a question from reporters about his plans to deal with the abuse crisis, and he announced that he would shortly be sitting down with victims. In a sign that his conversations with O'Malley and other members of the anti-abuse panel were having an impact, Francis also sharpened his rhetoric, comparing a priest abusing a child to celebrating a "black mass," which for a lifelong churchman such as Francis is tantamount to the ultimate perversion of a priest's role.

The meeting took place on July 7, 2014, with O'Malley selecting six victims—two each from Ireland, Great Britain and Germany. Back home, O'Malley took some flak for not including any Americans, but there was a logic to his choice: aside from the fact that Francis is likely to meet American victims when he travels to the U.S. in September 2015, O'Malley did not want to revive impressions that child abuse scandals are mostly an American problem.

Pope Francis first greeted the victims at the dinner table in the Santa Marta on the night of July 6, 2014, before celebrating a mass for them the next morning. He then sat down with each victim one on one, spending around three hours with the six victims.

In some ways, there was nothing revolutionary about what Francis had to say to the group. His plea for forgiveness wasn't original, since such apologies date back to 1993, when John Paul II voiced sorrow for the sins of "some ministers of the altar." The apologies became sharper under Benedict XVI, who first used the words "I'm sorry," in Australia in 2008. Nor was Francis's pledge of zero tolerance a novelty. The classic papal statement on the matter comes from an April 2002 speech by John Paul II to American cardinals: "There is no place in the priesthood and religious life for those who would harm the young."

Yet the 2014 meeting did break new ground because Francis had something to say on accountability. "All bishops must carry out their pastoral ministry with the utmost care in order to help foster the protection of minors," Francis told the victims. He added the single most important phrase he has uttered to date on the abuse crisis: "And they will be held accountable."

At least one of the victims came away convinced that the pontiff is in earnest. "I believe him to be a sincere man. I believe him to be someone who wants to do this right," said Peter Saunders. Today, Saunders heads a London-based group called the National Association for People Abused in Childhood (NAPAC), which for the past two decades has been helping other victims overcome their suffering by providing a support system. "I don't think [the man I met] would let us down," Saunders told the *Boston Globe*. "He's a different kind of pope . . . a pope of the people. I trust him, and I can only hope that he doesn't betray that trust."

WHILE SAUNDERS IS PREPARED to give Francis the benefit of the doubt, other victims and critics of the Church's response to the abuse scandals are far more skeptical. SNAP, for one, issued a statement calling the July 7 meeting nothing more than a "disturbing placebo" and a "public relations event." The organization elaborated, "We're asking for prevention, not symbols, gestures, pledges, or meetings. . . . A dozen popes could meet with 100 victims, and very little will change."

Sadly, there is a precedent for abuse victims being excited by encounters with a seemingly sympathetic pontiff, only to become disillusioned when progress appears to stall. Bernie McDaid, for instance, was 11 years old in the late 1960s when he was molested for the first time by Fr. Joseph Birmingham at St. James Parish in Salem, Massachusetts. (Birmingham died in 1989, so he was never tried.) McDaid was among the first five victims ever to meet a pope, taking part in an April 2008 encounter with Benedict XVI in Washington, D.C. At the time, McDaid expressed optimism that the wheels were turning. He was later disappointed, however, by what he regarded as stalling and hollow assurances from Church officials and helped to organize a large victims' protest at the Vatican in 2010. In July 2014 McDaid said he's not optimistic that Francis's legacy will be any different. "Despite the media hype about what a nice guy this pope is, it took 16 months for him to reach out, and that alone says a lot to me," McDaid said. "[Church officials] talk about moving on, but when you see them doing the same old things, it's almost like getting abused all over again."

Two episodes during the early stages of Francis's papacy have fueled concerns. First is the case of an Argentine priest named Fr. Carlos Urrutigoity, who served in the early 2000s in the diocese of Scranton in Pennsylvania, where he was named in a highly public sexual abuse lawsuit in 2002 and where he is still identified on the diocesan website as a "serious threat to young people." Incredibly, Urrutigoity made his way to Paraguay, where, despite the charges against him, he rose to the position of vicar general of the Ciudad del Este diocese, meaning he was effectively second-in-command. In July 2014 Francis dispatched investigators to the diocese and soon afterward announced that the priest had been removed from his position as vicar general and that the local bishop had been temporarily barred from ordaining anyone. The diocese released a long defense of both Urrutigoity and the bishop, all of which did not save the bishop from being removed by Francis in September 2014. The Vatican said at the time, though, that the bishop wasn't being removed on the grounds of his handling of the Urrutigoity situation but for other offenses. By late 2014, Urrutigoity was still in Paraguay and it was unclear whether he would be charged with a criminal offense. He has not commented on the allegations. The obvious question remains: Why did Urrutigoity's superiors let him evade charges in the U.S. for 12 years? To date, Francis has not required him to return to the U.S.

The second case concerns Archbishop Józef Wesolowski of Poland, a former papal ambassador to the Dominican Republic, who in late June 2014 was defrocked by the pope following charges of molesting teenage boys during his diplomatic assignment. In August 2014 the *New York Times* carried a front-page story by veteran religion writer Laurie Goodstein detailing how the former papal official lured young shoeshine boys in Santo Domingo to various discreet locations around town, where he reportedly paid them to perform sexual acts. The piece quoted outraged Dominicans wanting to know why the Vatican hadn't turned Wesolowski over to authorities there for prosecution. Catholic bishop Victor Masalles, who had been stunned to see Wesolowski walking freely down the streets of Rome during a recent visit, said, "The silence of the Church has hurt the people of God." In response, Vatican spokesman Fr. Federico Lombardi said that Wesolowski, who has not commented on the allegations, will face a criminal trial under the laws of the Vatican City State that could lead to a prison term of several years once an appeal of his defrocking verdict is exhausted. Lombardi also said that the former diplomat has been stripped of his diplomatic status, so that if either the Dominican Republic or his native Poland want to make an extradition request for prosecution, the Vatican will comply. Still, critics could not help but wonder why all this hadn't happened much earlier, before the pressure of public opinion compelled officials to act. As of December 2014, the criminal trial against Wesolowski had not yet begun.

More broadly, victims wondered why the new anti-abuse commission seemed to move at a slower pace in its early stages than other reform vehicles. It took almost nine months merely to name a secretary for the commission and to confirm O'Malley as its president. Officials such as Fr. Robert Oliver, one of O'Malley's key aides on addressing the abuse scandals in Boston and now Scicluna's replacement at the Congregation for the Doctrine of the Faith, say great progress has been achieved behind the scenes, particularly in identifying capable new members from various parts of the world, but it's fair to ask why the group hadn't made a bigger splash in its opening phase in order to show that the fight against child sexual abuse is a priority.

On the other hand, defenders of the pope's commitment hailed the September 2014 appointment of Blase Cupich as archbishop of Chicago as another victory for the reform position. Cupich had previously been the bishop of Spokane, Washington, and since 2008 had served as chair of the U.S. Bishops' Committee for the Protection of Children and Young People. In that role, he was seen as a champion of the zero-tolerance approach to clerical abuse and spent considerable time meeting with abuse survivors.

The single most debated point about the Church's response to sexual abuse is full accountability. Catholicism may now impose stern punishment on clergy who abuse, but there's no equally strong consequences for bishops and other superiors who fail to act when abuse complaints surface. Even Francis sometimes lapses into the view that accountability is only about the abuse itself. In a press conference after his trip to the Middle East, Francis claimed that three bishops were facing Vatican inquiries as proof of accountability, but they were all prelates charged with the crime itself, not with sweeping others' offenses under the rug. Francis's language in his meeting with the victims in July 2014 implied that he's ready to embrace a more expansive notion of accountability, holding bishops responsible not just for their personal conduct but for their administrative obligation to enforce zero tolerance. There is no shortage of candidates with whom Francis might demonstrate his resolve.

Francis seemed to take an important step in that direction in September 2014, when news broke that the pope had commissioned an investigation of Bishop Robert Finn of the Kansas City–St. Joseph, Missouri diocese. In September 2012 Finn became the first U.S. bishop to be criminally convicted after pleading guilty to a misdemeanor count of failure to alert police of charges against one of his priests, Shawn Ratigan. After admitting to taking pornographic images of children, Ratigan was sentenced in 2013 to 50 years in prison and also laicized—expelled from the priesthood. The indictment against Finn charged that he learned about images found on Rattigan's computer in December 2010 but only sent him away for counseling and ordered him to have no contact with children. Police were not informed until May 2011, after Finn was told by a diocese official that Rattigan was still taking lewd pictures of minors and Finn authorized notifying the police. Finn was sentenced to two years of probation for his delay in reporting, and has remained bishop of the diocese. The belated Vatican investigation is being led by Archbishop Terrence Prendergast of Ottawa, Canada. As of late 2014, the review of Finn's conduct, known as an apostolic visitation, was still pending.

Despite that step forward, Francis sent a somewhat mixed message on accountability at around the same time when he appointed retired cardinal Godfried Danneels of Brussels, Belgium, as a special member of an October 2014 synod of bishops on the family. Francis wanted Danneels there in part because he's an erudite veteran churchman and is associated with a more liberal stance on the question of whether divorced and remarried Catholics ought to be able to receive communion, a position that Francis wanted to ensure was heard at the synod. In Belgium, however, Danneels is also associated with a scandal surrounding retired bishop Roger Vangheluwe, who in 2010 admitted at a press conference to announce his resignation that he had sexually abused two of his nephews over a 15-year period while serving as a priest and then as a bishop. Because the statute of limitations for those crimes had expired in Belgium, he was never charged. As revelations surrounding the affair surfaced, a taped conversation came to light between Danneels and one of Vangheluwe's victims in which the cardinal appears to pressure him to keep quiet about the abuse and allow Vangheluwe to retire without incident. Danneels has acknowledged taking part in the conversation that was recorded. Two priests came forward to say they had tried to warn Danneels about Vangheluwe in the 1990s, but he had not taken action. For many Belgians, the fact that Francis chose Danneels for a specialVatican role without at least acknowledging his dubious involve-ment in theVangheluwe case raised questions about what accountabil-ity means for Francis.

Marie Collins said that after the pope's encounter with victims, as well as the second meeting of the anti-abuse commission, she finds herself hopeful that Francis will do the right thing. "I know there are many survivors around the world who are hoping and have great expec-tations" that the pope will act, Collins said. "What I can say so far is you can't make concrete promises. But as a survivor myself, I am hopeful that we are going to achieve [progress on accountability]." She said she feels a special responsibility, as a tribune for abuse victims everywhere, to remain vigilant. She also issued a thinly veiled warning to Francis that if he flags in his commitment, "I'll be the first one to speak out."

As with Pope Francis's language about promoting new roles for women in the Church, his verbal pledges of sexual abuse reform, combined with his outreach to victims, have elicited high expectations. While there have been steps forward, it's clear that much work remains to be done. Pope Francis will be evaluated by how much he follows through, because he has again set the bar himself, saying publicly that the Church has to "keep moving forward" and committing himself to zero tolerance. People everywhere, most of all victims of abuse, will be watching to see if the pope's deeds match his stirring words.

8

The Paradox
of Power

IN AUGUST 2013 the phone rang at the home of Stefano Cabizza, a 19-year-old information technology and engineering student in Padova. The person calling asked for Stefano. Cabizza's sister, who had answered the mid-morning call and figured it was his soccer coach, answered that he wasn't home but would return at "around 5 p.m." She then hung up. Promptly at 5 p.m., the phone rang again. Cabizza was home this time and answered it. But it wasn't his soccer coach on the line.

Previously, Cabizza had brought a personal letter for Pope Francis to a mass in Rome and approached a cardinal to hand it to him, but he had not expected a response. To Cabizza's astonishment, a response came in the most direct way possible: it was Pope Francis calling. The pope chatted with the teenager for about eight minutes, dispensing some basic pastoral wisdom. In a characteristic touch, Francis also implored Cabizza to pray for him, which the young man vowed to do.

Pope Francis has gained a reputation as the "cold-call pope," for his love of phoning people directly. It expresses his populist streak, his determination not to be sealed off from ordinary people that's part of his appeal. It also neatly illustrates one of the paradoxes of power of Francis's papacy. He's a pope who has said he wants to govern in collaboration rather than imposing his own will, who has called for a "healthy decentralization" of the Church but who nevertheless blows past established systems of communication and sometimes sets off a media storm by acting entirely on his own.

Sometimes, as with Stefano Cabizza, the impromptu telephone conversations are on everyday subjects; at other times, they carry a heavy sadness. Ten days before he called Cabizza, Francis phoned Michele Ferri, the 14-year-old brother of Andrea, a gas station operator in Pesaro, Italy, who had been killed during a robbery. Ferri had written to Francis saying that he was finding it impossible to forgive the killers, and the pope called the teenager to tell him the letter had made him cry and that he would pray for his brother and his family. Usually the writers include their contact information, and Francis simply makes the call himself. In other cases, he hears about someone in distress through the media or a friend and decides to reach out. It's part of his strategy to avoid fencing himself off from contact with ordinary people.

In both cases, Francis insisted on using the informal Italian *tu* rather than the formal *Lei* in speaking to the youngsters. He reportedly asked Cabizza, "Do you think the apostles called Jesus '*Lei*' or 'Your Excellency'?"

Famously, Francis picked up the phone not long after his election to call Daniel del Regno, who runs a newspaper kiosk in Buenos Aires that used to deliver the daily paper to the cardinal. "Hi, Daniel. It's Cardinal Jorge," he said. Del Regno suspected a prank, but it was actually the new pontiff calling to cancel his delivery. According to del Regno, who said he broke down in tears, the pope thanked him for providing good service over the years and passed along his best wishes to his family.

In January 2014 Francis called an Italian woman named Filomena Claps, reaching her at her husband's bedside in a hospital in Potenza, Italy. After the by-now familiar opening act—"This is Pope Francis." "Sure, it is. Who is this really?" "No, really, it's the pope. . . ."—Francis explained that he was calling in response to a letter Claps had sent imploring him to help her find out what had happened to her daughter, Elisa. Elisa had disappeared in 1993 at the age of 16, and her body was eventually discovered in a church. A local man by the name of Danilo Restivo was convicted for the murder, but the Claps family believes Church officials knew Elisa's body was in the church long before they reported it, suggesting that perhaps the pastor, who has since died, was somehow involved. The family has demanded an answer from the bishop but has never been satisfied. According to Claps's account of the call from the pope, Francis invited her to visit him in Rome and promised that "light will be shed." (As of late 2014, the family was pressing Italian police to reopen the investigation into Elisa's disappearance, fueled by the publicity generated by the pope's call. Magistrates were looking into it, but the case has not yet been reopened.)

Imagine, now, that you are a traditionalist Catholic writer and you've recently published a critical essay in a national newspaper with the heading "Why We Don't Like This Pope." When the phone rings, you might well be startled to hear the subject of your criticism promising prayers for your recovery. That's what happened to Mario Palmaro, who received a call from the pope in November 2013 when Palmaro was gravely ill in a hospital. When he tried to bring up the critical essay he and another writer had penned, the pope cut him short. "I know you wrote that out of love," Francis apparently told him, "and they were things I needed to hear."

Perhaps the most amusing result of one of Francis's calls happened when he phoned a convent of cloistered Carmelite nuns in Lucena, Spain, to pass along New Year's greetings. When no one picked up the phone, Francis left a voice mail message. "What are the nuns doing that they can't answer?" he joked. "I am Pope Francis, I wish to greet you in this end of the year. I will see if I can call you later. May God bless you!" The sisters passed the audio message to a Spanish Catholic radio network, and it quickly went viral. (The radio outlet reported that the nuns had been praying when the pontiff called.) A few hours later, Francis rang again, and this time the nuns gathered around the speakerphone to chat with the pope about the community's upcoming 400th anniversary.

Only Francis knows how many such calls he makes; these are just the ones we know about because the recipients chose to go public. Aides say he works the phone virtually every day. In general the calls are pastoral in nature, with Francis responding to a personal situation or celebrating a special occasion. He also makes a point of staying in touch with old friends. Bishop Jorge Eduardo Lozano of Gualeguaychú in Argentina, a close Bergoglio ally, said in early 2014 that he has become accustomed to walking down the street or riding in a subway when his cell phone goes off, and when he answers, he hears, "It's Jorge."

Once in a while, however, Francis does dip into policy. In April 2014 Francis called Jacquelina Lisbona, an Argentine woman who had written to the pontiff the previous fall to complain that her local parish priest had denied her communion. Lisbona's husband had divorced her and then remarried without an annulment; in the Church's eyes, this meant that Lisbona should be barred from the sacrament. As she later told the story to a Buenos Aires radio station, she received a call, and the voice on the other end of the line said, "It's Father Bergoglio calling," an indication that Francis understood himself in that moment to be acting as a priest rather than as the pope.

According to Lisbona, Francis advised her simply to go to a different parish and take communion, saying that "there are some priests who are more papist than the pope." He also supposedly told her that he would use her situation to help set the table for a debate at an October 2014 synod of bishops on the family, where the issue of divorced and remarried Catholics would be front and center.

News of the call spread, creating a firestorm in the Catholic world because it seemed to offer a very clear indication of where the pope stands on that issue. Vatican spin doctors swung into action, insisting that such calls "take place in the context of Pope Francis's personal pastoral relationships" and "do not in any way form part of the pope's public activities." In addition, the statement said, reporting on the content of the call "cannot be confirmed as reliable, and is a source of misunderstanding and confusion." Yet the statement never actually claimed that Lisbona's account of the exchange was dishonest, only insisting that "consequences relating to the teaching of the Church are not to be inferred from these occurrences."

Although Francis has vowed to be a collegial pope—in Catholic argot, a leader who governs in collaboration with others rather than simply imposing his own will—the calls he makes are actually unilateral acts. He doesn't check with anyone before making them, and he certainly doesn't vet what he intends to say with a team of theological advisers. His own communications staff are generally the last people to know they've happened, usually learning about them when a reporter calls seeking comment. Once the call is made and its contents broadcast, Fr. Federico Lombardi, the Vatican's official spokesman, is forced to contact one of the pope's aides or Francis himself to find out if the call actually happened and if the pope did indeed say what has been reported.

Given that the Vatican has little control over these conversations, Francis is effectively licensing the recipients of these calls to tell the world what he said, creating an entirely new outlet for papal commentary. That's delightful for the people he calls, but some Church insiders argue that those filters exist for a reason, namely to avoid confusion. Francis has said on several occasions that he wants Catholics to take risks in trying to spread the gospel and even to "make a mess," which some aides and bishops privately say is a great sound bite unless you're the one who has to clean it up. In any event, it's not really collaborative when a whole team of experts works for months crafting a position on something, only to see the pope upset the applecart with an impromptu five-minute phone call. One person's spontaneity is another's caprice.

The Lisbona call illustrates another paradox. The pope's most ardent fans sometimes seem to want a contradiction in terms: a collegial, decentralized Church in which Francis nevertheless makes all the decisions and compels everyone else to follow his lead. Many of the people who cheer loudest when Francis says he wants to decentralize Catholicism—take power away from the papacy and Rome and spread it around the lower levels—don't seem to mean it if it prevents the pope from pursuing policies and initiatives that they support. In this case, they applauded the pope's compassion in his call to Lisbona, which seemingly encouraged people to end-run Church rules that bar those in irregular situations from receiving communion. Yet Francis has called two synods to discuss this issue, in October 2014 and October 2015, saying it needs "careful study" and promising not to make a decision before deliberation had taken place. In the eyes of some critics, it was improper for him to dispense pastoral advice on the fly that could be seen to pre-empt the synod's conclusions. At a minimum, it certainly wasn't the sort of diplomatic and political caution typically associated with papal conduct.

THERE ARE A FEW ISSUES in Catholic life that seem incapable of ever being resolved but can always be counted upon to spark a good fight. Somewhere near the top of that list is the debate over collegiality, the proper distribution of power in the Church. Before the Second Vatican Council, few thought to question it, but since the mid-1960s it has become a thorny subject. Complaining about authority is often the favorite sport of the Catholic Church, since everyone seems to have an opinion not only about what the bishops should be doing but how they should be doing it. In the words of mystery writer

John Sanford, whose fictional detective Lucas Davenport explained the difference between Catholics and Bible-thumping Evangelicals thus: "Catholics don't scream about Jesus. They scream about the bishop."

For Americans, the argument over collegiality is a counterintuitive one. The traditional dichotomy in the American political system defines liberals as the champions of a strong central government and conservatives as those who believe that government is best when it governs least. Generally speaking, the federal government has taken up progressive causes such as the civil rights movement, while the states have resisted—think governor George Wallace standing in the doorway of the University of Alabama in 1963, defying an order from President John Kennedy to compel the enrollment of two black students.

In Catholicism, collegiality works in exactly the opposite way. The central government, meaning the Vatican, is the great defender of tradition, while progressive reforms typically take shape at lower levels of authority. As a result, liberals tend to favor decentralization, and conservatives support a strong papacy. (The latter position is sometimes known as ultramontanism, or "beyond the mountains," a term used after the Protestant Reformation to refer to the pope who lived beyond the Alps mountain range in Rome.) In 19th-century England, W.G. Ward, a theologian, mathematician and former High Church Anglican who converted to Catholicism, famously said with the typical zeal of a new believer that he'd like to have a papal encyclical every morning with his breakfast in which the pontiff would definitively pronounce on whatever the question of the day happened to be. Compare that position with the one held by John Henry Newman, another convert from Anglicanism who eventually became a cardinal, who resisted an 1870 proclamation of the dogma of papal infallibility because he felt it would obstruct the natural development of doctrine in response to changing circumstances.

Technically, the debate over collegiality is about process—that is, how authority ought to be exercised—but it has almost always been tied up with substance—that is, Rome's line on a particular issue. One focus has been liturgy. Catholic liberals tend to favor a translation approach known as dynamic equivalence, in which the aim is to render the meaning rather than the exact words of the Latin original, using contemporary language that reflects the idioms and thought patterns of a given culture. Conservatives usually want a more literal approach, using sacral rather than colloquial language. For example, in the Catholic mass, at a certain point the priest addresses the congregation and says, "The Lord be with you." When the more liberal approach dominated in the years immediately after Vatican II, the response from the congregants was a fairly informal "And also with you." Under Benedict XVI, however, that changed to the loftier "And with your spirit," a more literal translation of the Latin base text.

In 2001 the Vatican's Congregation for Divine Worship issued an instruction titled "Liturgiam Authenticam," which tightened Rome's control over the process of translating liturgical texts. Howls of protest arose from critics such as Bishop Donald Trautman of Erie, Pennsylvania, a former chair of the U.S. Bishops' Committee on the Liturgy, who published an essay charging that "the congregation has missed a decisive moment to model collegiality for the church" by failing to trust local bishops to sort these things out for themselves. Trautman also objected on principle to the Vatican's disapproval of inclusive language, for instance translating "man" as "person" or "people" in order to make it gender-neutral.

In the argument over collegiality, some Church leaders from the developing world charge that the Vatican is excessively European, or Western, in its outlook and doesn't understand what life is like elsewhere. At a more basic level, some bishops wonder how Rome can even collect enough information to make intelligent decisions. In the 1990s, for instance, the bishops of Japan issued a stirring call for greater collegiality in the run-up to a 1998 synod of bishops about Asia. Among other things, they argued that proclaiming the gospel of Jesus Christ in the context of Asia, where religious harmony and social cohesion are key values and silence is often more respected than speech, is very different than in Latin America or Europe. Aggressive and triumphal techniques, they argued, will backfire and end up cementing impressions that Christianity is a Western faith rather than a universal creed equally at home in Asia. They pushed the Vatican to provide them greater latitude but felt their pleas sometimes fell on deaf ears.

At other times, the fault lines on collegiality reflect institutional dynamics. Vatican personnel tend to defend a robust concept of papal power, partly because they're the ones who wield it. Residential bishops around the world, even those who tend to be theologically conservative, generally don't like being told what to do by Rome. One American cardinal who didn't want to be identified put it this way: "Nothing will turn you into a reformer more quickly than sitting in the waiting room of some Vatican congregation and being read the riot act by a wet-behind-the-ears priest who barely speaks English and who's probably 30 years younger than you are."

Based on his experience and philosophy, Pope Francis is inclined to sympathize with those calling for greater collegiality. He served as a residential bishop for more than two decades—six years as an auxiliary bishop in Buenos Aires and 15 as the archbishop—and had never previously worked a day in his life in the Vatican. Such a background disposes him to the view that Rome ought to show more restraint in overriding the judgments of local leaders. As a Latin American, Francis also appreciates that Rome, for all its cosmopolitanism as a city, is still a place where European experiences and priorities have a disproportionate impact on shaping impressions, which means Church leaders from other parts of the world often have a hard time making themselves understood.

The future pope occasionally felt the sting of being reprimanded or overruled in Rome during his run in Buenos Aires, notably the 2006 episode in which he was pressured to cut his spokesman loose for criticizing Pope Benedict XVI's remarks on Islam. Since his election,

Francis has expressed nostalgia for the "old curialists"—Vatican personnel who did their jobs and never sought fame or power. By situating such figures in the past, Francis clearly meant to imply that today's Vatican mandarins leave something to be desired.

The life experience of Jorge Mario Bergoglio also disposes him to embrace a collaborative and shared model of wielding authority, since he now looks back on his period as a Jesuit provincial in Argentina in 1973 as an object lesson in the dangers of an excessively rigid style. He reflected on that period of his life at length in his September 2013 interview with *Civiltà Cattolica*. "My style of government as a Jesuit at the beginning had many faults," the pope said in a conversation with fellow Jesuit Italian Fr. Antonio Spadaro. "I had to deal with difficult situations, and I made my decisions abruptly and by myself. . . . Eventually, people get tired of authoritarianism."

The pope said he carried those lessons into his period as the archbishop of Buenos Aires. "Over time, I learned many things," Francis said. "The Lord has allowed this growth in knowledge of government through my faults and my sins. So as archbishop of Buenos Aires, I had a meeting with the six auxiliary bishops every two weeks, and several times a year with the council of priests. They asked questions and we opened the floor for discussion. I believe that consultation is very important."

Another Jesuit from Argentina, Fr. Humberto Miguel Yáñez, is today the head of the department of moral theology at the order's Gregorian University in Rome. He was received into the order by the future pope back in 1975, growing up under him as a scholastic during a time when Bergoglio was rector of the Colegio Máximo in San Miguel. Yáñez can testify to his old friend's penchant for working the phone, since Bergoglio called him in April 2013, not long after his election, and the two men have been in semi-regular contact since. In an April 2013 interview, Yáñez said that Bergoglio got caught up in the tensions between left and right in Latin America and within the Jesuit order in the 1970s and sometimes tried to settle things by the imposition of his own will. He cited Bergoglio's introduction of a fixed schedule at the college and his decision to integrate manual labor into formation training. "Whatever one might think about it, he didn't really talk to anybody before doing it," Yáñez said. But he added that Bergoglio is now passionate about hearing other points of view. "He's well adapted to face the most difficult situations facing the Church today," Yáñez said. "Above all, he's a person of dialogue, and I think all the various sectors of the Church will be able to talk with him."

The Jesuit imprint on Pope Francis may cut in the opposite direction, though, toward a style of government that perhaps can be described as consultative, in the sense of listening widely, but not really participatory or shared, because in the end it's still very much the pope who makes his own decisions. That's how things work within the Society of Jesus. A superior is expected to listen carefully to the views of the order's members and to consult widely among experts on the matter at hand. In the end, however, there's no vote before a decision is made and no veto power or referendum procedure once it's made. A superior is expected to decide alone and carry the weight of whatever choice he makes.

All these impulses—from the residential bishop instinctively hostile to Roman diktat to the former Jesuit superior accustomed to deciding on his own—coexist to some degree in Pope Francis.

TWO FIGURES PUT A FACE on the paradox of power in the Francis era. The first is Bishop Nunzio Galantino of the tiny southern Italian diocese of Cassano all'Jonio, who was a surprise pick by Francis in December 2013 as the secretary-general of the powerful Episcopal Conference of Italy (CEI). The other is Fr. Greg Reynolds, a popular liberal priest in Melbourne, Australia, who was excommunicated over his support for women priests and gay marriage in September 2013.

Northern Italy is the country's financial and political hub, while large parts of the south remain agrarian and chronically underdeveloped, with a youth unemployment level in excess of 60 percent and one of the lowest rates of university attendance in the entire European Union. In recent years the per capita GDP of the *mezzogiorno*, as many Italians call the south, has actually crept up slightly, but that's largely because the region is depopulating at a dizzying clip. Southern Italians often feel neglected and disadvantaged relative to their northern countrymen.

That cultural divide is very much reflected in the country's bishops. Speaking broadly, northern Italian prelates tend to be concerned with the politics of the Church, while southern bishops are usually modest men of the people, concerned above all with poverty and the corrosive influence of the Mafia. (The cultural predominance of the north is reflected in the fact that in the 20th century the See of Venice produced three popes, Milan two and Bologna one, but there wasn't a single pontiff from south of Rome.)

Bishop Nunzio Galantino is changing that perception. A vintage prelate of the *mezzogiorno*, Galantino was born in 1948 in Cerignola, a town in the southeast that was the birthplace of the father of Fiorello La Guardia, the legendary 1930s and 1940s New York City mayor. Galantino had a largely unremarkable career in the Church for most of his life, serving as a seminary professor and vice-rector in the Apulia region and as an adviser for the southern branch of Catholic Action, the country's largest lay Catholic movement. He was named the bishop of Cassano allo Ionio in December 2011, a diocese about as far off the usual ladder to advancement in Catholicism as possible. (As one American Catholic blogger put it, "Cassano allo Ionio is to Italy what Biloxi, Mississippi, is to these United States": a nice place but not traditionally a major center of power.)

Galantino—generally considered a kindly, self-effacing man—has something of Francis about him, especially when it comes to leading a modest life. When he was named to the episcopacy he asked that people not buy him any gifts but instead donate money to the poor and also insisted on being called "Don Nunzio" rather than formal titles such as "Your Excellency." He declined to name a priest secretary, handling his appointments himself; turned down a chauffeur; and opted to continue living in a modest room at the seminary rather than moving into the bishop's residence.

This seeming kinship probably explains why Pope Francis named 65-year-old Galantino to the position of secretary-general of CEI in late December 2013. Earlier in the year, Francis had asked the once-powerful president of the conference, Cardinal Angelo Bagnasco of Genoa, to poll the country's bishops and submit a list of candidates for the secretary's position. The pontiff had already limited Bagnasco's influence by removing him from the Congregation for Bishops, assigning his place to Archbishop Gualtiero Bassetti of Perugia, whom Francis later made a cardinal. Bagnasco, despite his removal, dutifully complied with Francis's request for names, offering him a complete list of all the Italian bishops and the people they had flagged as possible contenders. Galantino had only one vote from his almost 500 Italian colleagues. Francis surprised everyone by ignoring the rest of the list and opting for Galantino. Francis also went against statutory protocol by making the appointment without a green light from the permanent council of the conference and then underlined his affection for Galantino by making a day trip to Cassano allo Ionio in June 2014 to thank the locals for letting him borrow their bishop.

Galantino has played to terrific reviews since gaining national prominence. He got high marks for the way he handed the pope's brief trip to his home diocese, insisting that both Church and civic officials should avoid exploiting it as an excuse for "unjustified expenses." Instead, Galantino called for preparations to be marked by a spirit of "sobriety" and "attention to one's neighbor," especially the most needy. Galantino's position was that if money was to be spent, it ought to be used to build infrastructure in poor areas, even in neighborhoods the pope wasn't planning to visit. Such development, Galantino said, would capture the real sense of the pope's visit.

Playing off Francis's joking apology to the people of Cassano allo Ionio for taking him away, Galantino said the trip also ought to prompt locals to ask forgiveness "for the poor left alone in our streets, for the nonbelievers to whom we continue to propose our religion without asking if it means something to them too, to our youth for whom we've abdicated being credible role models, to our young adults when we've done nothing to sustain their dreams, and to our territory reduced solely to a place to exploit." Privately, bishops around the world said that Galantino had created a template for how to host a papal visit.

It's true, however, that Francis's much-vaunted commitment to collegiality was missing when it came to Galantino's elevation. In April 2014 Italian journalist Sandro Magister wrote that Galantino's appointment signals that the Italian bishops' conference effectively has a new president, one who rules the roost by his own lights and without much consultation with the membership: that new president is Pope Francis.

THE REYNOLDS CASE in Australia represents an entirely different side to Francis. Seemingly hesitant to impose his own judgments in the face of contradictory advice from leaders on the ground, "collegial Francis" won the day. Technically, the decision to excommunicate 61-year-old Fr. Greg Reynolds came from the Vatican's Congregation for the Doctrine of the Faith, but most observers in Australia believe the behind-the-scenes protagonist was likely Cardinal George Pell, the former archbishop of Melbourne and Sydney, the pontiff's all-powerful finance czar and a man keenly committed to doctrinal orthodoxy. Adding weight to rumors, the decision to cast Reynolds out of the priesthood and out of the Church was communicated to

Reynolds by Archbishop Denis Hart of Melbourne, a former seminary classmate and friend of Pell's. Reynolds was the first priest of Melbourne ever to be excommunicated and the first priest in Australia to be laicized for a reason other than sexual abuse.

Hart wrote to area priests that the reason for the action against Reynolds was his support of women's ordination to the priesthood. Talking directly to the press, however, Hart had a somewhat different story, claiming in media interviews that in addition to the priesthood issue, the expulsion also had to do with Reynolds's advocacy of gay rights. Reynolds was well known for having attended rallies advocating same-sex marriage and officiating at mass weddings of gay couples, all in defiance of Church authorities. Conservative bloggers asserted that Reynolds had also presided over an illicit mass in which a visitor offered a consecrated eucharistic host to a dog. If true, it would be a deep shock to the sensibilities of ordinary Catholics, even those who see eye to eye with Reynolds on other matters. Reynolds insisted that if any such offense occurred, it was without his knowledge.

Reynolds was cast as a victim in most media coverage, partly reflecting an instinctive Australian sympathy for the underdog and partly because Reynolds is a bespectacled, frumpy character who hardly seems anybody's idea of public enemy No. 1. Reynolds had resigned as an active parish priest in 2011 to form his own breakaway community, Inclusive Catholics, which attracts only around 100 people, mostly aging, and hardly seems the basis for a French Revolution in Catholicism. The *Sydney Morning Herald* ran a long profile of Reynolds shortly after his excommunication, featuring his battles with pneumonia as a child, his spiritual quest in India and Nepal in the 1970s and his early service as a priest with the rural poor (he is said to have lived for a stretch in "a one-room brick hut built for potato diggers"). Reynolds is quoted by the newspaper as striking a note of defiance, saying of the Catholic Church, "How can they, who are so big and so powerful, be so frightened of me?"

The process against Reynolds began before the election of Francis to the papacy, yet liberals nevertheless wondered why Francis had allowed it to reach its ultimate conclusion. Laicization and excommunication are considered a death penalty under Church law. Despite the fact that Francis has said no to women priests, many expected the pope of mercy to let bygones be bygones, especially given that Reynolds was already effectively out of the fold and hardly a threat to officialdom (he was technically still on the books as a priest but without any real power). Defenders of the pope suggested that Francis was acting collegially, since both the Australian bishops and his own doctrinal department had recommended bringing the hammer down. But a well-known theologian at Melbourne's Australian Catholic University summed up another view in July 2014. "What's the point of being pope," he asked, "if you can't stop the system from doing something stupid once in a while?"

FRANCIS'S FIRST SUBSTANTIVE DECISION after his election was to create a Council of Cardinal Advisers, made up of eight prelates from around the world, representing every continent. The body's role is to advise Francis on Vatican reform, but Francis has widened the mandate to include helping his "government of the universal Church," which basically means the council is involved in every decision the pope has to make. It was within this Council of Cardinals that Francis worked out his idea to call a synod of bishops devoted to the family, and it was also the council—led in this case by Archbishop O'Malley of Boston—that pressed Francis to create a new papal commission devoted to reforming the Church's sexual abuse scandals. In other words, its influence runs well beyond tinkering with the structures of Vatican departments.

The council, which was proposed by the cardinals who gathered in Rome prior to Francis's election, is now a permanent institution. It has dislodged the Secretariat of State as the most important decision-making force in the Vatican. In effect, the choices that matter in Francis's Vatican are no longer being made exclusively by Vatican officials but by residential cardinals too.

In his first round of appointments to the body, Francis clearly signaled that he wanted to hear all voices in the Catholic Church, since the people he chose were far from like-minded acolytes. Ideologically, the group stretches from the progressive Rodríguez Maradiaga to the arch-conservative Pell, with a number of centrists such as Boston's O'Malley in between. They are strong-minded men, none more so than Cardinal Laurent Monsengwo Pasinya of the Democratic Republic of Congo. Pasinya was once president of a transitional governing council in the former Zaire as the troubled country found its way following the departure of the authoritarian president Mobutu Sese Seko, who ruled from 1965 to 1997. Pasinya has remained a voice of conscience in Congo's newly formed state, sometimes putting his life at risk. In 2010 two men dressed as priests showed up wanting to see him at his office, and when their stories didn't check out, the police were summoned and found handguns hidden beneath the men's cassocks.

This pope's commitment to collegiality is crystal clear in how seriously he takes the synod of bishops, an institution created by Pope Paul VI in the wake of the Second Vatican Council and billed at the time as a sort of "council in miniature." Generally, a synod brings together about 300 bishops and other participants for an annual three-week gathering in Rome. There are three different kinds of synods—ordinary, extraordinary and special—and 26 have been held since 1967. However, the synod has never really lived up to its promise as an organ of collegiality; preparations for the synod often don't foster real consultation, and the results have been anemic and often predetermined. During the John Paul II years, the pontiff sometimes came to sessions of the synod and sat on the dais reading a book while bishop after bishop delivered a seven-minute speech on whatever the topic happened to be. (The running joke was that the book in John Paul's hands was the apostolic exhortation containing the conclusions from the synod, which had already been worked out before the meeting began.)

Francis is a synod veteran, having taken part in a 1997 synod on the Church in the America and served as the relator, or chairman, of a 2001 synod on the role of the bishop in the Church, at which he presented the final report. As pope, he seems determined to make the synod live up to its original mission. Accordingly, in September 2013 he handpicked a new secretary for the synod. Lorenzo Baldisseri had previously been the No. 2 official for the all-important Congregation for Bishops, so by appointing him as secretary, Francis signaled that the synod matters to him. When Francis made Baldisseri a cardinal in February 2014, his name appeared on the official list of new princes of the Church ahead of any other Vatican official, another small but telling indication of where the synod ranks in the pecking order under this pope.

Francis's personal engagement in the synod's work has been extraordinary by recent papal standards. Prior to Francis, the synod had passed its conclusions to a papal aide, usually without even consulting the boss. In an act akin to the U.S. president heading over to Congress to sit in on a meeting of a House committee, in October 2013 Francis decided to walk down the Via della Conciliazione—the broad Roman street leading away from St. Peter's Basilica—to join one of the synod meetings. Francis spent six hours over two days with the council, impressing members not only with his commitment but his informality. Cardinal Timothy Dolan of New York said members of the council had been briefed that the pope was coming but were told that he didn't want anyone downstairs making a production out of his arrival. He arrived by himself, with no aides or security personnel, carrying a briefcase. "He came over like it was just another day at the office, with his lunch box," Dolan said in an interview with the *Boston Globe* in early 2014. "We couldn't believe it."

Francis led the council that day in overhauling procedures for the synod of bishops, including shortening the period devoted to speeches, increasing the periods set aside for informal conversation and enhancing consultation with the grass roots via a special questionnaire bishops were encouraged to use to get feedback from ordinary parishioners. Francis has also made the synod on the family a two-stage affair, with an extraordinary session in 2014 and an ordinary meeting in 2015. The idea is to allow ideas to percolate for a year, fueled by reaction to whatever emerges from the first meeting, before reaching final conclusions.

These moves reflect the vision of papal restraint that Francis laid out in "Evangelii Gaudium," the November 2013 apostolic exhortation expressing his program of governance. "The papal magisterium should [not] be expected to offer a definitive or complete word on every question which affects the Church and the world," the pope wrote. "It is not advisable for the pope to take the place of local Bishops in the discernment of every issue which arises in their territory." He added, "In this sense, I am conscious of the need to promote a sound decentralization."

DESPITE THOSE WORDS, there have been multiple occasions on Francis's watch when he has seemed indifferent to the usual channels of consultation and vetting papal decisions, setting the process aside in order to do whatever he thinks needs to be done.

Saint-making is one such example. Many theologians believe that canonization—the formal act of declaring someone a saint—invokes the pope's infallible authority over faith and morals, and no one wants to deploy that power in a cavalier fashion. Accordingly, Catholicism has developed an elaborate procedure for canonization, in part because the Vatican doesn't want to be embarrassed again as it was in 1969 when it had to remove St. Christopher, the famous patron of travelers, from the official list on the grounds that he probably never existed.

Sainthood generally begins when a group of people, such as a religious order or a lay movement, nominate a candidate. The bishop of the diocese where the person lived or worked authorizes someone to conduct an investigation, and if the results are positive, they're sent off to the Vatican's Congregation for the Causes of Saints, where a team of theologians examines the spiritual and moral virtues of the candidates. If the nominee passes that step, then evidence of performing one miracle is ordinarily required for beatification, the next-to-last step, and another for canonization. A bank of scientists—usually medical doctors—scrutinizes alleged miracles. A body of bishops then votes on the cases, and only then is a candidate submitted to the pope. The intentional cumbersomeness of the process helps explain why some causes languish for years, even centuries, often waiting for a miracle to pass examination.

In December 2013, however, Francis canonized Frenchman Peter Faber, a 16th-century co-founder of the Jesuits. Technically, the pope exercised what's known as "equivalent canonization," meaning he bypassed the usual procedures for someone long venerated. Faber had been beatified in 1872, and his case had since been in a holding pattern in the Congregation for the Causes of Saints. There's no serious question about whether Faber meets the usual tests for being recognized by the Church, since he was a noted theologian and a deeply pious believer. Moreover, he was also known as a man of dialogue and moderation, qualities Francis cited when announcing the decision to make him a saint. Francis canonized Faber without evidence of a miracle—the second time he had moved somebody across the finish line in that fashion. The first came when he canonized Pope John XXIII along with Pope John Paul II in a massive Roman ceremony in April 2014.

Despite the fact that both Faber and Pope John XXIII are Catholic icons, the pope's disregard for protocol left a mixed impression. Journalist Andrea Gagliarducci wrote that Francis's mode of governing can sometimes be "anything but collegial," citing his new saints and charging that his Council of Cardinals had become a closed shop.

Gagliarducci even suggested that Francis was acting as if he was still living under the military dictatorship in Argentina, conducting deliberations in secret and playing his cards close to his chest until springing a decision on an unsuspecting world.

Francis's approach to media relations is another good example of what some critics have called "government by surprise," in which the pope acts on his own and leaves his subordinates scrambling to keep up. When his interview with *Civiltà Cattolica* appeared in September 2013—the one in which he vowed to dial down the papal rhetoric on matters such as abortion and homosexuality—it hit the newsstands at the same time that the Vatican's Pontifical Council for Social Communications (basically, its media think tank) was holding an annual plenary assembly just down the street on the Via della Conciliazione. The day the interview went public, a surreal scene unfolded inside the hall. The approximately 200 participants in the meeting—which included Vatican officials and a cross-section of cardinals, archbishops and bishops from around the world, as well as the cream of the crop of the Church's media advisers—were discussing how to make the Catholic message relevant in the 21st-century media environment, when the room erupted in a cacophony of smartphone beeps. None of the heavy hitters present had any idea Francis's comments were coming, and the meeting essentially dissolved into gasps and cries of "Have you seen this?" One flustered cardinal found himself sitting on a street bench outside the hall for the better part of two hours, fielding phone calls from media outlets back home. In between interviews, the cardinal looked up at a passing friend and asked, "How in God's name is it possible the media had this before we did?"

Since that conversation with *Civiltà Cattolica*, Francis has granted several other sit-down interviews, none of which have been arranged through the Vatican's usual gatekeepers. The pope has come across as refreshingly candid and accessible, although not all observers have been happy. Italian journalist Sandro Magister published an essay in

December 2013 chronicling the "monocratic, centralizing form in which Francis is . . . governing the Church," the headline of which was "Highly Centralizing and Hardly Collegial."

ALTHOUGH FRANCIS HAS SAID he does not envisage sweeping changes in Catholic doctrine, there is one area in which he has opened the door to reconsideration: the rule that bars divorced and civilly remarried Catholics who did not obtain a Church annulment of their first union from receiving the sacraments.

The pope has made no secret of his own bias. He took a question on the subject during a July 2013 press conference, saying "this is the season of mercy" and pointing to the Eastern Orthodox practice of permitting a second marriage under certain circumstances. In tapping German cardinal Walter Kasper to deliver the opening address at a February 2014 meeting of cardinals, Francis knew that Kasper would roll out an argument for admitting the divorced and remarried to the sacraments. (Kasper first floated this idea back in 1993, and since then the more lax approach has became quasi-official policy for some German bishops.) Francis made his inclinations sufficiently obvious that the Vatican had to issue a public plea to bishops and other Church officials around the world not to get ahead of the pope, begging them instead to "conduct a journey in full communion with the Church community."

Any move to change existing discipline would encounter fierce opposition, of course. Several cardinals have said publicly that such a move is unthinkable in light of Christ's clear teaching on marriage in the New Testament: "What God has joined, let no one separate." Across the world, Catholic opinion is split, with one wing of the Church urging Francis to act and another insisting he shouldn't because it would be an abuse of his authority.

What's a maverick pope to do? In light of his own promises of collegiality, Francis might conclude that in the absence of consensus, he has no basis to impose his will on a divided Church. In keeping with his policy of decentralization, however, he could compromise and allow local bishops or bishops' conferences to make their own decisions (possibly resulting in a permissive standard in, say, Germany and a tough no-communion position in Nigeria). Or, perhaps fueled by a sense that divine providence has ordained his papacy as a kairos of mercy—a special moment in God's plan for the world—he could decide to pull the trigger and change the rules. (Francis described the present time as just such a kairos in his answer to a question about divorced and remarried Catholics during a July 2013 press conference.) No matter what happens, the question of divorce and the sacrament of communion will be one of the biggest decisions he's likely to face during his reign.

9

Backlash

CATHOLICISM IS LIKE POLITICS—no one in power ever plays to unmixed reviews. Popes always experience resistance, and their success is often related to how well they cope with this backlash. Pope John XXIII—the "good pope" who led the reforming Second Vatican Council in the 1960s—had to navigate around a cluster of Vatican traditionalists. Chief among them was Cardinal Alfredo Ottaviani, the powerful doctrinal czar whose motto was *Semper idem*, "Always the same," an ideological program in miniature. John XXIII's successor, Pope Paul VI, struggled for 15 painful years to hold the Church together, as one wing thought the liberalizing changes of Vatican II weren't going fast enough and the other believed things had already gone too far. His occasional indecisiveness between these two impulses earned him a reputation as the "Hamlet pope."

Despite ruling for almost 27 years, Pope John Paul II never fully succeeded in bringing the Church's bishops around to his evangelical style of leadership, focused on mission rather than maintenance, and to some extent his reign was seen in Rome as a Polish interlude, an anomaly. During the Pope Benedict XVI years, speculation abounded about which prelates sought to undercut his stern defense of Catholic identity—expressed, for instance, in his attempts to revive the Latin mass.

There's a backlash against Pope Francis too. At the grass roots and senior levels, some Catholics aren't on board with what some derisively characterize as "Francis mania," describing the view that the pope is more talented at eliciting applause outside the Church than at defending order and tradition within. What's different about the early 21st century is that new communication technologies allow this resistance to go viral in a short arc of time. Because Francis has generated so much positive buzz outside Church circles, there's a tendency for an equal and opposite push on the inside, especially among Catholics who are leery of too much popularity. They worry that since the outside world has rejected a large portion of Church teaching, its affection can only mean that the Church has gone soft or lost its way. To date, there's little evidence that the backlash has slowed Francis down, but there's also no reason to believe he has seen the last of it.

THE CASA DEL CLERO, a clerical residence on the Via della Scrofa, across the Tiber River from the Vatican near the trendy Piazza Navona, is a destination of choice for cardinals, bishops and priests visiting Rome. An unprepossessing, if beautiful, peach-colored three-story building, it's known for having a better-than-average kitchen, at least by the standards of clerical lodgings, and an entertaining mix of permanent residents and visitors. It's close enough to the Vatican—a 15-minute walk from St. Peter's Square—but far enough away to be less formal and stiff. (It's also a steal in terms of pricing for Roman hotels: a room and full meal service generally runs to about 85 euros, or $115, per night.)

Until recently, Casa del Clero—as well two other lodgings, including the Domus Santa Marta in the Vatican—was being run by Monsignor Battista Ricca. Originally from Brescia, as a young priest Ricca had been part of the Vatican's diplomatic corps, serving in overseas postings including Congo, Colombia and Switzerland. Such a trajectory usually leads to a papal ambassador position and thence the red hat of a cardinal. But for years, Ricca was merely an innkeeper, dressed in Dockers and a sweater.

Among the VIPs who liked to stay at the Casa del Clero during their Roman sojourns was the Jesuit cardinal of Buenos Aires, Jorge Mario Bergoglio. Over the years, Ricca became one of Bergoglio's favorite Roman contacts, and the two men often grabbed a table together at dinnertime. They had a natural bond, since Bergoglio considered himself an outsider in the Vatican and saw a kindred spirit in Ricca, someone who had once been on the fast track but had somehow fallen off. In addition, Ricca was deeply plugged in to the current gossip about Vatican goings-on, so he could catch Bergoglio up on whatever drama he'd missed between trips.

What no one anticipated, however, is that running hotels for clergy afforded Ricca a key advantage in scripting an improbable second act in his career. The naturally gregarious clergyman was able to strike up friendships with a wide swath of the power structure of Catholicism outside Rome, a fact that turned out to be decisive in casting him for a leading—albeit controversial—role in the Francis era.

When Bergoglio arrived in Rome in February 2013 to take part in the final meeting of the College of Cardinals to elect a successor to Pope Benedict XVI, he stayed at the Casa del Clero. There, Ricca was able to fill him in on fellow princes of the Church he didn't know well and give him the political lay of the land. Later, one of the first things the new pope did that charmed the world was return to the Casa del Clero to pay his own bill, though insiders also perceived a tip of the papal *zucchetto* to Bergoglio's old friend. Ricca figured prominently in pictures from that stop, for once actually wearing his black clerical cassock with the purple piping signifying his status as a monsignor—ironically, a title that Francis later all but abolished.

Coincidentally, one of the first challenges Francis took up after his election was the fate of the Vatican Bank. Francis knew he needed his own eyes and ears inside the place. Ricca seemed the natural choice, in part because by then Francis had decided to live permanently at the Domus Santa Marta, where he and Ricca were once again spending time together over meals. The Argentine pope calculated that the job required an Italian, since the inner workings of the bank were still heavily dominated by an Italian old guard.

In June 2013 the Vatican press office announced that Ricca had been appointed to the position of prelate of the bank, a previously defunct role that made him the pope's personal representative. Although a prelate is usually a spiritual role, akin to a chaplain, in this case it promised to be a position of real power, because everybody who worked at the bank knew that if they talked to Ricca about bank business, they'd also be talking to the pope. The appointment made Ricca a player, but it also made him a target.

One month later, Italy's most widely read Vatican writer penned a salacious exposé about Ricca, alleging homosexual activities while he served in the papal embassy to Uruguay in the late 1990s and early 2000s. In his weekly column on Church affairs in *l'Espresso*, Sandro Magister described how Ricca's behavior "scandalized numerous bishops, priests and laity of that little South American country, not least the sisters who attended to the nunciature" (the term for a papal embassy). According to Magister, these escapades were reported to Ricca's Vatican superiors, who chose to turn a blind eye.

When the Vatican issued an anemic denial calling the report "not credible," Magister stood by his story and insisted that it had been "confirmed by primary sources." *L'Espresso* issued its own response, basically daring the Vatican spokesman, Lombardi, to visit their offices to consult documentation for the story, including copies of police reports from Montevideo. Ricca never commented on the reports, which did not include any suggestion of abuse of minors or criminal activity. He was never charged by authorities in Uruguay.

The veracity of the reports aside, it seemed apparent that Magister wasn't motivated by breaking news. He is associated with a traditional wing of Catholicism that viewed Benedict XVI as a hero and suspected that he was sabotaged by liberal elements in the Church. Magister has close ties to the conservative former vicar of Rome, Italian cardinal Camillo Ruini. Magister's article about Ricca struck many insiders as an early sign of discontent with the new pope.

Francis didn't blink. During his return flight from a July trip to Brazil for World Youth Day, he said a preliminary investigation had found "nothing of what had been alleged." The pontiff went on to describe his general attitude when dealing with gay people, a reflection that produced the single most celebrated line of his papacy, "Who am I to judge?"

Not only did Francis keep Ricca at the bank, but the prelate continues to wield real influence. In May 2014 a critical letter from Ricca about bank president Ernst von Freyberg, complaining that von Freyberg was not providing enough information about bank operations, played a key role in the German businessman's decision to step down.

Sources close to the pontiff provided two reasons for his resolve to keep Ricca in a position of power. First, he came to the conclusion that whatever may have happened in Uruguay 15 years ago, the Ricca he knows today is worthy of trust. Second, Francis did not want to set the precedent that his reform could be blocked by character assassination.

The Ricca affair was a turning point. On one hand, Francis made clear that he's not going to cut people loose just because they find themselves under attack. On the other, his refusal to jettison a cleric with Ricca's alleged history of homosexuality soured a chunk of Catholic opinion, becoming a standard reference on Catholic blogs and in some media commentary. Magister has gone on to become something of an in-house critic, occasionally implying that Francis's popularity in secular circles may come at the expense of standing tall behind Church teaching. It was the start of some significant resistance to the pope of mercy.

IN THE CORRIDORS OF THE VATICAN, the argument "This is how we've always done things" packs a solid punch. While any new pope must therefore expect a degree of reluctance from others to follow his lead, Andrea Riccardi—a Church historian and founder of the influential Community of Sant'Egidio, a lay association dedicated to evangelization and charity—says that because Francis is leading the Church in a dramatic new direction, "no pope of the 20th century ever experienced as much resistance." Riccardi argues the resistance isn't just percolating inside the Vatican but at the grass roots of the Church as well. Sant'Egidio is generally classified as belonging to the Church's center-left camp, with a special emphasis on interfaith dialogue, peacemaking and poverty relief, making Riccardi an unabashed Bergoglio enthusiast and giving his analysis a special poignancy.

In political life, one reliable way to detect opposition to a new administration is when somebody starts claiming to be persecuted by it. By that standard, no outfit in Catholicism is more of a canary in the coal mine than the Franciscan Friars of the Immaculate, a small offshoot of the vast Franciscan family of priests, brothers and nuns. The community was founded in 1970 in the wake of the Second Vatican Council. Seen as a destination of choice for orthodox and often zealous young believers, the Friars of the Immaculate have a special attachment to the Latin mass. Although they claim only about 400 members worldwide, since the ascension of Bergoglio to pope, their community has become the first casualty—some would say martyrs—of Francis's reign.

The crackdown on the order began swiftly. In 2013 the Vatican department that oversees religious orders issued a decree, with the authorization of the new pope, dissolving the friars' leadership, appointing a special papal commissioner and requiring any friars who want to celebrate the older mass to obtain special permission from their new superiors. (That last edict was seen as an especially clear break with the policies of Benedict XVI, since Benedict's 2007 ruling on the Latin mass specified that priests don't require anyone's permission to say it.) Eventually, a theological institute run by the order was also closed, with seminarians ordered to attend the same papal theological faculties in Rome as everyone else. Although Vatican officials insisted the intervention was not about Church politics, the move was seen as part of a broader agenda to steer away from Benedict XVI's doctrine. About 40 members defected in protest, most of them moving to other like-minded communities.

The pontiff, noting the backlash he faced, attempted to make peace by sitting down with 60 members of the order in June 2014. Francis was visibly ill during his meeting, having canceled most of his appointments the previous day due to a severe cold, but he told aides that he was determined to be there because he knew that the fate of the order had become a symbol of broader tensions in his papacy. And although he assured the friars of his goodwill, two more members broke away in the aftermath.

Later that month, Italian Catholic commentator Marco Tosatti described the crackdown on the Friars of the Immaculate as the leading edge of a wider "witch hunt" directed at conservatives, calling it "an internal war ... being waged in the name of the pope." Tosatti, who's seen as slightly conservative, asserted that in Francis's Church, young priests who are judged too conservative are not being allowed to profess final vows in their religious orders, and candidates for the seminary seen as too traditional are being rejected. He claimed that chances for advancement in Vatican departments are now being shaped by whether the official is sufficiently open-minded and progressive, while conservative bishops aren't being promoted to the most important dioceses that would put them in line to become cardinals. Certainly, some of Francis's highest-profile appointments—such as the choice of Carlos Osoro Sierra for Madrid and Blase Cupich for Chicago—give credence to Tosatti's last point, because these prelates were previously seen as representing the moderate sector of their national bishops' conferences and not the conservative camp.

Among other instances of what he saw as a witch hunt, Tosatti cited the case of Fr. Justin Wylie, a South African priest who had been serving at the Vatican's embassy to the U.N. in New York. After he delivered a homily critical of the archdiocese of New York for considering closing a local parish in which the Latin mass is celebrated, Wylie lost his position at the papal embassy and ended up returning to South Africa, making him in Tosatti's eyes a victim of the "bergoglisti"—Francis enthusiasts engaged in a nasty campaign to suppress perceived enemies of the revolution.

So despite Francis's strong poll numbers, there is a spreading sense that he's as much a disturber of the peace as an agent of unity, and perhaps what Tosatti captures best is the perception of forces being arrayed for battle.

Francis is a savvy Jesuit politician, and he has been quietly taking steps to cope with the blowback. One example was his phone call to Mario Palmaro, the writer who co-penned the article "Why We Don't Like This Pope," as Palmaro lay seriously ill. While such generosity might disarm some, it may not be enough to overcome deeply entrenched resistance. It also remains to be seen if Francis's greatest obstacles will come from his critics or from friends and allies who celebrate the pope's agenda but find themselves incapable of actually implementing it.

Francis faces three main types of resistance. The first is ideological, which in his case means conservatives who find his political and theological stances too progressive. The second is institutional, referring to people invested in the current structures and patterns of doing business in the Church who feel threatened by change. The third is existential: the basic human tendency to avoid unnecessary effort, which for a missionary pope determined to shake things up may prove the greatest obstacle of all.

IN POLITICAL TERMS, Catholicism could be described as a continuum of opinion from the far right to the far left, loosely united by a body of core beliefs and worship practices. An American Tea Party member, a Colombian Marxist guerrilla and everyone in between can go to mass, take communion and regard themselves as good Catholics. Believers form a motley crew, and reactions to a new leader are therefore predictably wide-ranging.

Outside the Church, ideological opposition tends to be especially virulent among neoconservatives and advocates of free-market economics. Along with Rush Limbaugh's "pure Marxism" jibe, Fox News senior judicial analyst Andrew Napolitano said the pope's rhetoric revealed a "disturbing ignorance" about economic realities, while business analyst Stuart Varney accused Francis of trafficking in "neo-socialism."

It's not just those on the right who are unhappy. Secular leftists regularly conclude that Francis is rebranding rather than reforming. John Bloodworth, editor of the popular leftist British political blog Gentleman Crafter, said in late 2013, "Pope Francis's position on most issues should make the hair of every liberal curl." He continued, "Instead we get article after article of saccharine from people who really should know better." Segments of the more radical Catholic left—those who support the ordination of women priests, gay marriage, birth control and abortion—are also far from pleased with Francis. Jon O'Brien, president of the pro-choice group Catholics for Choice, reproved Francis in March 2014, describing him as "not exactly Che Guevara for the Church," and complained that Francis has a "blind spot" about women because of his refusal to rethink the possibility of female clergy.

Inside the Church, opposition tends to be spread across a wider set of issues. At the margins, there are hard-core Catholic traditionalists openly calling Francis a heretic, usually for his belief in interreligious dialogue, unity with other Christians and decentralizing the power of the papacy. Some of these dissenters, such as American priest Fr. Paul Kramer, best known for his 2002 book *The Devil's Final Battle*, believe that Benedict XVI remains the real pope. It's a camp prominent enough to merit its own name: resignationism (the belief that Benedict's resignation was invalid). These voices are often loud, but they are generally far from the levers of real power.

Catholicism is in many ways still a monarchy, with the pope at the top of the pyramid. As in other monarchies through the ages, it's easier for insiders to criticize courtiers rather than go after the king himself, or insist that the king has been misunderstood rather than wrong. In that guise, it's not difficult to spot a rising tide of indirect, unorganized resistance to Francis.

Cardinal Carlo Caffarra of Bologna, Italy, is one such person questioning Francis's approach. Caffarra is the former president of Rome's John Paul II Institute for Studies on Marriage and Family, a perch from which he emerged as one of the premier right-leaning culture warriors in global Catholicism. So strict is Caffarra about sexual ethics that he once said condom use to prevent HIV/AIDS could never be justified because "even the smallest moral harm is so much greater than any physical harm." He also opined that any Catholic politician who supports gay marriage should automatically be cut off from the Church. Although his formerly jet-black hair has gone gray in recent years, none of the intensity has gone out of Caffarra's eyes, which gaze out over crowds through thick black glasses when he's reading one of his typically dense texts.

It's natural that conservatives look to Caffarra to draw some lines in the sand in the Francis era, and he has been happy to oblige. In

February 2014, after the pontiff invited Cardinal Walter Kasper, who favors communion for divorced people, to give the opening talk at a meeting of cardinals on the family, Caffarra went on the offensive. In an essay and a series of interviews, Caffarra insisted that the Church's ban on divorced and remarried believers receiving communion is part of a teaching on marriage that comes from Christ himself and that "the pope has no power" to change it. Given that Francis has already signaled that he's considering just such a move, Caffarra's commentary was seen as a warning to Francis that the divorced and remarried issue is a red line for some in the Church's power structure and that he might want to curtail his non-collegial instincts.

Francis's popularity lends him some insulation from such criticisms. For one, he has greater support at the grass roots in Caffarra's own backyard, given that the city where the 76-year-old serves as archbishop is known in Italy as "Red Bologna" for its progressive political climate (Bologna was once at the heart of the Italian Communist Party). One can still find such downtown intersections as Workers' Avenue and Stalingrad Street, and in today's Bologna those areas are likely to be festooned with images of Francis and quotations from his texts, especially the pope's rhetoric on the "savage inequalities" of capitalism. Yet Caffarra has a significant following in pro-life circles and among doctrinal purists around the world; Francis can't dismiss him altogether, because his supporters are destined to remain important voices.

Another folk hero for ideologically disenchanted Catholics is American cardinal Raymond Burke. A former Church lawyer who served as a judge for a canon law court in Rome from 1989 to 1994, he was the president of the Apostolic Signatura, effectively the Vatican's Supreme Court, from 2008 to 2014. It's tough to find a more ferociously committed pro-lifer than Burke. He has publicly described the Democrats in the U.S. as the "party of death," saying pro-choice Catholic politicians should be denied communion (he also explicitly said that no Catholic in good faith could vote for President Barack

Obama). Burke once blasted a Catholic hospital for hosting a Sheryl Crow concert because she's pro-choice, and has even warned parents against letting their kids read J.K. Rowling's *Harry Potter* series because the novels might encourage an interest in witchcraft. When a group of vociferously pro-life Italian Catholics organized a rally in Rome in the fall of 2013 to protest a bill in parliament outlawing homophobia, not a single Italian prelate showed up, but Burke attended.

Even in the way he dresses, Burke's difference from Francis is clear. Burke favors clerical finery, often wearing a train of watered silk, fine scarlet gloves and jeweled red hats. He's an aficionado of the Latin mass, embodying an ornate and highly traditional "smells and bells" approach to worship that leaves Francis cold. Burke has become a go-to figure for devotees of the older liturgy; he's considered the "big get" whenever a major event is being organized anywhere in the world devoted to what is now officially called the "extraordinary form" of the mass.

Burke's disagreements with the pope came to the fore in an interview he gave to the conservative American Catholic TV network EWTN. Asked about Francis's apparent determination to dial down the Church's rhetoric on the culture wars, Burke said, "One gets the impression, or it's interpreted this way in the media, that he thinks we're talking too much about abortion, too much about the integrity of marriage as between one man and one woman. . . . But we can never talk enough about that."

As a Church lawyer, Burke knows canon 331 of the Code of Canon Law, which says the pope wields "supreme, full, immediate and universal" authority in the Church. In other words, Francis can clip the wings of Burke or anyone else he wants. Nevertheless, Burke was said to be caught off guard when the news broke in December 2013, just days after his EWTN interview, that he had not been reappointed to the Congregation for Bishops. He had been replaced by Cardinal Donald Wuerl, a centrist from Washington, D.C. At just 65 years old, Burke would have expected 15 more years at the Congregation (the retirement age is 80)—enough time to shape the choices of bishops, especially in the English-speaking world. Privately, Burke told friends he was "stunned." A month later, Burke was reassigned from the Apostolic Signatura, the highest judicial authority in the Church, to become the patron of the Order of Malta, which today functions mostly as a Catholic philanthropic organization. In a December 2014 interview with an Argentine journalist, Francis insisted the move was not a punishment, saying he wanted a "smart American" in the role.

Another outspoken critic is Bishop Rogelio Livieres Plano, formerly of the diocese of Ciudad del Este in Paraguay and a member of Opus Dei. He was removed as the head of the Paraguayan diocese in September 2014 for allegedly dividing the bishops' conference in that country. During the synod of bishops, Livieres Plano wrote on his personal blog, "Inside the Church, and recently from some of its highest circles, new winds blow that aren't from the Holy Spirit. . . . The situation is very grave and I'm not the first to notice that, regretfully, we're facing the danger of a great schism." He added a scathing reference to the "propellers that lead this confusion in Bergoglio's church."

One could chalk up the comments from Burke and Livieres Plano to sour grapes. Yet it would be a mistake to think they're the only ones who feel this way. In October 2014 Robert Royal, a respected American Catholic commentator who is usually on the conservative side of Church debates, reported hearing subterranean grumblings in Rome about Pope Francis. Royal wrote that some were calling the pontiff "a Latin dictator" and "a Peron," someone who likes to be center stage. Royal said he had heard more than one disenchanted person comment, "His health is bad, so at least this won't last too long."

Yet politics is hardly the only source of pushback against Francis. On a warm Roman day in June 2014, a veteran Italian cardinal voiced another opinion while sitting at a table in the garden of the Cecilia Metella restaurant on the Via Aurelia, across the street from some of the city's most famous catacombs. Because of its out-of-the-way setting and reputation for discretion, Cecilia Metella is a favorite haunt for prelates looking to fly below the radar. In between courses, the cardinal held forth on the reform of the Vatican's central administrative bureaucracy, the Roman Curia. The fate of the Curia has been the subject of fevered speculation since Francis announced shortly after his election that he was creating a council of cardinal advisers to help him make significant changes to its structures and operations. The sense of drama has been exacerbated by hints of a shake-up from the man Francis chose to lead the body, Cardinal Óscar Andrés Rodríguez Maradiaga of Honduras, a plane-flying, saxophone-playing iconoclast who is unabashed about thinking outside the ecclesiastical box.

Speaking off the record, the veteran Italian cardinal was of the view that talk of reform is likely to turn out to be sound and fury, signifying very little. Some minor departments of the Curia may be closed or consolidated, he predicted, and some personnel may be shuffled around, but the underlying culture will endure. Pressed to explain why, he put the point simply: "Bergoglio won't be here forever, but we will." The "we" in that sentence didn't refer to any individuals but the Church's entire apparatchik class, who are more loyal to the system than any particular inhabitant of the papal throne.

It was a classic example of Italian ideological flexibility. With few hard and fast views on substantive matters in the Church or any real theological or political resistance to Francis, the cardinal was happy to live with however things shake out, praying only for a moderate resolution that doesn't rock the boat. In fact, he said, he was thrilled with the popularity of the new boss, largely because it has made his daily life easier. Now when he walks into a restaurant, boards a plane or speaks to a Catholic audience, he no longer has to worry about running into people wanting to vent their spleens about the pope or the Church. Instead, he said, he's more likely to find delight.

But the cardinal was also adamant he doesn't expect the Vatican he has known for almost five decades to evolve significantly on Francis's watch. The old guard, of which he's a self-professed member, exercises too much gravitational pull for any pope to counteract. That's the nature of the institutional resistance Francis faces: those whose self-image and career prospects are invested in the status quo are determined to preserve established patterns of doing business.

In part, this institutional resistance expresses itself in doing things the way they've always been done until some external force compels change. Walk into any Vatican department nearly two years into the Francis era and ask what's different operationally as a result of the new pope, and the most common response is "Nothing." The same sort of documents are being drafted, the same meetings are being organized, the same decisions are being made, and the same kinds of people are being appointed to act as consultants, delivering basically the same advice. The attitude of many officials boils down to "Until the pope tells us differently, it's business as usual."

But the old guard doesn't only know how to play defense. A spate of articles in the Italian press in mid-2014 suggested that a shadowy Maltese lobby was wrapping its tentacles around the Vatican's financial operation. The alleged ringleader was Joseph F.X. Zahra, a former director of Malta's Central Bank and the vice-coordinator of the Council for the Economy, a body created by Francis. Zahra was said to be in cahoots with French financier Jean-Baptiste de Franssu and Italian academic Francesco Vermiglio, both fellow members of the council. The articles implied that the three men had ties to a Maltese company and might be exploiting their new positions to extract financial benefit from the Vatican's investment activities. (De Franssu was later named president of the Vatican Bank.) All three men denied the accusations but were compelled to provide materials to reporters proving that the company in question was defunct and had only been involved in market research, not investments. In any event, the men attested, they were serving pro bono as members of the Council for the Economy. No charges were ever filed.

The claims surfaced in an Italian newspaper that's part of the media empire of former conservative prime minister Silvio Berlusconi, a man who has strong ties to many senior figures in the Italian Church. The attack on Zahra and the other members of the Council for the Economy seemed like a classic example of the empire striking back, in the sense that some members of the old guard were trying to neuter the financial dimension of Francis's reform by sowing doubts about the credibility of the people overseeing it.

Australian cardinal George Pell, the pope's head of financial reform, dismissed the charges as "Alice in Wonderland stuff" and suggested that political and financial interests were behind them. "Quite often people don't like change, and I can understand that," Pell said. "What I can't understand is why anyone would bother to go to such lengths. I wonder whether there's significant money involved, [that] perhaps someone regrets that over the last few years the bank and the Vatican generally have cleaned up their act." Pell went on to say that Zahra and the other members of the alleged Maltese lobby had his "full support."

Pell had a taste of the same subterfuge in late September 2014, when a string of negative articles in the Italian press dusted off his record as archbishop of Melbourne in Australia from 1996 to 2001 with regard to the child sexual abuse scandals in Catholicism. Picking up on a Royal Commission hearing back home in which Pell had participated from the Vatican via a video link, the articles repeated complaints from victims that a compensation scheme Pell had adopted, one of the first such programs anywhere in the world at the time, was intended to limit payouts and keep victims quiet. Whatever the significance of the criticisms, they had been thoroughly aired in Australia for more than a decade and were undoubtedly well known to Francis at the time he appointed Pell to his council of cardinal advisers in April 2013 and as his finance czar in February 2014. The purpose of airing them in September 2014 seemed to be to link Pell to the brewing crisis regarding Józef Wesolowski, the former papal ambassador accused of sexual abuse in the Dominican Republic, and thereby weaken Pell's standing. Many Vatican veterans detected the old guard in action. "It's obvious Pell is making some people nervous," a senior official said at the time, asking that his name not be used. "That can't be a bad thing."

Whoever was behind the exposé, Francis now has to walk a fine line. Elected on a reform mandate, he hasn't shown himself to be bashful about bringing in a new cast of characters, but he also knows that running against the system is one thing, and governing against it quite another. He can't simply flush out the old guard entirely, which would devastate both the institutional memory of the Vatican as well as its operational capacity.

Take the cases of Cardinal Angelo Sodano and Tarcisio Bertone. Two giants of the Italian ecclesiastical landscape, Sodano was the secretary of state, effectively the Vatican's prime minister, under Pope John Paul II; Bertone held the same role under Pope Benedict XVI. At the peak of their power, the two men were considered rivals, but today they find themselves in the same boat. In Sodano's case, Francis's reformers are looking into his support for the controversial religious order the Legionaries of Christ. Its disgraced founder, the late Mexican Fr. Marcial Maciel Degollado, went into hiding following allegations that he sexually abused minors and young men. For his part, Bertone drew a round of negative coverage in the Italian press for his role in dispensing $20 million from the Vatican Bank to a film company owned by a friend.

But it's not easy to corral the old guard into obedience. Neither Sodano nor Bertone rushed to the pontiff's defense when he was under assault, for instance in the Ricca affair. Their protégés take thinly disguised glee in playing up any stumbles Francis makes, such as the fracas that broke out in 2013 when he tapped a young Italian PR expert named Francesca Immacolata Chaouqui for a panel on economic and administrative reform. When racy pictures of Chaouqui and her husband went viral, a number of Vatican veterans told reporters that it was what happens when you bring in untested outsiders and give them free run of the place. (For the record, Chaouqui is a PR professional who worked for Ernst & Young, and none of the criticism directed at her had anything to do with the substance of her contributions to the papal commission.)

THE FOREGOING FORMS OF RESISTANCE—politics and vested interests—may be more common among the pundit class in the Church and within the hierarchy than at the grass roots. At all levels, however, inertia can get in the way of Francis's desire to see the Church spring into action.

Francis has called for a missionary Church, one that gets "out of the sacristy and into the streets," as well as a Church that makes itself relevant to the experiences of ordinary people. Francis has implored Catholics of all stripes to imitate his example of reaching out to people alienated from the faith, embracing victims of the "throwaway culture": the poor, the elderly, unemployed youth, immigrants and refugees. Doing so requires sustained effort, including rethinking stale pastoral practices, launching new initiatives and generally being willing to think creatively. Even people who admire the pope's political line and have no personal interests at risk in his press for greater integrity sometimes simply don't have the energy to change.

Fr. Juan Isasmendi, an Argentine pastor groomed by the future pope to serve in his country's slums, said that Francis faced such resistance before. "Sure, there were some priests who had gripes about things Bergoglio said or did," Isasmendi said in a 2013 interview. "But the much bigger problem he faced is that many of us just didn't want to work as hard as it would have taken to be the kind of Church he wanted us to be. The problem wasn't with his vision but the effort required to get there. A lot of the time, ordinary human beings just aren't wired that way."

In early 2014, Italian journalist Marco Politi published a book, *Francis Among the Wolves: The Secret of a Revolution*. The title is a play on the legend of the pope's namesake, St. Francis, who supposedly persuaded a ravenous wolf that had been terrorizing the town of Gubbio to call off its rampage. Politi, a longtime Vatican watcher, was not so subtly suggesting that Pope Francis is facing some wolves of his own within the Church. Politi keenly noted, "At the same time that Francis is drawing thunderous applause from all quarters, he's finding great inertia within the ecclesiastical structures."

It's an assessment shared by Riccardi, the Community of Sant'Egidio founder. In March 2014 he published an essay in Italian newsmagazine *Famiglia Cristiana* about resistance to Pope Francis in the power structure of the Church and was pressed by reporters to elaborate. He acknowledged that there are some bishops nonplussed by the Argentine pontiff, prelates who like to play down the doctrinal importance of his commentary and exalt the contributions of Benedict XVI. Riccardi said that's not the most serious obstacle, however. The real roadblock is "the resistance of those who don't want to change, who don't want to live in a truly committed fashion, who simply don't want more work to do."

To date, efforts to quantify the "Francis effect" in terms of boosting attendance at mass or bringing more people to the faith have been largely unsuccessful. A November 2013 study by the Pew Forum in the U.S. showed that after eight months under Francis's leadership, the share of Americans who self-identify as Catholic, about 22 percent, was the same as it had been under Benedict XVI, and that the share of American Catholics attending mass on a weekly basis, 39 percent, was also unchanged. On the other hand, some pastors in such nations as Italy and Ireland have reported an uptick in mass attendance and demand for the sacrament of confession.

If Francis has made Catholicism cool again, why isn't that cachet translating into clearer missionary gains? It's partly because the decisions people make about their spiritual lives are driven by a host of factors beyond whether they happen to like the current pope. And Catholic personnel around the world will also tell you that while Francis may be a relentless missionary, the same drive doesn't always filter down to lower levels. Even if someone were to show up at Sunday mass on fire with enthusiasm for the pope's vision of the Church, they wouldn't necessarily find a priest with the same fervor, or people itching to join them on the front lines. Francis has called on Christians to revive the virtue of boldness alongside prudence, but the latter is often the more comfortable option. Sloth is considered one of the seven deadly sins, and it could prove to be the most hazardous to Francis's mission.

In April 2014 Francis delivered a homily during his morning mass at the Santa Marta touching on this point. "I think of many Christians, of many Catholics—yes, they are Catholics, but without enthusiasm, even embittered," the pontiff said. "This is the disease of sloth, the spiritual inertia of Christians. This attitude is crippling apostolic zeal. It makes Christian people stand still and at ease, but not in the good sense of the word; they do not bother to go out to proclaim the gospel! They are anesthetized."

With that in mind, the real trick for Francis may not be how well he handles disagreement but how thoroughly he's able to rouse those who agree with him. An inert majority, in the end, is every bit as threatening to a missionary pope as a dissenting minority.

10

Will It
Last?

POPE FRANCIS ENTHUSIASTS desperately want his papacy to succeed in overhauling Catholicism, while detractors fear that the longer it goes on, the harder it will be to roll back what they see as mistakes. Both camps tend to ask the same bottom-line question: "Will it last?" That is to say, will Pope Francis be a flash in the pan, a symbol of unrealized possibilities? Or will he permanently change the inner life of the Catholic Church and the way it presents itself to the outside world?

To some extent, the answer depends on how change is defined. If one means substantive alterations in Church teaching—for instance, acceptance of abortion; gay marriage; allowing couples to use contraception; and welcoming women priests—then the answer is no. Francis has made it clear that he's not a doctrinal radical and does not intend to upend the catechism (the official collection of Catholic doctrine). On the other hand, if one sees change as a reorientation of Catholicism toward the political center, the geographical and existential peripheries and the heart of the gospel, then it's possible Francis will leave an imprint on the Church that will outlive his own reign, however long or short it turns out to be.

Francis has moved aggressively to shuffle personnel in key positions. He has moved toward greater internationalization (dethroning Italians as the Vatican's financial power brokers) and chosen moderates as opposed to traditionalist hard-liners (for example, replacing the deeply traditional Cardinal Mauro Piacenza at the Congregation for Clergy, the body responsible for overseeing priestly life, with the veteran diplomat Beniamino Stella, a much more centrist and flexible figure). He has also started to appoint bishops around the world who share his views, notably the new archbishop of Chicago, Blase Cupich. Francis has acted with equal vigor on the legislative front, decreeing, among other things, a sweeping overhaul of the Vatican's financial operation in the direction of greater transparency and accountability and issuing a series of new laws that make it virtually impossible for any future pope to return to the *status quo ante*.

The Francis revolution is being felt at the level of in-the-trenches application of doctrine rather than the doctrine itself. The pope is trying to encourage the most generous, merciful and flexible application possible, making it clear that his Church wants to include rather than exclude and sees people living in less-than-ideal ways as souls on the path to redemption rather than enemies who need to be excoriated. While the tension between rigor and acceptance is a constant in Catholic life—and no pope can fully alter the balance—there's no question that in a remarkably short time, Francis has emboldened those who accent tolerance and discouraged those who want to battle with the outside world.

To what extent that new approach endures depends on a host of variables. For one thing, it may hinge on how long Francis is able to keep going at his current pace and to what extent he's able to curb his tendency to overextend himself. It may also depend on whether he imposes a term limit on himself, following the example of Benedict XVI and resigning from the papacy in order to make way for a new approach. It depends, too, on which side of his soul prevails: the go-it-alone pontiff who believes he was elected to lead, or the pope committed to decentralization who is reluctant to overrule a body of bishops that is not always eager to follow him. It also depends on whether he continues to amass political capital or whether his papacy is blindsided by an unforeseen scandal or crisis. Perhaps, most fundamentally, the shelf life of Francis's imprint will depend on how ready Catholics at the grass roots around the world are to embrace it and carry it forward, even when Francis himself is off the scene.

The key point to understanding Francis is this: beneath his humble, simple exterior lies the mind of a brilliant Jesuit politician. Francis is spontaneous and often unscripted, but he's never naive. Behind his seemingly impulsive and extemporaneous flourishes is a clear conception of where he wants to go and how to get there. His supporters believe he'll do whatever it takes to ensure that his vision for Catholicism is more than a beguiling but largely unrealized dream. Yet it's worth recalling that not every pope with a game-changing dream succeeds in transforming the Church.

CANON 331 of the Code of Canon Law says that the pope wields supreme power in the Church. Yet even the most ardent advocates of a strong papacy acknowledge that this power is not unlimited. For a start, popes are bound by already accumulated divine revelation: no pope is free to declare that Jesus Christ is not the son of God or that God is not a Trinity of persons. The pontiff is also bound by the truth: no pope can decree that 2 plus 2 does not equal 4. He is additionally bound by the authoritative teaching of ecumenical councils, so he couldn't simply rule that the Council of Chalcedon got it wrong in A.D. 451 when it taught that Jesus is "truly God and truly man."

Popes are also constrained by any number of exterior forces. Public opinion puts limits on what a pontiff can do, as does resistance from aides in the Vatican or from bishops around the world. The desire to not divide the Church, to hold people together, can limit how far and how fast a pope feels he can move. (As Pope John XXIII once said, "I have to be pope both for those with their foot on the gas and those with their foot on the brake.") Limited resources, both financial and human, can sometimes get in the way too.

So electing a new pope is not tantamount to flipping a switch in Rome and changing Catholicism all at once. Every pope faces obstacles to implementing his agenda, and the success or failure of a papacy generally depends on how successful a pope is in navigating those hurdles.

There are really only five ways a pope can institutionalize change in the Catholic Church, not just for the duration of his papacy but to reorient it in a decisive way for years to come. First, he can summon an ecumenical council, as Pope John XXIII did on Jan. 25, 1959, when he announced Vatican II. Second, he can appoint bishops who share his vision and who will translate it into practice in dioceses and parishes around the world. Third, he can change the law of the Church to make his way of doing things not merely a pious example but a binding requirement. (Pope John Paul II, for instance, issued a new Code of Canon Law for the Latin church in 1983 and a parallel new code for the Eastern churches in 1990.) Fourth, he can issue teachings that set the Church on a new path. And finally, he can create new structures in the Church as a permanent expression of a particular priority, as Pope Paul VI attempted to do by founding the synod of bishops in 1965 to give local Church leaders a stronger voice in governance in Rome. All these options are available to Francis, but he's more likely to exercise some than others.

The odds of Pope Francis summoning an ecumenical council are long. In a December 2013 meeting with Dutch Catholic bishops, Francis told them that "half of the work still has to be done" in implementing the last council, Vatican II. A full century passed between Vatican II and the previous council, Vatican I. Prior to that, three centuries elapsed between the Council of Trent and Vatican I. Most experts say it takes at least a century for the dust to settle on a council, so the thought of calling a new one is probably premature. There's also a logistical challenge to holding a council today. When Vatican II opened in 1962, it was the largest such gathering in the history of Catholicism (2,860 bishops took part). Today there are more than 5,000 bishops in the Catholic Church, and even if a pope wanted to bring them all to Rome, it's not clear where they would meet or be housed, let alone how one could possibly stage a constructive debate with such a large assembly. Many in the Church believe there may never again be a real ecumenical council, in the sense of a summit that brings together every prelate in the Church (a reformed synod of bishops might well take its place).

So without councils or dramatic changes in Catholic teaching, Francis's mission is likely to come to fruition through the bishops he appoints, the laws he issues and the structures he creates.

THERE'S AN OLD ITALIAN SAYING that captures the critical importance of the pope's role in appointing bishops: *Nella Chiesa, un vescovo bravo puo fare tanto bene, e un vescovo cattivo puo fare tanto male* ("A talented bishop can do a whole lot of good, and a bad bishop can do a whole lot of harm"). The Catholic system is such that the bishop is the closest thing left on the planet to a feudal lord. The Code of Canon Law makes the bishop the supreme authority in his diocese, and although bishops are ultimately subject to the authority of the pope, in reality it's impossible for Rome to exercise close supervision over the thousands of prelates around the world. Even when the Church tries to impose checks and balances, those limits are often more nominal than real. For example, Church law requires that a bishop have the approval of a diocesan finance council for certain types of expenditures, but it also allows the bishop to appoint the members of that council. If a bishop is so inclined, he can just pick people likely to rubber-stamp whatever he wants to do.

Even when Rome tries to rein in a bishop, it's sometimes unable to do so. In 2001 the head of the Vatican's office on liturgical policy tried to compel then-Archbishop Rembert Weakland of Milwaukee to alter plans for the renovation of St. John the Evangelist Cathedral, on the grounds that they didn't comply with the rules for church design. The verdict from Rome was that the new look was excessively modern. The building had been set up so that mass could be celebrated in the round, rather than from an altar in front of traditional pews, and the tabernacle—a gilded box containing consecrated hosts that Catholics believe to be the body of Christ—was relocated to a side chapel. Weakland, who later resigned in disgrace amid a sexual misconduct scandal (he was never charged), was known as a liberal on liturgical matters, while the Vatican prefect at the time, Cardinal Jorge Medina of Chile, was a champion of liturgical conservatives. After a brief back-and-forth, Weakland politely replied that since he was the one signing the checks for the work, he'd do it his way, and the renovation went ahead. (Today, there's a tongue-in-cheek Latin plaque inside the cathedral that says the remodeling was carried out "not without some difficulty.")

A pope can fire a bishop if he has a serious complaint about his performance, either by directly removing him from office or by informing him that his resignation is expected. Pope Benedict XVI did that a handful of times, dismissing Bishop William Morris of Toowoomba, Australia, for backing the ordination of women, as well as Bishop Jean-Claude Makaya Loembe of Pointe-Noire, the Democratic Republic of Congo; Bishop Francesco Miccichè of Trapani, Italy; and Archbishop Róbert Bezák of Trnava, Slovakia, all for alleged financial misappropriations (although Bezák and his friends believe he was brought down by conservative opponents in the hierarchy). Francis has already removed

German bishop Franz-Peter Tebartz-van-Elst (the so-called "bling bishop") from the diocese of Limburg in the wake of an overspending scandal. Considering the number of bishops in the world, however, such interventions remain rare. Everything about the culture of the Catholic Church assigns the benefit of the doubt to a bishop, and for the most part bishops have the power to govern their diocese as they see fit.

Bishops don't have to stand for reelection, so they stay in their jobs until they either reach the retirement age of 75 or are sent to a different bishopric. But even when that happens, Catholic theology holds that "once a bishop, always a bishop," and in those relatively rare cases when a pope ships a bishop off to a lesser assignment or forces him to resign prematurely, he remains a member of the College of Bishops with all its rights and privileges. As a result, bishops can carry forward a particular pope's agenda well after that pope is off the scene. In the 1970s, Pope Paul VI appointed a series of bishops known for reforming attitudes and a strong concern for social justice, an outlook that in the U.S. was most associated with Cardinal Joseph Bernardin of Chicago. Those "Bernardin bishops" are still a force in the U.S. bishops' conference today, more than 35 years after the death of Paul VI. Similarly, the generation of evangelical Catholic bishops appointed by Pope John Paul II, devoted to a strong defense of Catholic tradition and teaching and equally committed to a robust challenge to secularism, continue to be a presence in the Church and will be for some time to come.

The process by which a bishop is picked happens in three stages. When there's a vacancy somewhere, created either by the death or the resignation of the incumbent, the nuncio (papal ambassador) is supposed to survey everyone in the diocese—the clergy, the religious and the laity—about what they need in a new leader. The nuncio is also supposed to consult other bishops in the country about possible candidates. (In the U.S., bishops are organized into 15 regions, meeting periodically to maintain a list of possible picks for episcopal jobs.) The nuncio then puts together a list of three names, called a terna, along with accompanying documentation, and sends it to the Vatican's Congregation for Bishops. That department vets the paperwork, and its members from around the world—roughly 30 cardinals, archbishops and bishops—debate the proposed choices and put them to a vote. The congregation then proposes a revised terna to the pope, who is free to take one of those names or set it aside and pick someone else.

So much for the theory. The reality is that in more than 90 percent of cases, the pope simply chooses the top name on the terna, especially with regard to small- and medium-sized dioceses where he doesn't know the local situation or the people. In those routine cases, a pope has to rely on the system. The exceptions generally come in relation to major tone-setting appointments to large archdioceses around the world, as well as with nominations for a pope's home country. In those cases, pontiffs are much more inclined to become personally involved.

Pope Francis is hands-on with regard to most aspects of governance, and as a veteran churchman he knows how important the selection of bishops is in moving the Church in his direction. Francis laid out in black and white the sort of bishop he prefers in a June 2013 speech to his nuncios. He said that the first criterion for candidates is that they must be "pastors close to the people." He continued, "If he's a great theologian, a great mind, let him go to the university where he can do much good. But we need pastors! . . . They should be fathers and brothers, mild, patient and merciful. They should love poverty, interior [poverty] as freedom for the Lord and also exterior [poverty] as simplicity and austerity of life." (Interior poverty in Catholic spirituality usually means a detachment from worldly success or one's own importance.) In the most celebrated phrase of the speech, Francis insisted that bishops must not have "the psychology of a prince." Francis told the nuncios that if a priest seems to want to become a bishop, that's a strong indicator that he probably shouldn't get the job.

It's still too early to assess how successful Francis will be in finding men to lead the Church who fit this profile. As Cardinal Timothy

Dolan of New York said in a 2014 interview, "Let's face it, we're still in April of the baseball season with this pope," suggesting that there's no real point in checking the standings so early.

What's clear is that Francis takes the task seriously. For the most important choices around the world, Francis gets personally involved, reaching out to a wide cross-section of people, often by phone, to solicit candid opinions about what the diocese needs and who seems best suited to fill the slot. When he had to choose a new archbishop of Madrid in Spain in the summer of 2014, sources said Francis treated the task as a personal mission, with scores of Spanish bishops, priests and religious and lay leaders reporting that they had been contacted by the pope for a blunt assessment. Likewise, several American prelates said around the same time that they had been asked by Francis to offer opinions about a successor to Cardinal Francis George in Chicago. Strikingly, the prelates said that Francis often asked them to react to a perceived weakness of a particular candidate before they even brought it up, suggesting that he had studied the situation closely.

So far, there does seem to be a pattern in the leaders Francis selects. In July 2014 Francis named Cardinal Rainer Maria Woelki of Berlin as the new archbishop of Cologne, which is not only the largest diocese in Germany but among the largest and wealthiest Catholic jurisdictions in the world. Woelki, who turns 59 in 2015, took over from 80-year-old Cardinal Joachim Meisner, who retired in February. Generally seen as an archconservative, Meisner had been a close confidante of Pope Benedict XVI, with the two men typically speaking on the phone at least once a week. Born in Cologne, Woelki was cut from the same ideological cloth as Meisner—in fact, he was Meisner's protégé early in his career. In 2011 Woelki was criticized for referring to homosexuality as an "offense against the order of creation." With comments like that, there had been fears before he went to Berlin that he would be unsuited to the city's largely secular and highly diverse population. Yet leading the Church in such an environment seemed to have changed Woelki. He became an apostle of dialogue, holding meetings with leaders of the gay community, and said that while the Church believes marriage is between a man and a woman, it can also see that a long-term caring relationship between two people of the same sex deserves special moral consideration.

Woelki is generally thought of as humble, eschewing ecclesiastical finery and not taking himself too seriously. As someone who dialed down the rhetoric in the culture wars, Woelki developed into a Francis-before-Francis. "The Church is not a moral institution that goes around pointing its finger at people," Woelki said. "The Church is a community of seekers and believers, and it would like to help people find happiness in life." In 2012 the German Alliance Against Homophobia nominated Woelki for a Respect Award, saying he had promoted a "new cooperation with homosexuals in society." (Woelki expressed gratitude but politely declined the nomination.) He also emerged as a leader among German bishops regarding poverty relief and advocacy on behalf of immigrants and refugees, taking a special interest in the work of the Catholic charitable agency Caritas.

Meanwhile, in Spain there has long been a split between bishops who favor dialogue with secularism and those who want to fight it. For the past 20 years, Madrid has been led by Cardinal Antonio María Rouco Varela. He is seen as a stern conservative, fiercely opposing liberalizing currents in Spanish society, including the adoption of a gay marriage law in 2005, saying that in today's Spain, "not only is faith denied but also human reason itself." While Rouco embodied the confrontational option, Valencia's Archbishop Carlos Osoro Sierra—dubbed the "Spanish Francis"—was associated with a moderate line.

But when it came to making a change in Madrid, someone else was the clear favorite for the top job. Cardinal Antonio Cañizares Llovera had served for six years as prefect of the Vatican's Congregation for Divine Worship and the Discipline of the Sacraments, the office that sets liturgical policy. He is known as the "little Ratzinger," not only because he's short but because his theological and liturgical views are close to those of Pope Benedict XVI. Cañizares has expressed reservations about taking communion in the hand—arguing that receiving it on the tongue and in a kneeling position better expresses a spirit of adoration—and has robustly defended Benedict's decision in 2007 to widen permission for celebration of the Latin mass. During the Benedict years, it was widely believed that Cañizares would succeed Rouco. Instead, Francis dispatched Osoro to Madrid, making him the de facto leader of Spanish Catholicism, and sent Cañizares to Osoro's old job in Valencia.

In the U.S., the same logic applied when Francis tapped 65-year-old Cupich, previously the bishop of the small diocese of Spokane, Washington—and a figure who appeared on almost no handicappers' list—to take over the critically important archdiocese of Chicago. Chicago is one of a few large dioceses around the world whose leaders help set direction for the Church in their regions, and it has long been a symbol for deeper realignments. During the 1980s and 1990s, the late Cardinal Joseph Bernardin embodied the moderate, reforming spirit of the Second Vatican Council. Bernardin famously called for a "seamless garment" ethic in Catholicism, one that placed equal emphasis on resisting war and concern for the poor alongside opposition to abortion. The transition to Cardinal Francis George embodied the stronger emphasis on Catholic identity in the later John Paul II years, with resistance to the inroads of secularism the defining cause. George helped make the defense of religious freedom a signature cause for the American bishops, crystallized in the tug-of-war with the Obama White House over contraception mandates imposed as part of health-care reform. Both Bernardin and George served as president of the U.S. bishops' conference at different points, and both were seen as representing the broader spirit of their era in the American Church.

In Cupich, Francis found another defining prelate to take over in Chicago. On a personal level, Cupich is regarded as humble and open, a pastor who "carries the smell of his sheep" that Francis has often said he wants in a prelate. He is clearly a moderate, upholding Church teaching on abortion, contraception and gay marriage but, like Francis, shunning strong rhetoric on those matters. Cupich has been identified with the wing of the American bishops that has tried to steer the Church down a less confrontational path. He tends to place special emphasis on the social gospel—concern for the poor and for social justice. In 2011 Cupich dismayed some of the most aggressive pro-life forces in Catholicism when he discouraged priests and seminarians from taking part in an anti-abortion protest in Spokane. Cupich is also seen as an adept manager and an internal reformer. In his role as chair of the U.S. bishops' Committee for the Protection of Children and Young People, he helped lead the American Church's efforts to recover from child sexual abuse scandals. In 2010 Cupich said that listening to abuse victims is an "opportunity to recalibrate" the whole of a bishop's ministry, because it's a powerful reminder that "there are voices out there which the leadership doesn't usually hear." He explained, "We have to keep the connection with victims visceral and fresh," because doing so "will help us not to have amnesia."

Francis was personally involved in the selection of a successor to 77-year-old Cardinal George in Chicago, making phone calls to a wide variety of sources in and around the U.S. Church and consulting American prelates when they came to Rome. In those conversations, Francis asked for a blunt assessment of the strengths and weaknesses of a variety of candidates. One American cardinal said that he had been surprised when Francis asked him for an assessment of Cupich, since the Omaha native was not generally regarded as a front-runner for the position. It remains to be seen if Cupich will be the same heavyweight that Bernardin and George were in their day, but in a sense one could argue that the Francis era in American Catholicism began with Cupich's appointment on Sept. 20, 2014.

Adding it all up, the kind of man Francis seems to look for in key posts is someone orthodox in doctrine but committed to dialogue and outreach; a man who doesn't take himself too seriously; who emphasizes concern for the poor and those at the margins; and who gets out of the office and into the streets.

POPE FRANCIS IS THE SUPREME legislator of the Catholic Church, giving him the power to change laws with the stroke of a pen in what's known as a *motu proprio*, meaning a legal act under his own authority. But doing so is a less reliable way of making permanent change than appointing bishops, for the simple reason that laws can and are changed all the time, whereas bishops hang around for years. There's also no way for a pope to issue a law that will be binding on his successor, because the same provisions that protect his autonomy also apply to whoever holds the job next. That's why the Church can require bishops to submit their resignations at the age of 75 but can't demand the same of popes. Even if a pope were to adopt such a requirement, the next pope could simply repeal it. As a result, Church law is never eternal in the same way that doctrine is believed to be. (Laws can be changed, but doctrine is regarded as once-and-for-all, even though the Church's understanding of it can develop over time.)

Then there's the slippery nature of rules in the Church, which are always subject to pastoral application and interpretation. Take gays in the priesthood: despite the fact that a Vatican ban on admitting homosexuals to seminaries has theoretically been on the books since 2005, scores of gay men have been ordained to the priesthood in the years since. That's because bishops, seminary rectors and religious superiors decided that a particular candidate represented an exception to the rule. The example illustrates that in the Catholic Church, law is an inexact instrument to effect change, because the system affords fairly wide latitude to middle managers to decide what it means in their specific situation.

Issuing laws remains an important vehicle to institutionalize a new direction, however, because the Church favors precedent over willy-nilly change. Even though popes can theoretically overturn whatever edicts their predecessors issued, they're almost always reluctant to do so (in part, of course, because they realize the same thing could happen to them). And when a particular rule enjoys strong support inside and outside the Church, popes have to think carefully about whether it's really worth drawing down their political and moral capital to get rid of it.

There's little evidence that Pope Francis is contemplating a sweeping overhaul of the Code of Canon Law, although the Vatican has been working since 2008 on revisions to the penal section of the code, which, among other things, contains the provisions for disciplining a priest accused of child abuse. That project will probably be brought to a conclusion under Francis and is expected to narrow a bishop's freedom of action in these cases by requiring him to impose stronger penalties on clergy found guilty. Francis's impact as a legislator seems likely to come not so much in comprehensive revisions to the code but in one-off legislative acts to deal with specific situations.

It's striking that Francis's first two *motu proprios* were clear reform measures intended to deal with the two most persistent sources of scandal for the Vatican in recent years: sexual abuse and financial misconduct. In July 2013 Francis issued a *motu proprio* intended to bring Vatican law into compliance with the 1989 U.N. Convention on the Rights of the Child. The edict was aimed at defining and setting out penalties for specific crimes against minors, including the sale of children, child prostitution, the military recruitment of children, sexual violence against children and producing or possessing child pornography. Francis ruled that any Vatican employee can be tried by Vatican courts for violating those rules and that such crimes would be punishable by up to 12 years in prison. Giuseppe Dalla Torre, the presiding judge of the Vatican City court, said that the new laws make it much easier for the Vatican to cooperate with other governments and to extradite a person who committed the crime in a different jurisdiction and attempts to hide either in the Vatican itself or in one of its embassies around the world.

As it happened, a test of the system's teeth came quickly with the case of former Polish archbishop Józef Wesolowski, a onetime papal envoy in the Dominican Republic who has been accused of molesting minors there. (His case is described in Chapter 7.) Wesolowski was recalled in late 2013 and subsequently kicked out of the priesthood. After the *New York Times* ran a piece in August 2014 suggesting that Wesolowski's presence in the Vatican might be a way of evading civil prosecution, a Vatican spokesman insisted that not only would Wesolowski be tried under the new law and potentially subject to a stretch in a Vatican jail but that he had been stripped of his diplomatic status, so he could stand trial in the Dominican Republic or any other jurisdiction.

In August 2014 Francis issued another *motu proprio*, this one concerning the Vatican's Financial Information Authority (AIF), the anti-money-laundering watchdog unit created during Benedict XVI's reign. Under Benedict, the AIF had been almost exclusively a financial intelligence unit, responsible for investigating specific suspect transactions. Francis's edict expanded its powers, making it a prudential supervisor with the authority to monitor the capacities of Vatican departments to ensure financial transparency and accountability. The *motu proprio* gave the AIF purview over not just the Vatican's main economic centers but all departments, even nonprofit foundations with a financial footprint in the Vatican. The law gave the AIF real powers of supervision and made it clear that any hope of evading its reach was now gone.

THE LOGIC OF BUREAUCRACIES holds that the best way to signal that something is a priority is to create a department for it, with offices, staff and a budget. Such logic holds true in the Vatican as much as it does in the Pentagon or at General Motors.

When Pope John Paul II created a Pontifical Council for the Family in 1981 and a Pontifical Academy for Life in 1994, he emphasized the importance of fighting against what he memorably described as a spreading "culture of death," expressed in liberalizing currents around the world regarding abortion, contraception, gay marriage and other battles over sexual morality. In the years since, the Academy for Life in particular has emerged as the primary beachhead for the Church's most ardent pro-life forces, which was clearly the pontiff's intention when he founded the body.

The creation of structures, however, like changing Church laws, is an imperfect way of institutionalizing a pope's agenda. New bureaucracies depend upon the people running them to live up to their original purpose, especially in a relatively small world such as the Vatican, where changes to just a couple of key officials can dramatically alter the effectiveness of a whole department.

Francis has introduced three new permanent structures to the Vatican, aside from ad-hoc boards and study commissions that have a limited shelf life. The first is the Council of Cardinals, set up to advise the pope on governance of the universal Church, beginning with a reform of the Roman Curia, the Vatican's central administrative bureaucracy. The second is the series of new financial entities—including the Council for the Economy, the Secretariat for the Economy and an Auditor General—that report directly to the pope to review the work of the other departments. The third, so far, is a new Pontifical Commission for the Protection of Minors, intended to advise the pope on measures needed to combat the sexual abuse of children and to promote best practices in the global Church.

Francis's approach to structures appears to be predicated on the desire to create vehicles for reform on three fronts: money management, child sexual abuse and collegiality. No one yet knows how well these new institutions will perform. Francis and his Council of Cardinals are also pondering other reforms to the Curia that are expected to result in some downsizing and consolidation of the present array of nine congregations, three tribunals, 12 councils and a host of other commissions, offices, academies and other institutions.

To alter the impact of these departments, a future pope would only need to assign new leaders with a different approach. That said, over time, a department in the Vatican tends to build up a culture and a set of fellow travelers in the Church who can be stubbornly difficult to reorient. Even when the point of view they represent is no longer in favor, their presence means they still wield considerable power. In other words, the structures a pope creates and those he suppresses are a guide to his priorities. To date, it seems as if this reforming pope is determined to ensure that long after he has gone, someone will still be around to press the case for vigilance and accountability.

NO POPE, NO MATTER HOW magnetic his personality or how long his reign, has ever been completely successful at imposing his will on the Catholic Church. The Church is diverse, complicated and geographically and culturally far-flung. John Paul II's most significant resistance was always in-house, and he knew it—he was passionately committed to reaching out to young people but well aware that not all his middle managers shared his zeal. When asked about his vision for World Youth Day—the massive gathering of young people he founded in 1986 that's since become a sort of Olympic Games of the Catholic Church—John Paul replied that "they say it is to evangelize the young . . . but it is really to evangelize the bishops!"

It's unrealistic to believe Catholicism will uniformly embrace any new direction set by a pope, especially a maverick such as Francis. At the same time, there are three good reasons to believe that Francis may leave an important mark. First, Jorge Mario Bergoglio is not an ethereal monk indifferent to, or naive about, the realities of power. He has been a leader since the age of 36, when he became the Jesuit provincial in Argentina, and he has a track record of bending institutions to his will. Bergoglio is not shy about using his authority, and he knows that he was elected on a reform mandate, particularly with regard to making the Vatican's administration more accountable and efficient. He feels compelled to deliver, despite the naysayers.

Second, even if Francis's papacy ended tomorrow, he would never vanish into obscurity, because he has already achieved a level of celebrity that ensures people will remember him. He's good at quotes ("Who am I to judge?"), images of the smiling pontiff are everywhere, and he has become the person by which everything in Catholicism is judged. New York's Cardinal Dolan has said that whenever he faces a decision on whether to close a parish, the most frequent thing he hears from those wanting to keep it open is "This parish serves the poor, and Francis would never close it," while from the other side he gets "This place is bleeding money, and Francis says we can't do that." An entire generation of Catholics has already been trained to judge issues through the lens provided by Pope Francis and, while their conclusions may differ, his way of thinking will be hard to erase.

Third, the pace of change is quicker in the 21st century, even in Rome. Although the Vatican still lags in that regard—"Talk to me on Wednesday and we'll get back to you in 300 years," as the saying goes—the tempo has quickened notably in recent years, and more so under Francis.

Catholicism has never fully been the Church of Pope John XXIII, John Paul II or, for that matter, Gregory the Great or St. Peter himself. It has too much of its own mind—or rather 1.2 billion individual minds, all encouraged by Catholic tradition to bring their own reason to bear on what the faith means to them. The nature of the Church is that no one individual, not even a pope, can dictate its rhythms and its culture. That said, a handful of popes over the centuries clearly changed the Church forever, definitively closing some doors and kicking others open against all odds.

Francis's mission is to move the Church to the political center, the margins of the world and the heart of the gospel. Will he pull it off in a way that lasts? We can't be certain, of course, but anyone watching him at work knows the smart bet probably isn't against him.

Acknowledgments

WHILE MY NAME may be the one that appears on the cover, the truth is that a finished book is always a collaborative effort drawing on the insight and wisdom of a variety of people. Some are cherished friends and colleagues; others are people I've never met but whose work is almost as familiar to me as my own. That's certainly the case here, as *The Francis Miracle* benefited from the reporting, analysis and experience of others.

To begin, my gratitude knows no bounds for my wife, Shannon, who's also my business manager and agent. She is without a doubt the best-informed Jew on the planet about Vatican affairs, and she probably could have written this book by herself. I should also give a shout-out to our pug, Ellis, the most loving creature either one of us has ever known and whose simple pleasure in our company never fails.

Thanks definitely go to all those at Time Books who had the original idea for this project and who have been intimately involved in every phase of its writing and editing, as well as the people they brought on board to help out, especially Steve Koepp, Roe D'Angelo, Luke Dempsey, Christine Piper and Andréa Ford. This is my 10th book, and I've never been pushed as hard on the details as I was by this crew. Whatever the book's weaknesses, it's far better as a result of their contributions.

Because much of the content in these pages draws on reporting I've done for the newspapers I've worked for since Francis was elected, thanks also go to my colleagues at the *National Catholic Reporter*, Crux and the *Boston Globe*. My editors and colleagues tolerated occasional absences and delays in producing stories in order to allow me time and space to get this book done, and they also provided invaluable input along the way. Leaving *NCR* was one of the most difficult and painful decisions I've ever made, made easier by the fact that I've found a terrific new family at Crux and the *Globe*, and the imprint of everyone at both shops is all over this book.

I want to thank Inés San Martín, the Vatican correspondent for Crux and the *Globe*, who read the manuscript carefully and saved me from myself on multiple occasions. As an Argentine, she was especially critical in making sure the Argentine detail about Pope Francis is accurate and in the proper context. Before long, I'll be known as the guy who introduced Inés San Martín to the world, and I will be reading her manuscripts rather than the other way around.

Likewise, I want to thank my colleagues at CNN, where I serve as the network's senior Vatican analyst. Thanks for the friendship and support in what's now my 12th year under contract. I want to thank Hada Messia in Rome, the best producer in the business.

While there are far too many other people who helped with this project to mention by name, I want to say to my colleagues in the press corps; to all the Catholic bishops, clergy and laity I've had the privilege of knowing; to my audiences on the lecture circuit; and to my readers at *NCR* and Crux: you will never know how much your praise, criticism, observations and reactions have shaped my thinking and influenced this book.

Finally, I was raised in Western Kansas by three precious people: my mother, Laura Ileene Allen; my grandfather, Raymond Frazier; and my grandmother, Laura Frazier. All three have now made their way to Heaven, and I pray that news of this book, along with my eternal love, reaches them there.

About the Author

JOHN L. ALLEN, JR., covers the Vatican for the *Boston Globe* and Crux, a website specializing in news and commentary on the Catholic Church. For 16 years he was based in Rome as a correspondent for the *National Catholic Reporter*, and he is currently the senior Vatican analyst for CNN. The author of nine books on the Vatican and Catholic affairs, he also writes frequently about the Church for major national and international publications and is a popular speaker on Catholic affairs, both in the U.S. and abroad.

When Allen was called on to ask the first question of Pope Benedict XVI aboard the papal plane to the U.S. in 2008, a Vatican spokesperson presented Allen this way: "Holy Father, this man needs no introduction!" The London *Tablet* called Allen "the most authoritative writer on Vatican affairs in the English language," and renowned papal biographer George Weigel said he is "the best Anglophone Vatican reporter ever." Veteran religion writer Kenneth Woodward described Allen as "the journalist other reporters—and not a few cardinals—look to for the inside story on how all the pope's men direct the world's largest church."

Allen's work is admired across ideological divides. The late liberal commentator Fr. Andrew Greeley called his writing "indispensable," while the late Fr. Richard John Neuhaus, a conservative, called Allen's reporting "possibly the best source of information on the Vatican published in the United States." Allen's weekly column, "All Things Catholic," is widely read as a source of insight on the global Church.

Allen divides his time between Rome and his home in Denver, Colorado. He grew up in western Kansas and holds a master's degree in religious studies from the University of Kansas.

ALSO BY JOHN L. ALLEN, JR.

Cardinal Ratzinger: The Vatican's Enforcer of the Faith (Continuum, 2000)

Conclave: The Politics, Personalities, and Process of the Next Papal Election (Doubleday, 2002)

All The Pope's Men: The Inside Story of How the Vatican Really Thinks (Doubleday, 2004)

The Rise of Benedict XVI: The Inside Story of How the Pope Was Elected and Where He Will Take the Catholic Church (Doubleday, 2005)

Opus Dei: An Objective Look Behind the Myths and Reality of the Most Controversial Force in the Catholic Church (Doubleday, 2005)

The Future Church: How Ten Trends Are Revolutionizing the Catholic Church (Doubleday, 2009)

A People of Hope: Archbishop Timothy Dolan in Conversation with John L. Allen Jr. (Doubleday, 2011)

The Catholic Church: What Everyone Needs to Know (Oxford University Press, 2013)

The Global War on Christians: Dispatches from the Front Lines of Anti-Christian Persecution (Image Books, 2013)

Index